What People are Saying abou~ ~~~ ~~~~

The Original Jeeps is fascinating, insightful and loaded with information. [...] The amount of detail is amazing. [...] All in all, this is a job well done and a worthy addition to any Jeep enthusiast's library. —*Patrick R. Foster, Historian/Author, Foreword of this book*

Paul Bruno's fascinating book goes beyond describing the incarnation of the Jeep. It gives the reader an in-depth look into the inadequate state of the U.S. military following World War I and the great need for the Jeep. Paul then gives a detailed accounting of the development of the ¼-ton truck covering the creation of specifications and the roles of Bantam, Ford and Willys bringing the Jeep to life. This book will be an interesting read for the Jeep minded and history buffs alike. — *Bill Norris, editor of antique Jeep publications,* The Dispatcher Magazine *and* Holy Toledo! *wall calendars*

Paul was one of my graduate students more than 25 years ago. I am delighted to see his new work that highlights an important part of our American history. He has a gift for keeping the flame alive and he has done so brilliantly in *The Original Jeeps* showcasing an underdog story of triumph over all obstacles. —*William D. Danko, Ph.D., co-author of* The Millionaire Next Door, *and* Richer Than A Millionaire

The Original Jeeps by Paul Bruno is the story before the story of one of the most iconic American vehicles ever created. Most books about Jeep history start at WWII and usually tell the tale of how a military vehicle became a beloved civilian vehicle. Even the Jeep Corporation advertises that the Jeep Wrangler started in 1941. *The Original Jeeps* story starts well before WWII and answers the who, what, where and why. Where did the ideas come from for the Jeep? Who was involved in the design? Why did the Jeep windshield have to fold? Why didn't it have doors, why was it so small and light, why did it have four-wheel-drive? What was it called before it became known as the Jeep? If you want to know the complete back story read *The Original Jeeps* by Paul R Bruno. —*Steven Hoese, Past Fleet Management Specialist for Henderson, Nevada, and life-long "Car Guy"*

Paul Bruno's in-depth new book tells what radio legend Paul Harvey would call "the rest of the story." From humble beginnings in Western Pennsylvania, Paul follows the story of this U.S. icon as it weaves through military directives, production changes and manufacturers. The inspired story is nothing short of the definition of American entrepreneurial spirit, and Paul's unparalleled research and passion bring the dedicated individuals who changed the course of American and automotive history to life. — *Linda Harvey Burkley, Former President, Butler County Chamber of Commerce; Lecturer, Susquehanna University*

In my 40 years as an Economic Development professional, I have literally reviewed hundreds of start-up business plans and job creation strategies by the US government. However, the entrepreneurial spirit captured in this book is truly unique and a must-read for all small businesses and innovators needing a fresh inspiration. — *Bob Cooper, Certified Economic Developer*

As a former U.S. Army Major/Project Manager and Jeep owner, I was excited to have the opportunity to preread Paul Bruno's "The Original Jeeps" and was not disappointed. It is a fascinating read, intertwining the machinations of bureaucracy with the determination of a group of individuals to deliver a vehicle that would eventually win wars, save lives, and become an American icon. Paul does a brilliant job of putting all this into a historic context to provide the reader with, not just what, but also why things happened and had to happen, providing a rich and comprehensive view of the uphill battles this little vehicle faced and why it was imperative that it succeeded. While reading you may wonder how this project could have ever been successful, but as anyone that has ever driven or owned a Jeep can tell you, there is no obstacle too great for this tough little vehicle. Now you'll know that it is in its DNA! —*William P. Howlett, former Major, Military Intelligence, U.S. Army – HQ Training and Doctrine Command, Fort Monroe, VA*

Time Line—The Original Jeeps

1918–January 1940:	Project Genesis, research into a light vehicle
February–Mid-May 1940:	Discussions on light vehicle general characteristics
Mid-May–June 6, 1940:	Coalescing and documentation of vehicle general characteristics
June 6–June 20, 1940:	Initial work to develop a detailed vehicle specification
June 21–July 2, 1940:	Development and documentation of detailed vehicle drawing and specification
July 3–July 11, 1940:	Preparation and finalization of invitation for bids
July 12- July 21, 1940:	Bid preparation by manufacturers
July 22, 1940:	Bid opening and award to Bantam
July 22–July 24, 1940:	Willys given permission by QMC to build a pilot model at their own expense
July 23-August 5, 1940:	Finalization of bid award and contract award for Bantam
August 5-Sept. 21, 1940:	Bantam pilot model built and christened "Bantam Reconnaissance Car" (BRC)
August 15–November 4, 1940:	Willys pilot model built and named the Quad
September 23, 1940:	BRC delivered to Camp Holabird
Sept. 24-Oct. 23, 1940:	BRC tested at Camp Holabird
October 4, 1940:	Ford representatives, on invitation from the QMC, meet with QMC representatives who request they build and submit a pilot model

October 4–November 21, 1940:	Ford pilot model built and dubbed the Pygmy
October 4–December 3, 1940:	Order for 500 from each manufacturer becomes 1,500 from each contender
Oct. 23-29, 1940:	Inspection, test and final reports on Bantam pilot model completed
October 30, 1940:	BRC officially accepted and order for next sixty-nine placed
November 13, 1940	Willys Quad delivered to Camp Holabird
November 23, 1940	Ford Pygmy delivered to Camp Holabird
November 1940–January 1941:	Bantam builds the other 69 from original contract; Willys Quad and Ford Pygmy tested at Camp Holabird
January 6, 1941	Ford pilot model accepted and order for 1,500 vehicles commences
January 8–28, 1941:	Willys pilot model rejected and order for 1,500 cancelled
January 31–February 11, 1941:	Willys 1,500 unit order restored
February–June 1941:	Bantam and Ford build their 1,500
February 1941–May 1941:	Creation of the Willys MA
June 1941:	Willys MA goes into volume production
July 1941:	RFP for 16,000 vehicles
August 1941:	Award for 16,000 trucks to Willys-Overland Motors
August–October 1941:	Creation of the Willys MB
October–November 1941:	Formalization of agreement between, Willys, Ford and the QMC for Ford to build the MB under license

The Original Jeeps

By Paul R. Bruno

First Edition

MFM
PUBLISHING
LOS ANGELES

THE ORIGINAL JEEPS

FIRST EDITION

ISBN: 978-0-578-72175-0

Jeep is a registered trademark of FCA US LLC and Groupe PSA's merged corporate brand, Stellantis

Neither the Author nor any contributors to this work have any affiliation with FCA US LLC, Groupe PSA, or Stellantis

This Book: © 1999-2020 Paul R. Bruno, Henderson, NV 89012 U.S.A.

All rights reserved.

LCCN: 2020941640

Design of Cover, Layout, and Typography by M. Freedman

Published by MFM Publishing Division of Max Freedman Media, Los Angeles, California 90064, U.S.A.

Dedication

To the late Cathy E. Bruno, Ph.D., my beloved wife, companion and soul mate who supported me, and the telling of this story.

I am incredibly indebted to my parents, the late Miriam and Victor Bruno, and my brothers, Eric and Karl Bruno, for always being there for me and all my other family and friends who sustained me during the journey.

Acknowledgements

There is no "I" in "team" states a popular phrase and though "I" wrote this book many individuals comprised the "team" that assisted in the journey.

I wish to thank Manuel "Max" Freedman, writing mentor and dear friend, for sharing his wisdom, and for editing and publishing the book. Steven Hoese, best friend, and research partner. Bill Mertens, another best friend and research partner. Linda Morales-Kennon, friend and supporter for many years.

Vincent Appel, Maxine "Max" Duvall, Glenn Krause, Morio Lurenz, and Paul "Randy" Petty for being there for me during my darkest hours in 2012, and for all the other friends who helped along the way, too many to name, who provided encouragement and support to keep going.

Linda Burkley, of Butler, PA for her support of telling this story over many years. Robert Brandon also of Butler, PA for sharing the rare photographs of the building of the Bantam pilot model. Ralph Turner, Jr., namesake son of one of the four key individuals who built the BRC, for sharing documentation his father had kept and his own recollections of his dad's descriptions of events.

Hubert, Todd and the late Patsy Jordan, gracious hosts and my supporters in Bartow, Georgia, Roy Evans' hometown.

Patrick R. Foster, author and automotive historian, for providing the Foreword to this book and numerous photographs documenting Willys-Overland's history.

I am indebted to the archivists at the United States Archives, College Park, Maryland, who were always helpful and thoroughly professional as well as Bill Norris for sharing key documentation.

Last but certainly not least, my nuclear family, the late Miriam and Victor Bruno, parents who helped me become who I am, and the best brothers anyone could ever have, Eric and Karl Bruno.

Finally, deep thanks to my late wife Cathy E. Bruno, Ph.D. It was her love, support and encouragement that made this book possible.

—*Paul R. Bruno, Henderson, Nevada – 2020*

Contents

Time Line—The Original Jeeps 2

Dedication v

Acknowledgements vii

Contents ix

List of Figures xi

List of Tables xvi

Foreword xvii

Preface xix

Introduction xxi

Chapter 1: The United States Army between the Wars 1

Chapter 2: The American Bantam Car Company 11

Chapter 3: Genesis of a Legend 21

Chapter 4: What Do We Want? 47

Chapter 5: A Vehicle Takes Shape 61

Chapter 6: Bidding for the First Jeep 81

Chapter 7: Building the First Jeep 95

Chapter 8: Testing and Accepting the BRC 111

Chapter 9: Willys-Overland Motors, Inc. 119

Chapter 10: Willys Builds Pilots While Ford Emerges 137

Chapter 11: Competition 155

Epilogue 179

Time Line 183

Tables 185

Bibliography 221

Endnotes 223

Index 239

About the Author 263

About the Publisher 263

Premise of this Volume 264

List of Figures

FRONT

Figure A: Dedication...v

Figure 1: British Troops in World War I Trench—Battle of the Somme, 1916. 1

Figure 2: President George Washington. 1

Figure 3: Signing of the Treaty of Versailles, June 28, 1919.................................... 2

Figure 4: Signatories to the Kellogg-Briand Pact at the United States White House. 3

Figure 5: Edouard Daladier, Premier of France with French Delegation to the London Economic Conference, June 1933. 3

Figure 6: The Burning of the German Reichstag on February 27, 1933, was a catalyst to help Adolf Hitler consolidate his power after his appointment as Chancellor of Germany on January 30, 1933. 4

Figure 7: Location of the Rhineland circa 1936 when Hitler annexed it in violation of the Treaty of Versailles... 5

Figure 8: German Soldiers Passing the Arc de Triomphe in Paris on June 14, 1940, after the fall of France. Attribution: Bundesarchiv, Bild 101I-126-0347-09A / Gutjahr / CC-BY-SA 6

Figure 9: The United States' M1 Combat Car light tank used by the Cavalry in the late 1930s was no match for Hitler's Panzers. 6

Figure 10: Harking back to George Washington's Farewell Address a No Foreign Entanglements anti-war protest sign. 7

Figure 11: British Prime Minister Neville Chamberlain holding the Munich Agreement upon his return from that city on September 30, 1938. The agreement would hold for only six months when Hitler annexed the remainder of Czechoslovakia. 8

Figure 12: Soldiers of the United States First Army Prepare to Fire Large Artillery Piece During Summer Maneuvers in 1940. Used with permission from Town of De Kalb, New York Historian's Office.. 9

Figure 13: Sir Herbert Austin 11

Figure 14: 1926 Austin 7 Coupe— The Great Grandfather of the Jeep Prototype 12

Figure 15: 1931 American Austin Roadster—The Grandfather of the Jeep Prototype.

Photo used with permission from Dale Lynn James. 14

Figure 16: 1911 Maxwell Mascotte Touring Car. 15

Figure 17: 1939 American Bantam Roadster—The Father of the Jeep Prototype. Photo used with permission from Dale Lynn James. 17

Figure 18: 1940 American Bantam Hollywood Convertible Developed by Alex Tremulis. Used with permission from Conceptcarz.com. 18

Figure 19: Roy S. Evans (third from right and inserts) and the Bantam Team circa 1939. Sources (main): George Edward Domer, *Automotive Quarterly,* Fall 1976; (inserts): John W. Underwood, Heritage Press, 1965 18

Figure 20: The Mule—Primary Transport for Troops and Small Payloads the U.S. Army was Looking to Replace with A Small Vehicle. 21

Figure 21: 1930s era US Military Motorcycle with Sidecar Which Was Unsatisfactory for Modern Mobile Cavalry Uses. Used with permission from Auburn University Libraries Special Collections–Everett Leavins Papers.. 21

Figure 22: 1932 American Austin Roadster—Possibly the Model or a Similar Model Purchased by the Infantry for Testing in 1932. Source: sportscarmarket.com 23

Figure 23: Lieutenant Hamilton's Light Cross-Country Car. Source: United States National Archives, College Park, Maryland.. 24

Figure 24: Front View of the Howie Machine Gun Carrier. Source: United States National Archives, College Park, Maryland... 27

Figure 25: Side view of the Howie Machine Gun Carrier Powered by an Austin Bantam Engine, and using an Austin Radiator and Austin Steering Gear. Source: United States National Archives, College Park, Maryland.. 28

Figure 26: M2 Light Tractor Cat Model—The Marmon-Herrington TA30 Was Most Likely Similar to this Model. 33

Figure 27: A ½-ton Marmon-Herrington 4x4. 33

Figure 28: German Kubelwagen on Eastern Front circa 1943. Attribution: Bundesarchiv, Bild 101I-022-2926-07 / Wolff/Altvater / CC-BY-SA 37

Figure 29: A 1937 American Bantam ¼-ton Pickup Truck. 39

Figure 30: A German Panzer Mark IV Ausf C. Attribution: Bundesarchiv, Bild 183-J08365 / CC-BY-SA.. 45

Figure 31: Francis H. Fenn. 47

Figure 32: The Bantam Chassis with 4,500 pounds of sandbags—June 19, 1940. Photo taken in Shipping Department at the American Bantam Company Plant. Source: United States National Archives, College Park, Maryland 65

Figure 33: The Beasley-Brown Drawing—June 19, 1940. This is the very first sketch ever made of a Jeep-type vehicle. Source: United States National Archives, College Park, Maryland 67

Figure 34: Drawing QM 08370-Z–Note the Similarities to the Beasley–Brown Drawing Made at Butler on June 19, 1940. Source: United States National Archives, College Park, Maryland 80

Figure 35: George C. Marshall—Chief of Staff, U.S. Army, 1 September 1939-18 November 1945 81

Figure 36: Karl K. Probst. 87

Figure 37: Pilot Chassis Rail—September 3, 1940. Photo Courtesy of Robert Brandon, Butler, PA. 97

Figure 38: Chassis Coming Together—September 5, 1940. Photo Courtesy of Robert Brandon, Butler, PA. 98

Figure 39: Ralph Turner Examining the Engine. Photo Courtesy of Robert Brandon, Butler, PA 99

Figure 40: Body Tube and Rail Assembly—September 4, 1940. Photo Courtesy of Robert Brandon, Butler, PA. 99

Figure 41: Chassis Drive Train Under Construction. Photo Courtesy of Robert Brandon, Butler, PA 100

Figure 42: Chester Hempfling with the tin snips the German metal smith used to cut the rounded hood on the pilot model. Photo Courtesy of Robert Brandon, Butler, PA 100

Figure 43: Transmission and Transfer Case. Photo Courtesy of Robert Brandon, Butler, PA 101

Figure 44: The Clutch Throw Out Lever Original Blueprint for the Bantam pilot model. Source—United States National Archives, College Park, Maryland 103

Figure 45: Chassis Assembly as of September 10, 1940. Photo Courtesy of Robert Brandon, Butler, PA. 104

Figure 46: Body Added Sometime After September 10, 1940. Photo Courtesy of Robert Brandon, Butler, PA. 105

Figure 47: Bantam #1—The Very First Jeep—Minutes After Assembly Completed on September 21, 1940. Crist is driving, Bob Brown is in the passenger seat, Probst leans against the spare tire at far left. 107

Figure 48: A Quick Test Spin Around the Factory. Photo Courtesy of Robert Brandon, Butler, PA.. 109

Figure 49: Troops Testing the Bantam Pilot. Source—United States National Archives, College Park, Maryland 111

Figure 50: Bantam Pulling a 37mm Howitzer the exact weapons carrier role the Infantry had so long searched for in a lightweight vehicle. Source: United States National Archives, College Park, Maryland 114

Figure 51: The Bantam Proving Sergeant Ross Correct—it could do anything. Source: United States National Archives, College Park, Maryland 115

Figure 52: John North Willys c. 1917. 119

Figure 53: John North Willys c. 1927. Courtesy of the Patrick Foster Historical Collection... 119

Figure 54: 1904 Overland Model 15. Courtesy of the Patrick Foster Historical Collection. 120

Figure 55: 1911 Overland Roadster. Courtesy of the Patrick Foster Historical Collection. 120

Figure 56: 1914 Overland Model 79C Coupe. Courtesy of the Patrick Foster Historical Collection... 120

Figure 57: 1927 Willys Whippett. Courtesy of the Patrick Foster Historical Collection. 121

Figure 58: 1921 Overland Roadster. Courtesy of the Patrick Foster Historical Collection. 121

Figure 59: Ward Murphey Canaday... 121

Figure 60: 1937 Willys Sedan. Courtesy of the Patrick Foster Historical Collection. . 121

Figure 61: Delmar Roos. Courtesy of the Patrick Foster Historical Collection.......... 123

Figure 62: General Walter Short. 125

Figure 63: Joseph Frazer 1942. Courtesy of the Patrick Foster Historical Collection. 126

Figure 64: Go Devil Four. Courtesy of the Patrick Foster Historical Collection. 130

Figure 65: Willys HQ 1927. Courtesy of the Patrick Foster Historical Collection. 137

Figure 66: Willys-Overland First Pilot Model 1940. Courtesy of the Patrick Foster Historical Collection.. 141

Figure 67: Willys Pilot Model with Delmar Roos. Courtesy of the Patrick Foster Historical Collection.. 142

Figure 68: Willys Pilot Model Demonstration. 144

Figure 69: U.S. Army Takes a Ride in the Willys-Overland First Pilot Model. 147

Figure 70: Willys-Overland First Pilot Model 1940. 150

Figure 71: 1910 Model T Ford. 151

Figure 72: 1941 Ford GP. 277,000 units were manufactured by Ford for the War. ... 153

Figure 73: Lt. Gen. Edmund B. Gregory. The Quartermaster General During World War II. 155

Figure 74: Secretary of War Henry L. Stimson. 157

Figure 75: Brigadier General J. E. Barzynski, while a West Point Cadet in early 1900s. 158

Figure 76: Emory Sherwood Adams at the start of his assignment as Adjutant General, 1938. 160

Figure 77: Major General Richard C. Moore, deputy to Chief of Staff General Marshall. 163

Figure 78: John D. Biggers. 166

Figure 79: Quartermaster Drawing QM08501-Z, October 26, 1940. Source: United States National Archives, College Park, Maryland. 167

Figure 80: "The engineers tore it down and then rebuilt." Source: United States National Archives, College Park, Maryland. 174

Figure 81: 1941 Willys-Overland MA. 177

Figure 82: The Willys-Overland 1942 MB. 360,000 units were manufactured for the War. Source: jeep.com 180

List of Tables

Table 1: ¼-Ton Truck 4x4 Light – Specification ES–No. 475 185

Table 2: Bantam Main Bid and Two Alternative Bids.. 187

Table 3: Bantam's Response to Army Requirements 188

Table 4: Technical Analysis of Bids Submitted 192

Table 5: Contract—Additional Requirements 193

Table 6: Parts: ¼-Ton, 4x4 Truck ("Jeep").. 195

Table 7: Inspection Report on Pilot model ¼-Ton, 4x4 (Bantam) Chassis.................. 197

Table 8: Test Report on Bantam, ¼-Ton, 4x4, Pilot Model....................................... 200

Table 9: Final Inspection Report on Pilot model ¼-Ton, 4x4 (Bantam) Chassis 201

Table 10: Willys' Response to ES-475 Requirements.. 203

Table 11: Willys-Overland Motors, Inc. Key Pilot Model Parts 207

Table 12: Ford Pilot Model Test Report 212

Table 13: Willys Pilot Model Test Report 213

Table 14: Willys MA General Specifications 215

Table 15: Comparison Chart—General Specifications of Original Jeeps 220

Foreword

I approached this new book *The Original Jeeps* with a certain amount of skepticism. As one who has written six books about Jeep plus one on Willys-Overland, I know how hard it is to locate authentic information about Willys Jeep products from that era. To dedicate an entire book to just the early Jeep vehicles seemed to me to be an overly-ambitious undertaking. However, Paul Bruno has been able to accomplish the job well; *The Original Jeeps* is a very good book indeed.

The author has managed to take dry facts and breathe new life in them. *The Original Jeeps* is fascinating, insightful and loaded with information. It tells the entire story of the Jeep's birth, development, and the complex bidding and contracting fight that went on while a World War was rapidly arriving. It even gives a good bit of background history on Willys-Overland's early days. The amount of detail is amazing.

All in all, this is a job well done and a worthy addition to any Jeep enthusiast's library.

—Patrick R. Foster, Historian/Author
Milford, Connecticut
www.oldemilfordpress.com

Preface

Destiny. The dictionary defines it as "a predetermined course of events often held to an irresistible power or agency," and "something to which a person or thing is destined." It is a concept that only hindsight tends to illuminate, and only when seen through the rearview mirror of history.

The spring and summer of 1940 witnessed the resounding defeat of the French Army and British Expeditionary Force at the hands of a modernized German Army, designed to take advantage of the latest advances in technology. This included mobile vehicles, tanks used in formation to puncture enemy lines, as well as close air support of ground forces. The evacuation of the British from Dunkirk, and the final defeat of their French ally in June 1940, left only a thin line of English fighter planes between that island nation and total defeat.

While events unfolded rapidly in Europe, leaders of the United States Army, decimated by demobilization after World War I and budget cuts during the Great Depression, knew they were completely unprepared for this new type of mobile warfare, called Blitzkrieg or "lightning war." Experts in the Army had worked from the end of World War I to develop a combined light weapons carrier and command/reconnaissance vehicle—but with limited success. In June 1940 the military compiled a list of requirements for a revolutionary new truck to replace the cart and mule as the Army's primary method of moving troops and small payloads.

This book tells the story of the American Bantam Car Company, Willys-Overland Motors, Inc. and the Ford Motor Company, who all dared to meet the challenge to build pilot models of this vehicle. Their journey throughout 1940 and into 1941 comprises a story from which legends come. Overcoming incredible challenges and long odds these firms built the first ¼-ton truck 4x4 "lights", later known as the iconic Jeep.

Introduction

The story of the creation of the original Jeeps dates to the very beginnings of the automotive era in the early 20th century, long before the fateful events during 1940 and into 1941. This period represented a free-wheeling time when numerous entrepreneurs defined and redefined the industry. From 1900-1920 they established the industry, and during the next twenty years the business matured until their products became an indispensable part of daily life for billions around the world.

The story of the creation of the first Jeep pilot models, from the lineage that birthed each, to the final acceptance of the Willys MA in May 1941, represents the subject matter of this book. The story encapsulates the spirit of the individuals who made up the early automobile industry, those hands-on, get-it-done, no-challenge-too-great personalities who got their hands dirty. We owe a debt to them for many of the wonders of the automobile we take for granted today.

Chapter 1: The United States Army between the Wars looks at the state of the American military during the interim between World War I and World War II. Understanding the needs and reality of the Army represents an important component for the development of the first Jeeps. There were various players within the Army including the Infantry, Cavalry, Field Artillery, and the Quartermaster branches, which all had their own agenda vis-à-vis the creation of a light vehicle.

Chapter 2: The American Bantam Car Company presents the history of the company and individuals who contributed in some manner to the eventual development of the Bantam Jeep pilot model. These range from Sir Herbert Austin and his vision for small cars, to Roy S. Evans, who single-handedly kept the firm which built the first prototype afloat during the Great Depression.

Chapter 3: Genesis of a Legend examines the various attempts by the United States Army to develop a light weapons carrier/reconnaissance and command car during the 1930s.

Chapter 4: What Do We Want? tells the story of how the Infantry developed the general characteristics for the vehicle and then documented them in the now-famous June 6, 1940 memo, recognized as the first "official" documentation of the Jeep procurement.

Chapter 5: A Vehicle Takes Shape looks at how the Quartermaster Corps turned the general characteristics into specifications from which an automobile manufacturer could build a vehicle.

Chapter 6: Bidding for the First Jeep documents how the Army determined the process they would use to choose a manufacturer to deliver a prototype and how the American Bantam Car Company won the award.

Chapter 7: Building the First Jeep recounts the formalization of the agreement between the Army and the American Bantam Car Company, as well as their efforts to hand-build their pilot model in the incredibly short time of forty-nine days.

Chapter 8: Testing and Accepting the BRC relates how the military put the Bantam Reconnaissance Car through a series of trials which the durable little vehicle successfully traversed, and the final acceptance of the Butler manufacturer's product.

Chapter 9: Willys-Overland Motors, Inc. recounts the history of that iconic automobile manufacturer and their early endeavors in the ¼-ton truck 4x4 light procurement.

Chapter 10: Willys Builds Pilots While Ford Emerges details the extraordinary journey the Willys team travelled to complete and deliver their prototype, as well as recounts a brief history of the Ford Motor Company and the creation of their pilot model.

Chapter 11: Competition describes the momentous events surrounding the procurement in the latter part of 1940 and early 1941, the results of the Willys' prototype's testing, as well as a description of the birth of the Willys MA.

Epilogue looks at the mystery of how the name Jeep became applied to the ¼-ton truck 4x4 light, a brief "rest of the story" after February 1941, and conclusion.

Chapter 1: The United States Army between the Wars

The United States Army, a victor in World War I, declined dramatically afterward. The "peace decade" of the 1920s combined with a woeful domestic economy, and rapid changes in internal affairs in the United States during the 1930s, played a significant role in the readiness of the Army for war in 1940. However, the precipitating events that provided the impetus for the military to modernize and initiate a procurement to develop a vehicle to move troops and small payloads to replace the cart and mule revolved around the need to respond to international events that resulted from the aftermath of the Great War.

Figure 1: British Troops in World War I Trench—Battle of the Somme, 1916.

The nations of Europe blundered their way into a cataclysmic war in the summer of 1914. The aging leaders of these states, operating from a 19th century mindset, thought a short war was in the offing. "It will be over by Christmas" many thought, but instead, they were embroiled in a conflagration of unprecedented proportions, due to new technology meeting outdated strategy and tactics. By the time of the signing of the armistice in November 1918, the war had claimed twenty-five million casualties and billions of dollars. This tremendous price in blood and treasure left many with a firm desire to avoid another global war at all costs.[1]

The United States had initially profited greatly from the European conflict by selling armaments to the Allies. America, since the founding of the Republic, had studiously avoided

Figure 2: President George Washington.

being embroiled in foreign conflict, following a policy of isolation from Europe set down by George Washington in his farewell address in 1796. When Woodrow Wilson brought the country into the war, he did so based on lofty progressive ideals encapsulated in the phrase, "the war to end all wars." When the fighting ended, and the American public counted their sacrifice, a large segment of the citizenry believed the United States' involvement not worth the cost. To add insult to injury, many in America believed the European countries the USA assisted did not appreciate its efforts. This reenergized the isolationism movement in the United States, which would play a critical role in the readiness of the United States Army in 1940.[2]

When the major belligerent powers met in Versailles, France in 1919 to draw up a peace treaty, the aims and goals of the victors did not align. France, the country which had suffered the most during the war, desired to punish and blame Germany for the conflict, exact as much payment from their defeated foe as possible, weaken their former combatant both economically and militarily, and restore their premier position on the continent. Britain wanted to restore the "balance of power" that, at least in the minds of English leaders, existed prior to 1914, and protect their empire. The idealistic Wilson's objectives focused on his famous "Fourteen Points" as articulated in a speech to Congress on January 8, 1918. In the end a compromise resulted that satisfied no one. It did not leave

Figure 3: Signing of the Treaty of Versailles, June 28, 1919.

Germany in a long-term weakened state. Moreover, the "unfairness" of the treaty would become the cause de jure in Germany that essentially fertilized the ground for the Nazi Party's rise to power in the early 1930s. French General Ferdinand Foch postulated after the signing that, "This is not a peace. It is an armistice for twenty years." His prophecy came true when war came again to Europe in 1939.[3]

While Wilson worked to resolve the immediate issues at the conference, his major aim focused on the establishment of a League of Nations based upon the last element of the Fourteen Points.

"A general association of nations must be formed under specific covenants for the purpose of affording mutual guarantees of political independence and territorial integrity to great and small states alike."[4]

Wilson received the Nobel Peace Prize in 1919 for his work to create this institution; however, his tireless efforts during the summer of 1919 to have the treaty confirmed by the United States Senate ended when he suffered a debilitating stroke. That left him unable to support the accord's ratification effort and the pact met an ignominious defeat in the United States Congress' upper house in 1920, reflecting the first waves of reinvigorated isolationism. America never joined the League of Nations, seriously hampering that organization's effectiveness.[5]

World War I significantly changed the economic dynamic in world trade. Throughout the 19th century a hegemonic Great Britain, bolstered by its early industrialization, large overseas Empire, and lack of another country threatening its status, acted as the stabilizing force in the global economy. The costs of World War I seriously damaged Britain's economy. The United States, in contrast, by sitting out most of the war, and profiting from it, suddenly became a major world economic power. The American public, and many of its leaders, did not embrace that role. Warren Harding's election to the Presidency in 1920 on the slogan, "a return to normalcy," cemented a policy of trying to "turn back the clock" in both domestic and foreign policy.[6]

The United States had a history of maintaining a weak military other than in times of conflict. The nation followed this course once again after World War I, rapidly demobilizing after the conflict. This tradition, along with two major threads that weaved their way throughout the 1920s, one domestically, one internationally, eroded the level of preparedness of the United States military, even before the devastating years of the 1930s. Three successive Republican Administrations which believed in very limited Federal spending constituted the first thread. President Calvin "Silent Cal" Coolidge epitomized this thinking and pursued a minimalist interventionist government policy. He encapsulated his understanding of the nation's destiny as, "the chief business of the American people is business."[7]

The emergence of a strong desire for "peace" among the nations of the world represented the second thread. This resulted from the fact that during the 1920s there did not exist a powerful nation which threatened to, much less start, a major conflict. This "peace movement" saw its expression in a number of treaties including the Washington Naval Treaty of 1922, which limited the number of capital ships of the signatories; the Locarno Treaty signed in 1926, which attempted to secure the post-war territorial arrangements, as well as restore relations with Germany; and the most ambitious of them all, the Kellogg-Briand Pact of 1928 (or Pact of Paris, officially General Treaty for Renunciation of War as an Instrument of National Policy), where the participating nations

Figure 4: Signatories to the Kellogg-Briand Pact at the United States White House.

promised not to use war to solve their foreign problems. Unfortunately, economic events in the 1930s overwhelmed the international idealism of the 1920s and would bring the world to war once again in 1939.[8]

The global economic crash of the third decade of the twentieth century and the actions of America, as well as other nations in combating the economic dislocation, led to increasing international tensions, and finally, to the outbreak of fighting in Europe at the end of the

Figure 5: Edouard Daladier, Premier of France with French Delegation to the London Economic Conference, June 1933.

1930s. The United States' decision to impose prohibitive tariffs on imports in 1930 to boost domestic production quickly led to other nations' pursuit of the same policy.

In 1931, the international banking system teetered on collapse, and when England left the gold standard to devalue the pound, it shook world markets. U.S. President Herbert Hoover's decision to suspend German reparations payments in 1932 kept the global economy from utterly failing. With the United States unwilling to assume a leadership role in the world economy and international relations, a vacuum occurred that hyper-nationalism filled. When world leaders met in the summer of 1933 at the London Conference to try to craft a comprehensive response for economic recovery, newly-elected United States President Franklin Roosevelt signaled that America would go it alone. The conference broke up soon after America's chief executive's beliefs became known. For the remainder of the decade nations worked independently to revive their economies.[9]

The worldwide economic instability led to political instability across the globe as the 1930s progressed. Bolshevism triumphed in the Russian civil war fought immediately after World War I. From the early 1920s through the 1930s, the Soviet Union remained an international pariah even with admittance to the League of Nations in 1934. An economically backward agricultural nation in 1914, communist leader Vladimir Lenin's successor, brutal dictator Joseph Stalin, led his country on a difficult forced path to industrialization, starting in the late 1920s and lasting through the 1930s.[10]

Fascism took hold in Italy in 1922 under Benito Mussolini and the economic chaos of the next decade cemented his power. The greatest national change precipitated by the economic chaos of the 1930s occurred in Germany when Adolf Hitler, the head of the Nationalist Socialists Workers or Nazi Party, became Chancellor of that nation in 1933. The new head of government worked quickly to replace the Weimar Republic with a totalitarian regime.

Dedicated entirely to German national interests, and a policy of territorial expansion, even at the risk of war, the rise to power of the Austrian artist, and veteran of four years in the trenches during World War I, had dire world consequences. Lastly, in the Far East, a militaristic Japan invaded Manchuria in 1931, to little effective response by the League of Nations or western world governments. By the middle of the decade that nation had embarked on a policy of aggressive regional expansion to create the Greater Eastern Co-Prosperity Sphere under that ancient island's leadership.[11]

Figure 6: The Burning of the German Reichstag on February 27, 1933, was a catalyst to help Adolf Hitler consolidate his power after his appointment as Chancellor of Germany on January 30, 1933.

The second crisis to shake the world order occurred in 1935 when Italy invaded Ethiopia in its first attempt to recreate the glory of the long-dead Roman Empire. The League of Nations response, which Japan had left in 1933, after censure over its adventurism in Manchuria, proved so ineffective the organization became irrelevant for the rest of its existence. The western reaction to this and future provocations, led by Britain and France, both severely weakened politically, economically and militarily, but still perceived by themselves and others as dominant world powers, led to a policy of "appeasement." This doctrine believed that Germany, Italy and Japan had some legitimate grievances and that avoidance of another major war by mollifying these issues would maintain world peace.[12]

Appeasement has garnered historical disdain; however, in the context of the 1930s the policy appeared reasonable. The western powers' miscalculated by believing their opponents' aims rested upon rational national self-interest with limited scope. Italy might have a reasonable case to make vis-à-vis its historic role in Africa, and its second class status as a colonial power in need of markets for its goods, to invade Ethiopia to add it to its sphere of influence. Japan, in need of raw materials and markets, also received the benefit of the doubt to some degree, and she took advantage of western immobilization to attack China in 1937.[13]

Appeasement met with total failure when applied to Nazi Germany. Hitler's aims, as described in his autobiography, *Mein Kampf* (My Struggle), stopped nothing short of total continental European domination, especially in Eastern Europe and the Soviet Union, to produce Lebensraum (living space) for the German people. Starting in 1936, Hitler proceeded to create one international crisis after another in the quest for European territorial hegemony, believing that weak and morally corrupt western nations would not oppose him.[14]

At first Hitler's gambles paid off as he occupied the Rhineland in 1936 in direct violation of the Versailles Treaty and also publicly announced a program of German rearmament, again in open defiance of the agreement ending World War I. Western leaders reluctantly opposed Hitler for a number of reasons, including the correct belief that their nation's citizens did not want another war, and the fact that due to the depression these nations remained militarily weak. While Britain and France began their own rearmament programs in the late 1930s (as well as the United States) they perceived their military strength as deficient to Germany's, at least into the middle of 1939.[15]

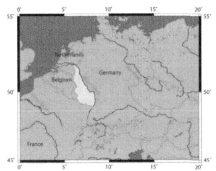

Figure 7: Location of the Rhineland circa 1936 when Hitler annexed it in violation of the Treaty of Versailles.

The policy of appeasement could entertain that Germany had some rightful argument in relation to the Rhineland, and its desire for Anschluss with Austria (completed in 1938), and for annexing the German-speaking Sudetenland of Czechoslovakia, which was done under the auspices of the 1938 Munich agreement. When Hitler annexed the rest of Czechoslovakia in March 1939, Britain and France had reached the end of their patience and what the policy of appeasement would allow. As the summer of 1939 wore on it became apparent that Poland fell next on Hitler's list, and the two former World War I allies issued public statements that war would result if Germany violated Polish sovereignty.[16]

The war that found England, France and the United States unprepared for erupted on September 1, 1939, when Germany invaded its eastern neighbor. The invasion came just weeks after a shocked world learned that Hitler and Stalin had signed a non-aggression pact. Later events would reveal the pact included a secret codicil that partitioned the Polish state between them. Britain and France declared war on September 3, 1939, but could not assist the Poles, who surrendered by the end of the month. Germany displayed its new tactics of mobile warfare, but the weakness of the Polish army took the blame for the resounding defeat. The conflict then entered a phase known now as the "phony war" in which neither side made any moves militarily, but during which time Hitler prepared his forces for an invasion of France.[17]

Figure 8: German Soldiers Passing the Arc de Triomphe in Paris on June 14, 1940, after the fall of France. Attribution: Bundesarchiv, Bild 101I-126-0347-09A / Gutjahr / CC-BY-SA

The denouement to the "peace movement" in the 1920s, and economic dislocation in the 1930s, came swiftly in the spring and early summer of 1940. Germany invaded Denmark and Norway in April and the British and French response proved weak and uncoordinated. Then, on May 10, 1940, Hitler unleashed his panzers against the Low Countries of the Netherlands and Belgium and then moved rapidly into France. Within weeks the British Expeditionary Force (BEF) fled the continent and the Third Reich defeated the French army by the end of June.[18]

These events shocked the American public and a Congress that had only recently begun to release funds for rearmament. The defeat of France, and new funds for the military, led to an initial burst of activity to modernize the United States' armed forces, actions that would lead the Army to seek a vehicle to replace the horse and mule.

Despite increasing world tensions in the second half of the 1930s, the American army in 1939 remained undermanned and ill-equipped from its low point in 1933. This was primarily due to public apathy during the peace period, parsimonious Presidents and Congresses during the 1920s, a lack of funds during the economically depressed 1930s, and ignorance on the part of the public, and by extension, its representatives in Congress and the Presidency, on the needs of a peacetime national defense.[19]

Figure 9: The United States' M1 Combat Car light tank used by the Cavalry in the late 1930s was no match for Hitler's Panzers.

The origins of the Army's deterioration began immediately following World War I. The nation, adhering to its tradition of no standing armies in peacetime, fell into an all too familiar pattern after demobilization as outlined in *Chief of Staff: Prewar Plans and Preparations*:

Prior to a war, insufficient military expenditures, based on the public's prewar conviction that war could not come to America;

Discovery that war could come after all;

A belated rush for arms, men, ships, and planes to overcome the nation's demonstrated military weakness;

Advance of the producing and training program, attended by misunderstandings, delays and costly outlay, but gradual creation of a large and powerful army;

Mounting success in the field and eventual victory;

Immediately thereafter, rapid demobilization and dissolution of the Army as a powerful fighting force; and,

Sharp reduction of appropriations sought by the military establishment, dictated by concern over high cost and for a time by the revived hope that, again, war would not come to America.[20]

Figure 10: Harking back to George Washington's Farewell Address a No Foreign Entanglements anti-war protest sign.

America again followed this paradigm after World War I, fueled by historic precedent, and aided by the public's perception of a seemingly wasted and underappreciated sacrifice during World War I. When Warren Harding won the American presidency on a promise of a "return to normalcy" the return to a weak military proved unstoppable. While the 1920 National Defense Act authorized a peacetime Army strength of 280,000 enlisted men, that figure was never attained during the interwar years.[21]

Harding and his extremely tight-fisted successor, Coolidge, would, along with a compliant Congress, significantly underfund the War Department during the decade of "peace." In 1929, newly inaugurated President Hoover ordered a review of the War Department's needs, but the stock market crash of the fall of that year and subsequent Great Depression effectively ended any opportunity to address the military's continued slide into decay and disrepair. The United States Army reached its lowest preparedness point in 1933, right when events birthed the leader (Hitler), and causes (German remilitarization and territorial expansion) that would eventually lead to the outbreak of war in 1939.[22]

The over-arching policy of a military force dedicated solely to defensive actions, combined with scant funding through the middle of the 1930s, seriously hampered the Army's ability to bring on line new equipment, especially any which appeared to enhance offensive operations. While inadequate and poorly trained personnel proved the norm during this period, obsolete and ill-repaired equipment also became standard operating procedure.[23]

This lack of motivation to bring newer military hardware on line rested on the belief in the public's mind, and especially in Congress, of the need to use the overwhelming amount of surplus leftover from World War I before investing in modern arms. This policy had two fatal flaws: 1) over time this stock would become obsolete as technology rapidly advanced during the period, and 2) aging equipment needs ever-increasing maintenance, making it ostensibly more expensive than new purchases. By the low point in 1933 the active strength of the United States Army ranked 17th in the world.[24]

While the world moved inexorably toward war as the 1930s progressed, the United States military continued to work under the handicap of the 1920s "decade of peace," which had

Figure 11: British Prime Minister Neville Chamberlain holding the Munich Agreement upon his return from that city on September 30, 1938. The agreement would hold for only six months when Hitler annexed the remainder of Czechoslovakia.

spawned a small, but politically powerful "pacifist" movement, that when combined with America's traditionally strong isolationism faction, created strong political opposition to anything "military." The decade of depression also starved the War Department of funds. During the middle of the decade the Roosevelt Administration and Congress made some minor adjustments in military spending, in particular authorizing some naval ship-building and munitions manufacture under the guise of making work for the unemployed. Political opposition to these moves ended any use of relief funds for "weapons of war" in 1937.[25]

While America's future enemies built modern, mobile armies, the United States fell further and further behind during Roosevelt's first two terms. A 1936 directive halted expenditures on research and development (R & D) for "unessential equipment" when "the Army needs large quantities of excellent equipment already developed." Caught between a rock and a hard place of investing in equipment that would produce improved weaponry in the future, or the bird in the hand of obtaining men and material that provided an immediate betterment of a force, but possessing obsolete and failing equipment, the Army made the difficult decision to deemphasize research and development. The Army Air Corps and general defense received priority for what little funds went into R & D.

Detection of the approach of hostile aircraft;

Development of fire-control equipment for antiaircraft artillery and aircraft cannons;

Rapid methods of aerial mapping and map reproduction;

Development of anti-mechanized weapons;

Development of aircraft and their propulsion; and,

Improvement of air navigation equipment.[26]

Four years later a different set of priorities would lead directly to the truck ¼-ton light procurement when the Blitzkrieg of 1940 demonstrably showed the need for a small mobile vehicle.

In 1938 the realization that Germany represented a serious threat to world peace became apparent in the aftermath of the Munich agreement. In October of that year a conference at the White House discussed increased military spending at the highest levels of government.[27] However, throwing money at the problem could not make up for the one deficiency that funds can't overcome: time. In 1939, outgoing Chief of Staff General Malin Craig warned,

> "...the sums appropriated this year will not be fully transformed into military power for two years. Persons who state they see no threat to the peace of the United States would hesitate to make that forecast through a two-year period..."[28]

In the early 1930s the United States had the time, but not the money or incentive to modernize its military; however, by 1939 the money started to flow, but time had run out.

The period between the fall of Poland and the beginning of the Blitzkrieg in Western Europe saw incremental movement in the direction for American military modernization and rearmament. Even with the outbreak of war in Europe, the strong isolationist and pacifist sentiments in the United States made a full-blown effort politically difficult. This proved especially true in the Presidential election year of 1940, with Chief Executive Roosevelt eyeing an unprecedented third term. Though America's 33rd President increasingly desired to assist the Allies, especially after the fall of France in June 1940, his own re-election effort that emphasized he kept America out of the war hamstrung his efforts. The various Neutrality Acts passed between 1935 and 1939 also hampered American assistance to England, the only country fighting Nazi Germany in 1940.[29]

Figure 12: Soldiers of the United States First Army
Prepare to Fire Large Artillery Piece During
Summer Maneuvers in 1940. Used with permission
from Town of De Kalb. New York Historian's

The low state of preparedness of the United States armed forces became apparent in maneuvers conducted during the summer of 1940. The National Guard division strengths listed on paper as 22,000 were actually at half strength; many divisions did not have newer mortars or antitank guns, and only 25% of its quota of rifles, some of the "cannons" just iron pipes, "tanks" simulated using trucks, and "bombers" just light observation planes.[30]

Professional judgment noted problems with:

1) Tank and plane formations as well as equipment;

2) Challenges in defense against modern weapons; and,

3) Low marks in experience, discipline, leadership, supply, communications reconnaissance, liaison, and sanitation.[31]

One American witness commented, "Just visited the maneuvers and thought they were lousy. The troops appeared deficient in fundamentals of minor tactics, could not maintain contact with hostile forces, permitted gaps in the line, etc. Combat intelligence very poor." More ominous still came the view from overseas. In particular, came the Soviet assessment, the country which found out in 1941 that their military could not match German arms. Mirroring General Craig's assessment, the USSR opined that America's military existed in a low state of training. They observed, prophetically, that, "the potential capacity of American industry is tremendous, but it is much more difficult to teach men to use arms in battle."[32]

The sudden and shocking Axis victory in May–June 1940 did open up an opportunity for increased appropriations to the United States military. The overwhelming display of mobility and mechanization led to issuance of directives on August 20, 1940, that greatly altered research priorities from the 1936 orders as follows:

Modification of antiaircraft guns and fire control for use against ground targets:

Development of tanks or armored vehicles for use as observation posts;

Further development of reconnaissance vehicles;

Development of personnel carriers;

Equipment for landing operations, including boats for installation on Army transports;

Antitank shoulder rifle; and,

Communications system for co-ordination of air support for ground units.[33]

Item number 3 provided official confirmation that the project to procure the truck ¼-ton 4x4 light begun in June 1940 reflected a top priority for the future.

Chapter 2: The American Bantam Car Company

The American Bantam Car Company played a critical role in the development of the Jeep. The background and history of that firm provide insight as to why this company figured so prominently in the initial stages of the Army's ¼-ton truck 4x4 light procurement.

American Austin Car Company

Figure 13: Sir Herbert Austin

Herbert Austin, born in England in 1866 to a farming family, led an entrepreneurial life. He immigrated with his uncle to Australia in 1884 and his interest in mechanics and engineering led him to work at the Wolseley Sheep-Shearing Machine Company, Ltd. His talent at improving sheep hand clippers persuaded many Outback shepherds to put down their trusted tool in exchange for a mechanized version the English transplant had developed.[34] By the age of 27, Austin became the firm's manager and his success brought him to the attention of the company's directors. He eventually came back to the mother country to oversee operations at the factory in Birmingham.[35]

Austin's inquisitive mind led him to the fledgling automobile industry before the 19th century ended. By 1901 he had designed his first automobile and he continued to improve upon his designs over the next two years.[36] In 1905 Sir Herbert and the board of directors disagreed over the vision for the future of the motor car division, with the board believing that larger cars with heftier engines were the future, while Austin believed the opposite. After the two parted ways he had a change of heart and over the rest of the decade, and into the 1910s, he built a bigger car with more cylinders. On the eve of the First World War, Austin's company, the Austin Motor Car Company of Birmingham, built and shipped primarily four-cylinder engines, about a thousand units a year.[37]

The war years saw Austin put his mechanical talents to use producing munitions, which resulted in knighthood. As the conflict ended Sir Herbert embraced his automotive future. His experience during the hostilities led him to conclude that mass production of one model represented the wave of the future. He designed, manufactured, and marketed the Austin Twenty, which had modestly successful sales.[38]

With the British economy in the doldrums after the war, Sir Herbert decided to downsize the vehicle, and he marketed a new version, the Austin Twelve, which also had modest sales. The English economy of the early 1920s continued to languish and that fact, combined with labor and raw material problems, led him to think even smaller.[39] During this time the motorcycle with a sidecar became popular in England and the essence of a small vehicle which could transport a few people and baggage germinated in the mind of Sir Herbert to compete with that product. The high price of gasoline, short driving distances, and an exponential increase in passable roads, also provided fertile ground for smaller vehicles.[40]

His mechanical skills still sharp in his 50s, Austin designed a brilliant small car, the Austin Seven, which debuted in July 1922. This car, about the same size as a motorcycle with a sidecar, proved immensely popular.[41] The Austin Seven fit the English market well with its high gasoline prices and the short driving distances. The Seven proved exportable to the European continent which had the same consumer dynamics. By the end of 1928 production in Germany and France had expanded the Seven's sales, but Sir Herbert had his eyes on an even bigger marketplace.[42]

Figure 14: 1926 Austin 7 Coupe—
The Great Grandfather of the
Jeep Prototype

The automobile industry in the United States had blossomed during the 1920s with—similar to Europe—an increase in traversable roads, but combined with two opposite dynamics than the Old World: low gasoline prices and long driving distances. Numerous manufacturers willingly produced vehicles for the motoring public and the general feeling of prosperity during the boom years following the 1921 – 1922 recession fueled rapid growth. The Ford Model T dominated the landscape, and later in the decade, the Model A would appear.[43]

General Motors and Chrysler would also grow dramatically during the decade and numerous niche players abounded. In 1929 the American market did not have a small car offering and the demand for one seemed non-existent. However, all these facts did not deter the irrepressible Sir Herbert from attempting to bring the Austin Seven to the United States.[44]

January 1929 saw Sir Herbert and his bride, Lady Austin, in New York City with the intent to show off his products at the New York National Automobile Show. He intended to raise the financing and find the partners to manufacture and sell Austins in the United States under the banner of the American Austin Car Company, formed in February of that year. 1929 saw the peak of the stock market run-up on Wall Street during the 1920s, and American Austin's initial public offering sold briskly.[45]

The search for a location for the home of the American Austin Car Company factory also proved fruitful with the selection of the small city of Butler, Pennsylvania. This city had a forward-thinking business community and a workforce with the skills to manufacture cars. Butler also possessed the additional advantage of having an idle automobile factory within its confines, the former home of the Standard Steel Car Company, which had gone bankrupt in 1923. Arthur J. Brandt, a former General Motors executive, purchased the buildings and became the director of the American Austin Car Company. The future appeared bright for a small car in the United States.[46]

Before Butler could produce cars in 1929, the Austin models needed redesigning to fit the United States market. Although the vehicles' mechanical structure would resemble its European cousin, including the engine and chassis, the English styling needed Americanization. Alexis de Sakhnoffsky of the Hayes Body Company, a leading custom coachwork designer of the time, submitted a model that improved the lines of the Austin, which helped mask the smallness of the car, undoubtedly a concession to the tastes of the American consumer.[47] While completing the final touches to the vehicle the company's infrastructure, including purchasing, marketing, production and engineering came on-line. All this effort took time, and 1929 slipped by without a single model rolling off the assembly line in Butler.[48]

1930 dawned and with it the cold winds of change. The American and world stock markets had crashed during the fall of 1929, dramatically altering the economic landscape. The transformed commercial conditions did not deter Sir Herbert, Brandt and the officers of the American Austin Car Company from visiting Butler on January 4th of that year to meet with city officials and inspect the factory.[49]

Sir Hubert displayed three prototypes in New York City in February 1930 and dealers lined up to sign on to sell the new economy car. It would take another five months to bring production up to speed, but the assembly line began to hum in May and the first product delivered to dealer showrooms in June.[50]

The vehicles delivered represented masterpieces in small car engineering. The basic Austin specifications of a 75-inch wheelbase, 40-inch tread, 122-inch and 53-inch length and width, 60.5-inch coupe height, 8.75-inch ground clearance with a total weight of 1,130 pounds remained even with American styling. The car measured sixteen inches narrower and twenty-eight inches shorter than any vehicle on the American market and had an astonishing turning ratio of sixteen feet. These Austin basics would prove extremely valuable ten years later when the Army needed a small vehicle weighing a quarter ton. Priced at a competitive $445 f.o.b. Butler, the company appeared poised for success.[51]

American Austin had a product and a distribution network, but customers remained another matter. With the market dynamics exactly opposite those of Europe (cheap gas and long driving distances), the leaders of the firm had to devise a compelling selling proposition for the American consumer.[52]

Their solution, which would remain consistent for the life of the company, argued that the American Austin was not built to replace an individual's larger car, but to provide a cost-effective alternative for local driving. This vision would attract Roy S. Evans to embrace the Austin line. The question remained, would the American buying public embrace the small car?[53]

The answer, similar to the 1970s during the initial oil crisis of the second half of the twentieth century, came back a resounding no. Even though Sir Herbert announced in the summer of 1930 pre-orders of 184,117 units and 19,300 dealers applying to carry the brand, these numbers had no basis in fact.[54]

While the American Austin received extremely favorable public relations, word-of-mouth advertising, and became a household word during 1930, the worsening Depression had a major impact on the American and world economies. Auto sales for 1930 tanked, and no matter how good the vision, advertising and public relations, the firm could not overcome economic reality. The America Austin Car Company sold only 8,558 units in 1930.[55]

At this juncture the company made a fatal error, common to many automotive manufacturers in dire financial straits, when they invested their financial reserves into extending the model line of a product that did not sell. An additional coupe line came on-line (standard and deluxe), a business and cabriolet coupe introduced, and the American Austin Roadster was retained.[56]

Figure 15: 1931 American Austin Roadster—
The Grandfather of the Jeep Prototype.
Photo used with permission from Dale Lynn James.

This strategy proved futile in igniting demand. Along with fighting market fundamentals, such as the American public's reluctance to embrace small vehicles, the availability of cheap gas and the long driving distances, the stark fact remained that the American Austin Car Company had the unfortunate timing of entering the American market at the beginning of the worst economic crisis that country and the world had ever faced. While many still did not understand the magnitude of the disaster facing them in 1930 Sir Herbert and his team faced strong headwinds in 1930 and 1931.[57]

American Austin sales tanked in 1931 to a paltry 1,279 units and as 1932 dawned liquidation of the company seemed the logical course. Reuben O. Gill came aboard to replace Brandt as President and General Manager, with his only duty being to preside over the organization's demise, including disposing of 1,500 unfinished vehicles. However, logic does not always sway a man with a vision, as well as the energy and the means to reach for that vision.[58]

American Bantam Car Company

The aforementioned Roy S. Evans possessed the skills of the consummate salesman. Born in 1900 at the dawn of the automotive industry, Evans grew up in the rural community of Bartow, Georgia, where he went to work at the age of eight due to the death of his father.[59] He started in newspapers, moved into shoe shines, then a peanut stand (a natural for Georgia!). In 1914 he started a taxi service where young Roy transported passengers around Bartow in a

Figure 16: 1911 Maxwell Mascotte Touring Car.

borrowed Maxwell touring car in which he agreed to get his hands dirty maintaining and repairing the vehicle in exchange for using it. This introduced Evans' to the automotive world.[60]

The young entrepreneur graduated from high school, operated a "news butch" venture on passenger trains, and eventually became a clerk for the Central Bank of Georgia. He raced motorcycles for a short time, but they proved too dangerous. He sold his two-wheeler, and with the proceeds bought a Model T, rebuilt it and fell in love with the automobile. He became a used car salesman, and after graduating from Georgia Tech in the early 1920s, he opened a used car shop. After disastrous experiences during the Florida land bubble in the mid-1920s, Evans settled down into the car business, and with his indefatigable energy, became the largest automotive dealer in the South by 1932.[61]

With the deepening of the depression many businesses found themselves with excess inventory. While difficult times present numerous challenges, opportunity often lurks among the distressing news. Roy Evans had learned this lesson, having bounced back from the Sunshine State land speculation debacle. With money in the bank, a substantial credit line, and the network to distribute the merchandise, the Bartow entrepreneur sat in a perfect position to take advantage of large supply and low demand to buy in volume at low prices.[62]

Evans had signed on early to sell the American Austin line and grew into the firm's biggest customer, accounting for eighty percent of sales. Evans noticed that when the American Austin appeared in 1930, the cars generated tremendous "buzz" among his customers. Most importantly, he truly believed in the small car concept for the American market and that the Austin fit that need. This belief drove Evans to single-handedly keep the small car alive during the 1930s.[63]

The opportunistic car dealer struck a deal with Gill where he purchased the excess inventory of 1,500, had the vehicles completed, and sold the whole consignment at the bargain-basement price of $295 per unit. Evans, the true believer in the small car, put his money behind the venture and agreed to assume management, as well as to finance the whole American Austin Car Company operation. Gill convinced suppliers that if the firm went under, their inventory would end up a total loss, as the components proved unusable in any other vehicles. In the age-old tradition of self-interest, they priced their merchandise competitively. The company had a pulse, if a faint one, as Roy Evans went all-in.[64]

Evans' resuscitation efforts appeared to pay off as sales in 1932 rebounded to 3,846 and 1933 saw a modest improvement to 4,726, truly remarkable figures given that the Great Depression bottomed out during those years. Franklin Delano Roosevelt assumed the Presidency of the United States in 1933 and his New Deal programs went into full swing as

1934 dawned and the future again appeared bright for the American Austin Car Company. Unfortunately these sales levels proved unsustainable and purchases plummeted in 1934 to the point the money ran out and the firm declared bankruptcy in June. Production continued to the end of the year with 1,300 units completed. In less than two years the firm returned to the land of the living dead.[65]

While some minor activity continued at the Butler factory maintaining the Austin market (parts and service), and the factory's excellent machine shop brought in some revenue filling odd jobs, the fact remained that the American Austin Car Company again faced oblivion, but fate hadn't met Roy Evans. The Bartow businessman remained committed to the vision of a small car in the driveway of every American, but he needed to dive further into the deep end financially to keep that vision alive.[66]

The man who in 1926 had traded his last valuable possession to buy, refurbish and sell one car that became the genesis of his business empire, took a gamble and rolled the dice. He arranged with the factory's mortgage holder to reduce the principal and interest as well as grant a two-year mortgage extension, and negotiated with Butler city officials to have back taxes and interest forgiven.[67] Lastly, in the fall of 1935, the United States Federal Court accepted Evans' token payment of $5,000 on an asset valued at $10 million, and the Georgia entrepreneur had bought the factory! If Evans had gone all-in during 1932, he now swam in the deep end without a life jacket![68]

The Bartow entrepreneur, now working with his key lieutenant, William A. Ward Jr., went to Wall Street during 1936 to raise capital, and two brokers signed up to handle the sale of both common and preferred stock. During 1936 a serendipitous association during the heyday of the early Austin models would enter history. When the initial cars appeared on the American market the term Bantam had become associated with the new vehicles, probably a reference to the miniature chickens of the same name, as the public viewed the cars as "miniatures."[69] The name stuck even though the company never produced an Austin Bantam. Evans, ever the pragmatist, decided to make lemonade out of lemons, and when he registered the new firm on June 2, 1936, he named it the American Bantam Car Company.[70]

Evans, installed as president and chairman of the board, went about creating an entirely new team to manufacture cars in Butler. Numerous individuals came and went, but one whom fate would slot for immortality, Harold Crist, became plant manager and chief engineer. Crist got his hands dirty, which would prove beneficial during the hectic days building the Jeep prototype.[71]

Before Crist answered destiny's call, American Bantam had to sell cars as soon as possible. The enterprising Evans reached into his network of contacts, which once again brought Alexis de Sakhnoffsky, the preeminent coachwork designer who had created the original "American" look for the American Austin Car Company, back to Butler. De Sakhnoffsky created new designs in just three days and charged Evans just $300.00 to cover his expenses. With de

Sakhnoffksy's designs relying completely on the original American Austin features, the Bantam team was able to retool to build the new models for a paltry $7,000. Evans and his team made up the playbook during the game, and to say they were operating on a shoestring would insult the shoestring.[72]

Figure 17: 1939 American Bantam Roadster—The Father of the Jeep Prototype. Photo used with permission from Dale Lynn James.

While the Bantam team frantically attempted to bring the factory on-line, bad news struck during the summer of 1937, when Evans found out that the two Wall Street brokers had swindled him by selling off their common stock and absconding with their ill-gotten gains. With the company once again on the brink Evans thought outside the box, and turned to the government for help.[73] He sent his trusted aide, Ward, to Washington, D.C. and secured a $250,000 loan from the Reconstruction Finance Corporation (RFC) with a lien against the factory to keep the lights on.[74]

The old adage states that "necessity is the mother of invention" and necessity dictated that the American Bantam Car Company find every way to save money. This led Evans to the fateful decision of eliminating the use of exclusive parts and building his vehicles from as many standard items as possible. It was this use of off-the-shelf parts that proved a critical skill when the Bantam team built their Jeep pilot model in 1940. Standardization would also rank as a major concern for the United States Army when they needed a new vehicle in the summer of 1940.[75]

All the effort paid off in the fall of 1937 when the first American Bantam models entered the market. Production ramped up, and by early 1938, the factory functioned again. The Bantam, thanks to Harold Crist and his team, proved a state-of-the-art small car, and the little company in Butler, Pennsylvania became the unlikely, and singular depository of expertise on economy automobiles in the United States.[76]

Initial orders appeared strong, and discussions held about entering foreign markets. The individuals who purchased Bantams, similar to their predecessors with the American Austin, raved about them; however, sales remained anemic in 1938 at a paltry 2,000 units.[77]

Similar to the American Austin Car Company, the American Bantam firm became the victim of another case of bad timing. While the demand for small cars by the American buying public remained lukewarm at best, it did not help that the first Bantam models appeared during the recession of the late 1930s. As the Roosevelt Administration slowed government spending in 1937 to ostensibly balance the Federal government budget, the private sector United States economy had not grown enough during the middle 1930s to absorb the reduction. The ensuing recession would make Bantam's already dim prospects of success virtually impossible. That would not stop Roy Evans from trying.[78]

The story of how the Bantam Hollywood convertible model came to being in 1939 perfectly illustrates the innovative culture instilled by the personality of Roy Evans into the

American Bantam Car Company that would prove so pivotal a year later. The Georgia businessman, among his many talents, was a pilot, having learned to fly in the 1920s. He used this skill to keep abreast of his far-flung dealership network which included outlets in Los Angeles. On a visit in the last year of the 1930s he went to see one Alex Tremulis, a custom body expert operating out of Beverly Hills, to have side curtains installed on his Bantam Roadster. While Evans wanted curtains, the Californian had other ideas.[79]

Figure 18: 1940 American Bantam Hollywood Convertible Developed by Alex Tremulis. Used with permission from Conceptcarz.com.

When Evans saw Tremulis and asked for his curtains the enterprising body man countered by proposing a "Bantam Convertible" and he could make one by being supplied with a coupe from which he would shear off the roof! Evans' go-getter, can-do personality couldn't resist the challenge, and he had one delivered in an hour. The innovator spent just one night designing the convertible, and when he presented the plans the next day to Evans, the Chairman of the Board of the American Bantam Car Company approved them on the spot. Tremulis told Evans he could build the car in ten days. He immediately returned to his shop and cut off the roof of Evans' coupe. Later that afternoon Evans visited and had intentions of backing out of the deal, but when he saw that his vehicle had no roof he rolled with the punches and changed his mind. Tremulis built the vehicle in ten days and delivered it to Butler shortly thereafter.[80]

Figure 19: Roy S. Evans (third from right and inserts) and the Bantam Team circa 1939. Sources (main): George Edward Domer, *Automotive Quarterly,* Fall 1976; (inserts): John W. Underwood, Heritage Press, 1965

Evans ordered the new convertible into production. Harold Crist and others worked diligently during 1938 and 1939 to improve every aspect of the Bantam's line engineering. The firm had excellent, high-quality products, which represented the state-of-the-art for small cars at the time, but nobody wanted them. Sales for 1939 came in at a meager 1,225 units, and while further aesthetic and mechanical improvements completed for the 1940 line, sales continued to plummet to only 800 units for that year. By June of the first year of the fourth decade of the twentieth century, the firm once again faced bankruptcy. All seemed lost until Roy Evans decided to roll the dice one last time.[81]

During 1938 and 1939, while American Bantam focused primarily on the commercial market, they did begin to mine another consumer that the American Austin Car Company had only cursorily explored. American Austin had supplied some vehicles to the United States Army in 1932, but this initial effort fizzled due to Austin's bankruptcy, and the Army's dire budget constraints caused by the Depression. With war not imminent, no urgency existed in the military to develop small vehicles.

That urgency changed in 1940 and with it immediately brought the American Bantam Car Company to the front lines of the truck ¼-ton 4x4 light procurement.

PAUL R. BRUNO

Chapter 3: Genesis of a Legend

Figure 20: The Mule—Primary Transport for Troops and Small Payloads the U.S. Army was Looking to Replace with A Small Vehicle.

Due to technological advancements during the period between the world wars the need for an all-terrain vehicle for reconnaissance, and to move troops and small payloads to replace the cart and mule as well as the motorcycle with sidecar became apparent to the military. The ½-ton truck, which represented the lightest truck in the United States Army arsenal at the time, did not fit the task. The tank had broken the stalemate of the Western Front in 1918, but rapid advances in mobility, especially by the Germans, pushed the envelope on vehicle technology and led to the need for a ¼-ton vehicle in the Army's fleet.

Increased mobility represented the most critical problem that confronted American military leaders after World War I. A lack of funds hamstrung the armed services in all areas of research and development, especially during the 1930s, and that included vehicle experimentation. The need to replace animal-based transportation which now proved too slow, cumbersome and vulnerable, became paramount. The motorcycle with sidecar proved dangerous to operate, and performed poorly in cross-country conditions. The need evolved into a desire for a light, highly mobile car that operated effectively in all circumstances.[82]

Figure 21: 1930s era US Military Motorcycle with Sidecar Which Was Unsatisfactory for Modern Mobile Cavalry Uses. Used with permission from Auburn University Libraries Special Collections–Everett Leavins Papers.

During the 1930s, the Infantry, despite a lack of funds, and in response to urgency on the part of the American public and its leaders that war loomed, expended the most effort of any service branch to solve the issue from their perspective. The Infantry Board, the committee tasked with developing and testing equipment for foot soldiers, had worked on the issue for many years. The Chief of Infantry summarized the issue in a July 26, 1938, memo from that office to the Adjutant General.[83]

> In the opinion of the Chief of Infantry, the lack of a suitable automotive carrier for the heavier Infantry weapons and their ammunition on the battlefield is the greatest deficiency in Infantry equipment today. Infantry weapons requiring transportation are the machine gun and mortars. The transportation provided at present consists of animal-drawn carts in those regiments in which the combat trains are animal-drawn, and 1½-ton trucks, supplemented by hand

carts, in those regiments which are completely motorized. The Caliber .50 Machine Gun with its transportation is to be replaced by the 37 mm Antitank Gun with prime mover … the type of mover included in the estimates for fiscal year 1940 is the four-wheel, four-wheel-drive, ½-truck chassis with pick-up body.

With the exception of the prime mover for the antitank gun, the present methods of transporting the heavier Infantry weapons with their ammunition show little improvement over the methods employed during the World War. They will not permit the weapons to advance as rapidly as, and to remain in close support of, the rifle elements due to the following limitations:

Attempts were made during the World War to use a mule cart but the vulnerability of the mule and leader, the size of the target presented, and the slow rate of progress across country, made this method entirely impractical under battle conditions. This resulted in the weapons having to be man-carried during forward displacements. It is reasonable to assume that similar conditions will exist in the next war if reliance is placed upon the mule cart as a weapons carrier.

The 1½-ton truck now used in motorized regiments is unsatisfactory for road movements, and it may be that these vehicles can be used in the early stages of development for offensive action. However, it seems certain that trucks of this size, due to their weight, conspicuous silhouette and limited cross-country ability, will be impractical in cross-country movements to assembly areas and subsequent movements to initial and to successive attack positions. To provide some means of transporting the weapons from the point where it is necessary to detruck to the forward positions, hand carts were adopted in lieu of a satisfactory automotive vehicle for the purpose. The use of hand carts entails the same disadvantages as the use of mule carts. While the carts themselves are light (90 pounds), the loads placed on the carts average between 250 to 300 pounds. To move these carts over rough ground at least two men are required to pull and, dependent upon the nature of the terrain, additional men must push. The rate of movement over long distances is not much more than a mile an hour. Progress necessarily is slow, and the men present a conspicuous target. While the use of hand carts may be practical in the advance to initial positions, man-carrying the weapons will be required in moving to successive attack positions.

Man-carrying these heavier Infantry weapons is a very slow, arduous procedure and is impractical except for short distances due to the weights involved. The average weight of the material that the members of the various gun crews must carry is 30 pounds in the Caliber .30 Machine Gun and the 60 mm Mortar squads; and 44 pounds in the 81 mm Mortar squad. Practical loads for the ammunition carriers of the various weapon squads are 42 pounds (2 boxes of 250 rounds each) in the Caliber .30 Machine Gun squad; 36 pounds (10 rounds in apron) in the 60 mm Mortar squad; 49–56 pounds (either 7 light shells at 7 pounds or 4 heavy shells at 14 pounds) in the 81 mm Mortar squad. Due to the type of material, the loads are necessarily unwieldy and cumbersome, and when man-carried, progress is slow and very fatiguing to the men.[84]

The Infantry's needs centered on weapons carrying; however, other branches had a need for a small vehicle, notably the Cavalry for reconnaissance patrol. The search commenced for a solution to this frustrating problem.

1932: The Austin

Figure 22: 1932 American Austin Roadster—Possibly the Model or a Similar Model Purchased by the Infantry for Testing in 1932. Source: sportscarmarket.com

In 1932 the Infantry Board requested procurement of an Austin roadster with oversized tires for testing at Fort Benning, Georgia, noting the problems with the motorcycle with sidecar. That group had heard reports that the British Army had used the car extensively with good results for "reconnaissance and messenger service." The Quartermaster General's office, while acknowledging the desirability of testing the Austin, replied that funds to make the purchase did not exist, "the Army Appropriations Act did not authorize the purchase of any automobiles for the Regular Army during the present fiscal year." Soon thereafter, the War Department did find the funding in the Quartermaster's budget to purchase "one or two Austin's of the reconnaissance truck type, carrying two passengers and having a pick-up body."[85]

The military purchased one Austin for $268.75 and sent it to Fort Benning for testing. While the Roadster did not meet Army requirements this interest in Austin products served as an initial performance indicator for small vehicles. Some of the parts from this car ended up in the Fort Benning salvage (junk) yard and in time into a key step in the process of solving the small vehicle mobility issue, the Howie Machine-Gun Carrier.[86]

1935: The Calvary—A Light Cross-Country Car

Another vexing issue facing the Army besides moving Infantry weapons revolved around finding a vehicle that could act in a reconnaissance role. Those considering the matter realized a vehicle with a low silhouette, which could carry a small crew of one to two soldiers along with their weapons and ammunition, and could go where the horse did and return safely, would prove critical for information gathering in a future conflict.[87]

While various discussions and informal efforts undoubtedly happened, the most likely first "official" recognition of the need vis-à-vis the reconnaissance role emerged in an article by First Lieutenant (later Colonel) Homer G. Hamilton published in the May / June 1935 Cavalry Journal. Colonel Hamilton joined the Army in June 1925 and served with the Cavalry for twelve years until he transferred to the Ordnance Department. In 1935 he moved to the Civilian Conservation Corps (C.C.C.) district headquarters at Fort Des Moines, and while there designed a number of items for light manufacturing, including a motor vehicle he thought suitable for army use.[88] He described the origin of the vehicle as follows:

> At that time (1935) I had had a good bit of experience with the Cavalry. At one time I had been assigned to headquarters troop of the 113th Cavalry. I had the Intelligence section of headquarters platoon. Their duties, in part, we would conduct reconnoitering missions and scouting and patrolling generally. The Cavalry had been given experimentally a very heavy car called a scout car, to use for scouting and patrolling. We found through experience and by "we", I mean the Cavalry, that that car was too heavy, too bulky to meet the Cavalry requirements. So I conceived the idea that the vehicle that would be best suited to Cavalry use should have certain characteristics. It should be a cross-country vehicle.

> The principal objection to the scout car that had been issued, it was so heavy it could operate only on fairly hard surfaced roads. It would bog down as soon as you would get on a secondary road or off the road on ordinary terrain. So by cross-country, I had in mind the vehicle should be able to go almost anyplace that mounted Cavalry could go. That is side roads, unimproved roads or cross-country.[89]

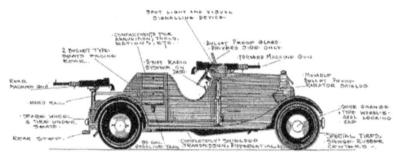

Figure 23: Lieutenant Hamilton's Light Cross-Country Car. Source: United States National Archives, College Park, Maryland

The other characteristics Lieutenant Hamilton envisioned in this vehicle included:

    a. low silhouette,

b. extended cruising radius,

c. lightweight,

d. communication either by signaling device or radio,

e. equipped with a machine gun,

f. sufficient undercarriage protection for operation across high center roads or ordinary obstacles that may be encountered,

g. driver's side shatter-proof, bullet-proof windshield,

h. radiator protected by a shield,

i. passenger payload of one to four,

j. fuel capacity to meet extended cruising radius,

k. compartments for tools, rations, equipment and ammunition

l. bucket type seats and,

m. commercial chassis.

Lieutenant Hamilton had certain specific uses in mind for this vehicle which he described as follows:

> In Cavalry there are three main characteristics, mobility, firing power and shot. As I told you a moment ago, in connection with scouting and patrolling, there are in general two types, reconnaissance patrol and a combat patrol. The mission of the reconnaissance patrol is to go out and secure your information about hostile forces. That information is of no value at all unless it gets back to the main body. Therefore, the combat patrol, rather than the reconnaissance patrol does not ordinarily offer combat, except as is necessary to ensure their return.

> On the other hand, the combat patrol has as its mission making contact with the enemy and actually engaging in the firing. The use of this car, as I visualized it, was principally for reconnaissance. In other words, it was not to be heavily armored, but it was to have sufficient on vehicle armament to permit its return and it was intended to be sufficiently maneuverable to make contact with hostile forces and secure information.[90]

He envisioned using a commercial chassis from Ford, Chevrolet or Plymouth to build the vehicle upon, all of which had a wheelbase of 100 inches, much longer than the eventual 80-inch wheelbase of the Jeep pilot models, and his vehicle did not have four-wheel-drive. His service arms leaders represented the Cavalry officer's primary audience for his article. He also knew from experience that in almost every post, camp or station, officer's club or officer's day room, there existed copies of all service publications. These places made the circulation of "Infantry Journal" and "Field Artillery Journal" readily available for reading by leaders from those branches.[91] Despite his efforts, support for the car did not materialize. Lieutenant Hamilton's article did not enter official channels for evaluation and he failed to pursue a patent on his idea. The Calvary officer made no effort to approach a commercial manufacturer or the Quartermaster Corps (QMC) to interest them in building the vehicle.[92] Later, though, he became convinced that his car factored in the development of the Jeep:

> Well, I certainly feel there are so many, many points of similarity, both in general appearance and in specifications and in specific statements of equipment and fittings, and knowing that this article was quite widely publicized throughout the services, that the similarities are way beyond the realm of just pure coincidence [...]
>
> I had hoped it (the article) would influence official opinion for the same reason that any, let us say, any manufacturer who produces a product advertises it in a magazine, he hopes to get people favorably impressed with his product and he hopes that the greatest number of people will see it and that their thinking will be influenced by what they have seen and read. So I feel reasonably certain that at least any of the service people who have been actually connected with the design and development, manufacture or any other phases pertinent to the Jeep, may have very conceivably have been influenced by this article [...]
>
> I could see perhaps one or two points of similarity might be a matter of some coincidence. But if you would take the drawing, its general appearance, specific appearance, the location of certain features, the textural matter and compare that with any Quartermaster drawings or specifications of the Jeep, you would find there was perhaps as much as eighty percent that was exactly similar.[93]

While the exact influence, if any, Colonel Hamilton's article had on the events of 1940 remain speculative, the piece shows that as early as 1935 individuals attempted conceiving and combining, as never before, features such as a short wheelbase, low silhouette, lightweight, high mobility, compartments for ammunition, tools, rations, some firepower, etc. into one vehicle.[94]

1937–1938: The Howie Machine-Gun Carrier

At the time Lieutenant Hamilton focused on the aspect of mobility and reconnaissance in a car, the Infantry worked on the issue of a small weapons carrier that would provide fast and close assistance to troops on the attack. The Infantry branch authorized a test in 1936 to formulate characteristics for such a vehicle:

- o suitable chassis for Infantry cross-country cars and for trucks, reconnaissance, eight-passenger,

- o type of body which should be placed on the chassis for Infantry cross-country cars and for trucks, reconnaissance, eight-passenger and,

- o fuel capacity for at least 300 miles, no armor, ½-ton or light touring car chassis, phaeton in body with folding top and windshield, cut down fenders, eliminate running board, provide for radio use.[95]

Figure 24: Front View of the Howie Machine Gun Carrier. Source: United States National Archives, College Park, Maryland.

The three vehicles tested against these characteristics included a Ford, a Marmon-Herrington truck and an International Harvester model. These tests did not lead to any further efforts to pursue these particular items for military use (other Marmon-Herrington products would later receive evaluation). The Infantry's dire need for a vehicle did provide the impetus for the creation of the Howie Machine-Gun carrier.[96]

Captain Robert G. Howie led the team that built the vehicle named after him and completed the prototype in April 1937. His vehicle remained a far cry from the eventual Jeep prototype, but proved a valuable evolutionary step. To maintain the low silhouette the builders had the soldiers lie in a prone position which differed significantly from the Jeep pilot models. The overall height of 33¼ inches ranged only slightly lower than the first Jeep, the wheelbase 75 inches—5 less than Bantam's creation—the weight of 1,000 pounds less than half of the standardized Jeep, and its top speed of 28 miles per hour a far cry from the top pilot model speeds.[97] Captain Wendell G. Johnson wrote about the project that created the Howie vehicle in a 1937 Infantry Journal article, describing the problem as follows:

> Almost everybody agrees that truck-hauled machine guns give no closer support to attacking riflemen than do mule-towed guns, once they're in action and reduced to hand-hauling. Which is admitting that the front-line mobility of machine guns hasn't been accelerated materially during these lush years of military renovation. Trucks, in fact, because of their size are really worse off than mules, up where grazing fire persuades bay-windowed noncoms to belly down like worms.
>
> So we still have pulling privates snaking guns along per TR 420-55 from one firing position to another—torment enough with the "thirties," and plain hell with the "fifties." And what is more serious, the muscle power of the best of them isn't up to the task. Whether creeping, crawling, or bounding, machine-

gunners can't lug their loads fast enough to get them where needed in time to hold a captured knoll or break up counterattacks. So there we are—right where we've been for years.

But not for many more, it is hoped. There is a growing clamor from the chorus of speeder-uppers decrying this immobility of supporting weapons on the battlefield, and advocating low-silhouette motorized carriers as the cure. Not baby tanks or tankettes as now used in several European armies, for such vehicles are too costly, too complicated for quantity production, and too conspicuous. What is wanted is merely a gasoline-propelled conveyance not much higher than a man crawling (or is it creeping?), that will be able to carry a one- or two-man crew, a grin, and plenty of ammunition, and scoot from one firing position to another at five to ten miles an hour.

Of course there are many who demand more, and propose a lot of trick characteristics and odd accessories for these scooters. Some would run them on wheels, others on tracks, and still others would make them convertible wheel-and-trackers—and thereby run their weight up into tons. One proponent would make this machine with a sharp nose of ponderous fangs to cut through wire entanglements. Another has it armored against .30-caliber AP, virtually a tank. There are backers of jack-of-all missions contraptions which would out-rube Goldberg.

Their Buck Rogerisms probably could be put on S.D. as lawnmowers and street sweepers in garrison, and might even carry retractable plows for use in company gardens.[98]

Figure 25: Side view of the Howie Machine Gun Carrier Powered by an Austin Bantam Engine, and using an Austin Radiator and Austin Steering Gear. Source: United States National Archives, College Park, Maryland

Captain Johnson then described the project that resulted in Captain Howie's carrier.

The more practical-minded limit their proposals to a simple, lightweight, low-silhouette carrier with no complicating contrivances. This is exactly what we find the recently constructed Howie Machine-gun Carrier to be.

The building of this vehicle was initiated by Brigadier General Walter C. Short while he was Assistant Commandant The Infantry School.

Of course the Fort Benning salvage pile was put on tap.

General Short specified that a vehicle be constructed for the sole purpose of transporting two men, a caliber-.30 machine gun, tripod, and ammunition. Other requirements were:

The gun not to be mounted for firing from the carrier.

The vehicle to be light enough for four men to lift into a 1-1/2-ton truck and across small obstacles.

To present as low a silhouette as possible—sacrificing ground clearance therefore, if necessary.

Dimensions to be such that it could be carried in the 1-1/2-ton truck issued to machine-gun companies.

Speed no object—as low as 10 mph maximum.

Units to be commercially available as far as possible.

The job of designing and building the carrier was given to Captain Robert G. Howie, then an instructor in the Tank Section. The Infantry School. Another long-time tanker and expert mechanic, Master Sergeant M. C. Wiley, was his partner in production. Assisting in the final assembly was Sergeant G. L. Rush, also of the Tank Section. Work began late in 1936 and ended in April of '37.

Captain Howie described the fabrication of the carrier.

It was decided to build a wheeled vehicle. . . . A track vehicle would greatly exceed the weight limitation. It was also decided that, in order to provide a low silhouette, the crew should be placed in the prone position. This should assist in determining the feasibility of this feature for future designs.

Several types of engines were considered... A light air-cooled engine would be ideal. However [it] would require an additional cooling medium inasmuch as it [the carrier] would he run at low vehicle speed a great deal of the time.

The Austin Bantam engine... including... clutch and transmission, complete without radiator weighs 155 lbs. A new unit was purchased for the job.

The radiator used is the conventional Austin radiator, taken from salvage.

The propeller shaft, universal joints, and rear axle assembly were retrieved from salvage. The shaft was modified by shortening, and the rear axle assembly was reversed in order to provide for the reversal in drive.

In view of the nature of the vehicle, the engine was placed in the rear, the rear axle to form a jackshaft mounted amidships, a sprocket (11-tooth) fitted to the end of the shaft upon which to operate a standard Motorcycle chain to a motorcycle sprocket (21-tooth) on the rear wheels. This provided for an additional and necessary gear reduction of 2 to 1 ... An additional wheel can be mounted on each jackshaft to be either driven or floated.

A salvaged Austin steering gear was used and was modified by shortening, mounting crosswise, and the installation of a crank [like a tiller] instead of a steering wheel.

Inasmuch as no springs were provided for the vehicle, and to take advantage of a standard commercial product, it was decided to use a 6.00 x 9 tractor tire with a ground-grip tread ... A tractor-type cast-iron wheel was purchased. A [lighter] wheel which weights 16 to 20 pounds can be obtained.

Standard motorcycle brake drum assemblies were mounted on the rear wheels and operated mechanically through linkage to a conventional foot pedal.

Frame 1-1/2 x 1-1/2 x 3/16-inch channel steel ... Aluminum alloy ... is more expensive ... and steel was used to reduce cost.

DIMENSIONS:

Height overall (radiator cap)	33-1/4 inches
Width overall	61-3/4 inches
Length overall	124 inches
Tread	49-3/4 inches
Wheelbase	75 inches
[Ground] clearance	7-3/4 inches
Weight (less machine gun and equipment)	1,015 pounds
Speed (maximum)	28 mph
Climbing ability (with traction)	45 degrees

That, in word and figures, is the Howie carrier.[99]

As with all vehicles built or procured by the Army the Howie Carrier underwent rigorous testing.

Now let's see what it had done in a few of the tests made by Lieutenant Charles R. Kutz and personnel of Company D, 29th Infantry.

The [sic] found that although this puddle-jumper wouldn't jump puddles, it could run through then [sic] without balking or stalling. Its light weight and broad tires carried it skimming in high or second over the top of sand in which other vehicles would sink or wallow. It charged through light underbrush in a fashion that made even designed [sic] Howie's eye pop. Everywhere it had ample power to climb up or plow through, provided it could get traction.

Where it was stopped, as by a ditch, the two men forming the crew usually could lift it out, over or through.

The two-man crew could dismount the gun from the carrier and set it up on the ground as rapidly as a three-man crew could do it from a Matthew's Mount.

It was able to carry the 81-mm. mortar, its bipod, and 20 rounds of ammunition; likewise the .30 caliber machine gun and the 47-mm. gun. The 27-mm. gun also was easily towed by the carrier.

A pedestal was constructed on the front end of the carrier, and from it the caliber 0.30 machine gun fired with remarkably accurate results, both in stationary and moving fire. The slick feature in firing from the carrier was the ability to fire a whole and from one chassis–defilade position, back up when simulated enemy fire came close, and pull up again into another firing position. Moreover, this was done in far less time that normally is required to go out of action from one ground position and setup again elsewhere.

Of all the admirable features of the Howie carrier, the one that was outstanding in the tests was its invisibility even on flat terrain with little vegetation to provide cover. Given a modicum of grass, weeds or ground furrows, this midget was easily concealed from even closer observation.

Here's what a machine gummer [sic] of the 29th Foot and [sic] said on seeing the carrier perform. "Jees, she's lower in the grass. You can't hardly see her even when she's going."

As would be expected, driving belly-buster without benefit of spine-rubber cushions has a tendency to trade tail troubles for tummy aches. But after a little practice one soon finds a reasonable degree of comfort by turning the body so as to rest on the side, rather than on the stomach. In this position the manipulation of the foot pedals aft, and of the gear shift lever and the tiller forward, is soon mastered. At least that is what an experienced automobile driver should find.

All in all, the testing people–and most of the observers who have chanced to see it–consider this unpretentious looking little cruiser a pretty swell job.[100]

Captain Johnson concluded that the vehicle had a future, but most likely did not represent the answer to the vexing issue of creating "the" vehicle to solve the Army's light payload and personnel mobility issue.

Not that they rate it superior either as a road or cross-country vehicle. That couldn't be expected in an experimental machine, especially one that was designed largely to determine the feasibility of building such a vehicle.

And, naturally enough, containing plunder from salvage piles, they have found bugs in it. But what new product comes out of Flint or Detroit without a few bugs?

So it is not intended to hold up this carrier as the ideal in motor mounts. Perhaps it should be stronger, larger, faster, more suited to long moves, so as to eliminate the 1-1/2-ton truck. Or possibly it should be even smaller, lighter and slower. Maybe it should have an armor shield for frontal protection. Maybe.

Many, many questions remain to be answered in the difficult [sic] of determining how to move heavier-than-can-be-handily-handled Infantry weapons. Merely to pronounce "motor mounts" as the panacea isn't enough.

This machine and its modifications, other types of motor driven vehicles, truck-carried hand carts, all have to be tested to ascertain just what is wanted– and also what is practicable from a procurement viewpoint–for caliber .30 guns, for heavier guns and for mortars. Of course it would be ideal if a vehicle similar to this could be produced with characteristics that would fit it for general utility with all Infantry supporting weapons, both on the road and in action. But that is asking almost too much.

At any rate, just as the early tanks were a beginning in the field of armored fighting vehicles, so is the Howie Machine-Gun Carrier a start in the field of support-weapon carriers. And judging from its early achievements, a might good start too![101]

In a bit of historic irony the builders of the Howie Machine-Gun Carrier used salvaged Austin parts, most likely from the vehicle purchased in 1932, and installed a new American Bantam engine in the contraption.

1938: Vehicle Testing

As 1938 dawned the Infantry still wrestled with the issue of finding a lightweight weapons carrier, as described earlier in the July 26, 1938, memo from the Chief of Infantry to the Adjutant General that concluded, "the lack of a suitable automotive carrier for the heavier Infantry weapons and their ammunition on the battlefield is the greatest deficiency in Infantry equipment today."[102] This judgment came after significant effort expended earlier in the year testing numerous vehicles to solve the problem although the Infantry, through this testing, believed they had found a solution. The intrepid staff at Fort Benning evaluated an assortment of trucks, tractors and cars.

Cargo Carrier T-2

1. Angleworm Tractor (Commercial)
2. Silver King Tractor (Commercial)
3. Marmon-Herrington Half-track Truck T-9
4. Light Tractor T3E4 (Ordnance)
5. Marmon-Herrington Tractor TA-20
6. Marmon-Herrington Tractor TA-30
7. G.M.C. 1-1/2-ton Truck 4x4
8. Marmon-Herrington ½-ton truck 4x4
9. Dodge ½-ton Truck 4x2
10. Howie Carrier
11. Marmon-Herrington Trailer (Ford)
12. Quartermaster Trailers (4)
13. Academic Department Cross-country Car[103]

Figure 26: M2 Light Tractor Cat Model—The Marmon-Herrington TA30 Was Most Likely Similar to this Model.

The conclusions reached from these tests as documented in a February 12, 1938, memo from the Office of the Infantry Board at Fort Benning to the Chief of Infantry included:

Figure 27: A ½-ton Marmon-Herrington 4x4.

> Careful analysis of the results of tests conducted to date show but three of the ten vehicles tested as possessing characteristics and showing performance which justify their consideration as possibly suitable for the purposes for which tested, i.e. the Marmon-Herrington tractor TA-30, the ordnance tractor T3E4, and the Marmon-Herrington truck ½-ton 4x4. Of these three vehicles the greater weight, cost and silhouette of the Ordnance tractor T3E4 and the fact that this is a specially built vehicle makes it undesirable for Infantry use as a cross-country carrier. The tests indicate, however, that this tractor may prove highly desirable in Infantry organizations in limited quantities as a trouble vehicle. Further tests along this line will be conducted. Of the two remaining vehicles the Marmon-Herrington truck ½-ton 4x4 outperforms the Marmon-Herrington tractor TA-30. While the performance of the TA-30 has fallen below the standard considered desirable for Infantry use as a cross-country carrier the Board desired to conduct further tests of the vehicle before definitely recommending rejection. In addition to its better performance the

Marmon-Herrington truck ½-ton 4x4 has the added advantages of carrying a satisfactory pay load on the vehicle, equal performance when trailing an additional gross load of about 1000 pounds, a general type vehicle which can be procured commercially in large quantities and at a price about one-half the price of the tractor TA-30, simple in construction, easier and more economical to maintain and with considerably better strategic and tactical mobility.[104]

These tests, while unknown at the time, narrowed the field for the Infantry to a vehicle that weighed a ½-ton and included 4x4 that might possibly be purchased commercially. The field would narrow in less than a month when a March 1, 1938, Infantry Board report issued on the Howie Carrier exposed its weaknesses:

The vehicle has excellent mobility across dry terrain. It is unable to negotiate mud, loose sand or steep hills. Its low silhouette causes it to hang up on small obstacles such as stumps, logs, etc. It is light enough when lightly loaded to be readily lifted over small obstacles by its normal crew of two men. When one man is replaced by a load the vehicle cannot be man-handled by the driver alone. It is low in silhouette. It has great maneuverability. It is as sturdily constructed as is desirable in a carrier for cross-country use. It lacks strategic mobility. It is not commercially produced and it is not available in quantity production ...[105]

The Infantry Board considered the Howie invention for two possible uses, as a weapons mount and/or as a cargo carrier and found it unsatisfactory for both. The report stated an eerie foreshadowing of many of the characteristics that would find their way into the bid specification for a solution a few years later that would constitute "a mean between the two vehicles in question," a quarter ton 4x4 truck.

It is considered that the Howie Carrier basically presents many commendable ideas. However, if a specially designed vehicle of this general type were to be authorized for development for Infantry use certain modifications and improvements would be desirable. It is believed that when the necessary improvements are embodied in a unit of this type the result would closely resemble the chassis of the presently commercially available one-half ton truck.

The Infantry Board is at present engaged in a test the purpose of which is to develop characteristics for a satisfactory cross-country carrier for Infantry. Because of its low silhouette its lightness and maneuverability the Howie Carrier is being continued in the test for purpose of comparison. The most suitable vehicle for the purpose sought yet observed by the Board is the Marmon-Herrington truck ½-ton 4x4. Unless some track laying vehicle subsequently furnished the Board outperforms this vehicle it is quite likely that the Board will consider this vehicle as the point of departure for the development of a suitable four-wheel-drive tractor or truck for use as an Infantry cross-country carrier. The Howie Carrier which represents one extreme of a wheel cross-country vehicle will be used as a desirable standard in silhouette, lightness and maneuverability. Characteristics will probably be written contemplating for development purposes a mean between the two vehicles in question.

The Infantry Board recommends no further immediate development of the Howie Carrier and that Captain R. G. Howie, Infantry, and Master Sergeant M. C. Wiley, Infantry School Detachment, be commended for their work in developing and building the Howie Carrier.[106]

Through this testing process the Infantry formed a picture of the type of vehicle they would require as detailed in a July 26, 1938, memo.

Since the World War the lack of a suitable carrier for the heavier Infantry weapons has been of paramount interest to the Infantry, and all means of transporting have been investigated or tested. Until recently, no vehicle has proved satisfactory, either due to the lack of cross-country ability or because of excessive weight and cost. Tests conducted by the Infantry Board in compliance with 1st endorsement, AGO, June 3, 1937, and reported upon in attached Infantry Reports Nos. 980 and 1014, have proved conclusively that the four-wheel, four-wheel-drive commercial truck chassis, ½-ton, with pick-up body, is the most satisfactory vehicle of all types for the purpose of a weapons-and-ammunition carrier. This vehicle, a purely commercial type, has outperformed all vehicles including hand carts, power carts, commercial tractors and tanks. During the tests it has negotiated all types of terrain and terrain in which tanks have been stuck. It is capable of being man-handled in that, if temporarily bogged, men are able to lift and move one end to firmer soil. It is of low silhouette, possesses remarkable cross-country ability, has sufficient cargo capacity, and withal, is procurable commercially. It is adaptable for use as a carrier for the Caliber .30 Machine Gun, 81 mm Mortar, 60 mm Mortar, communications equipment, and as a prime mover for the 37 mm Antitank Gun. It is considered that this vehicle will fully meet Infantry requirements in a weapons-and-ammunition carrier better than any vehicle developed to date.

Adoption of this vehicle would eliminate the necessity for mule carts, hand carts, or 1½-ton trucks now used for special weapons. In the Caliber .30 and 81 mm animal-drawn machine-gun companies or mortar companies, it would replace two mules, two carts, and two hand carts per gun squad. In motorized regiments the automotive carrier would replace one 1½-ton truck and hand carts now prescribed for each machine-gun squad. From the economical point of view alone, savings thus effected are well worthy of consideration.

In war, one weapons-and-ammunition carrier is required for each gun squad to carry all essential equipment and ammunition prescribed; in time of peace, one carrier per two gun squads is practical as the full war-time allowance of ammunition is not required for training purposes.

It is not contemplated that the automotive weapons carrier will eliminate entirely the necessity of man-carrying weapons and ammunition. The point will finally be reached somewhere near the front line where man-carrying becomes necessary irrespective of the type of carrier employed. However, the use of the automotive weapons carrier should permit weapons to be brought to the first cover in rear of the front line in the most expeditious manner and with the least fatigue to personnel. Due to its ability to cross-country more quickly and to negotiate rougher terrain, and because it presents a smaller target than a mule-drawn cart or a hand cart pulled and pushed by men, it is reasonable to assume that the automotive carrier can approach nearer the front line than either the mule-drawn or hand carts, thereby reducing the distance that the weapons must be man-carried.

Criticism of the four-wheel, four-wheel-drive vehicle has been presented by some on the grounds that such vehicles are not a commercial item and are not in general use in the automotive world. It is submitted that such vehicles are being used more frequently each year in commercial activities; Marmon-Herrington Company, GMC and Chrysler Corporation all produce 4x4 vehicles. Attention is also invited to the purchase by the War Department about two years ago of 39 extra light, 4x4 vehicles for experimental purposes at Fort Benning. At the time invitations for bids were issued the Marmon-Herrington Company only was making a truck of this kind. However, General Motors Corporation immediately undertook development of the type of vehicle desired and secured the bid. Demand by the War Department for 4x4 vehicles would unquestionably augment present commercial activities in production of that type of vehicle.

The Chief of Infantry recommends that a motor vehicle of characteristics equivalent in the tested Marmon-Herrington ½-ton, 4x4 truck, with the additional characteristics listed below, be adopted standard for Infantry use for the purpose of a weapons, ammunition and communications carrier, and as a prime mover for antitank guns:

1. Be equipped with 7.50 X 15 Chevron type tires with non-puncture inner tubes, single front and rear.
2. Have open cab with folding top.
3. Have folding windshield.

4. Heavy front bumper capable of pushing down saplings and brush.

5. Have rear bumperettes.

6. Have double windshield wiper.

7. Have towing pintle.

8. Have towing hooks at two front corners of frame.[107]

The Infantry had come to the conclusion that they needed the Marmon-Herrington ½-ton 4x4 truck; however, in reality their "perfect" vehicle would consist of a cross between the ½-ton truck and the Howie Machine-Gun carrier. While this solution met Infantry needs for a weapons carrier, it did not take into account Cavalry, Field Artillery or other branch's requirements. Yet the Infantry's testing had spelled out key requirements for the ultimate answer in a lightweight military vehicle: a weight of ½-ton or less, low silhouette, and four-wheel-drive.

The German "Jeep"

While the United States Army moved cautiously into mechanized warfare the principle that competition drives innovation in business applied also to the military. Numerous wars have resulted from arms buildups based upon superior technology and a global contest to possess the strongest and most modern navy represented a leading cause of World War I. In the 1930s major powers again began competing to develop superiority in military capacity. Germany, under the Nazis, reignited the rivalry with an aggressive rearmament program which included research and development in light reconnaissance vehicles.

Figure 28: German Kubelwagen on Eastern Front circa 1943. Attribution: Bundesarchiv, Bild 101I-022-2926-07 / Wolff/Altvater / CC-BY-SA

Hitler had made the development of the Volkswagen or "People's Car" a priority of his regime declaring that, "the automobile must become the means of transportation for the people" and he pushed for production of a car, "at a price which would make it affordable to the broad masses." With the dedication of the new Volkswagen plant on May 26, 1938, the Nazi leader had turned his vision into reality.[108]

Beginning in 1934, discussions opened up to develop a military version of the vehicle designed to solve the same issues the United States Army wrestled with during the late 1930s, i.e. develop a vehicle to transport troops and small payloads while also acting as a weapons carrier.[109]

The Germans worked slowly and the design of this vehicle took shape in early 1938 with a proposed weight of approximately 2,000 pounds significantly heavier than the 1,200 pounds the U.S. Army would require in a few short years. That weight met by liberally using aluminum wherever possible. Developed during 1939 and 1940 the vehicle christened the Kubelwagen (Bucket Car) a generic name derived from the shape of all German Army vehicles. Eventually the term came to apply to the highly successful Kubelwagen built by Volkswagen, which became the sole military car for German forces in November 1941. The vehicle saw action and acquitted itself well in all theatres. In a testament to the superiority of the vehicle created by the United States, it eventually became known as the "German Jeep."[110]

1938–1939: Bantam Strikes Out

Roy Evans and the team at the American Bantam Car Company struggled to sell vehicles in the commercial market. Evans, always the salesman, looked for other markets and he realized that the Army had a need for a small, light, mobile vehicle, just what his firm in Butler manufactured. He would work to interest the Army in Bantam products with no success.

In late 1937 the Army continued its cautious movement toward a small motorized vehicle authorizing the purchase of three truck chassis ¼-ton for testing. Early in 1938 procurement authorized to secure the items, and through competitive bidding, the award went to the American Bantam Car Company. [111]

The overall objective of obtaining these units included, "the development of a suitable self-propelled vehicle of the wheeled type, consisting insofar as practicable, of standard commercial units and parts and of the least possible weight and size for the purpose of transporting two (2) men, a caliber .30 machine gun, tripod and ammunition over c/c terrain as may be expected to lie between opposed Infantry and Infantry machine gun positions." The June 2, 1938, memo outlining the program also contained detailed specifications, marking one of the earliest lists of characteristics for a light reconnaissance vehicle.[112]

While American Bantam had made an inroad into the military market, their initial efforts turned out unfavorably. The Infantry reported in August that they "no longer require the development of a vehicle of the subject type for the purpose mentioned in the subject project, this project is hereby cancelled" and recommended incorporating the chassis into a "truck master's vehicle."[113] This decision most likely resulted from the fact that the Infantry had settled on the Marmon-Herrington ½-ton 4x4 for their needs.

The Cavalry conducted a detailed test of the chassis.

> The vehicle was equipped with two seats in front and with a light "pick-up" type of wooden body. It was then issued to the Headquarters Troop, 2nd Cavalry, for test. This troop used it in lieu of a motorcycle to accompany the Scout Car Platoon and, at times, the Transportation Platoon during all garrison and field training conducted by the unit until the end of the test

period. It accompanied the troop of the Cavalry School spring march during which the regiment operated over wet clay roads. It was also used on the reservation on several occasions to transport a caliber .50 machine gun, with ammunition and one man in addition to the driver.[114]

Unfortunately for Evans and Reuben O. Gill, the general manager of the company, who approved the sale of the units, these tests also went against American Bantam's product. The Cavalry Board concluded in November 1938, "that the subject vehicle is not suitable for any tactical use in Cavalry, either horse or mechanized" and that, "the Bantam chassis be considered unsuitable for any tactical uses in Cavalry either horse or mechanized."[115]

Figure 29: A 1937 American Bantam ¼-ton Pickup Truck.

In addition, also during 1938, Bantam furnished a ¼-ton 4x2 truck for testing by the Infantry against the remaining vehicles from the February 1938 evaluation: the Marmon-Herrington Tractor TA30, Light Ordnance Tractor T3E4, Marmon-Herrington ½-ton 4x4 truck as well as a new entrant, the General Motors 1½-ton 4x4 truck. How Bantam had their entrant considered remains unclear, but the truck in question represents the first ¼-ton item included in any of the tests.[116]

The Bantam vehicle furnished consisted of, "the standard Bantam chassis on which a ¼-ton body and open cab was mounted by the local Quartermaster. The vehicle is powered by a 4-cylinder, 4-cycle engine which develops 20 horsepower at 4000 revolutions per minute. The maximum torque developed is 31 foot-pounds at 2000 revolutions per minute." The report stated that the tests conducted against the requirement, "that the vehicle visualized as an ideal cross-country carrier for Infantry was one of the small tractor type, of low silhouette, inconspicuous, without armor and capable of moving rapidly across country and on roads, as well as at the slow speeds approximating the march of foot troops."[117,118]

Once again, Bantam failed, as the report concluded, "It was the unanimous opinion of all concerned with the test at its commencement that a vehicle of the above-stated characteristics would be desirable. As the test progressed and as the capabilities and limitations of the vehicles under test began to be disclosed, opinion gradually changed until it became completely and unanimously crystalized in favor of the ½-ton truck as a cross-country vehicle" and the Marmon-Herrington ½-ton 4x4 truck became the clear favorite. The discussion section of the report went into great detail on advantages of the ½-ton 4x4 truck over the other vehicles examined and dismissed Bantam's entry at line 29 of a 30 line discussion, "the Bantam ¼-ton truck proved to be entirely unsuitable for use as a cross-country carrier and no requirement is known for Infantry use of this vehicle. This vehicle lacks adequate power, performance and capacity for use as a cross-country carrier," or in other words, Bantam was laughed off the field.[119]

Nearly a year would pass and with an executive change at American Bantam, the Butler car manufacturer would make another effort to interest the Army in a small reconnaissance vehicle based on their product. Frank Fenn replaced Gill as President and General Manager in 1939. He immediately penned a detailed letter to Lieutenant Colonel Herbert J. Lawes (though Lawes was actually a Major) of the Holabird Quartermaster Depot (the focal point of all vehicle procurements of the Army) to reignite the Army's interest in his products.

Fenn began by acknowledging the chassis failure, as he wrote, "Some months ago this company made the error of selling three Bantam chassis chasses [sic] to the Quartermaster Corps for trial, which was a serious mistake inasmuch as these cars in no way came up to the government requirements. In fact they were the first series of cars manufactured by this company and had I been connected with the company at that time I would not have permitted the sale." Fenn then made his pitch, "Since then, however, our entire unit has been redesigned and our 1940 models will, in my opinion, provide anything and everything demanded for army use up to their carrying capacity."[120]

Fenn described the improvements, marking another milestone in the evolutionary development of the specifications that would emerge for the first Jeep prototype in June 1940, as follows:

1. an improved three-bearing engine with 25% more horsepower;
2. two-way springs and hydraulic shock absorbers;
3. a frame and radius rod assembly in front greatly strengthened;
4. can cover hills within a hundred-mile radius of Butler at speeds of 45 to 60 miles per hour fully loaded with a level ground speed of 70 miles per hour;
5. can shift through gears from a dead stop to 30 miles an hour in 30 seconds;
6. new self-equalizing brakes stop the car in twice their own length from 30 miles an hour; and,
7. no oil usage and gallonage consumed in ordinary work is from 40 to 50 miles per gallon.[121]

The American Bantam President and General Manager then stated his objective, "and the thing we are after, Colonel, is an opportunity to demonstrate these cars again at our expense" and he used the tried and true testimonial (an early example of the love troops would have for the Jeep) referencing a contact to buttress his case:

During the Maneuvers at Manassas, Majors Eggers and Leetch used one of these cars for reconnaissance purposes and found them far more satisfactory than a motorcycle and sidecar. They could go anywhere the foregoing vehicle could go and many places where they could not because of their power. The use of these cars is in no way confined to highways. They followed marching troops everywhere, over any trail which the troops chanced to follow. The cars were extremely well-liked with the result that Major Eggers has given me your name, together with several others in the War Department, in the Quartermaster Corps, because he is of the opinion that there is a definite place for our equipment in the service.[122]

Fenn closed his sales letter by again making his offer, "if it is possible to arrange a demonstration of the new 1940 car anyplace which you may see fit, we will gladly take the necessary equipment to whichever spot may be designated, together with any instruments which may be required to prove out compression, mileage, etc." and humbly asked for a second chance, "I realize that it is pretty difficult to get a second trial on any product but we feel our present cars will be extremely useful and would like very much to conduct a second test for you. Thanking you for whatever consideration you may see fit to show us, I remain…"[123]

Lawes succinctly responded on December 12, 1939, that, "it is suggested that in the event favorable consideration is given to this request of the Bantam Car Company by higher authority that one or more of these vehicles be assigned to the Streamlined Divisions. These organizations undoubtedly could, and would give a more positive answer to the utility of this vehicle than any other in the Army."[124] Fenn's effort may have failed; however, rapidly changing events only months away would bring the military to Butler and would make the words of the long-forgotten Major Eggers prophetic, "that there is definitive place for our (American Bantam's) equipment in the service".

1940: Evolution of a New Vehicle

1936–1939 saw numerous attempts by various using arms of the Army, especially the Infantry and Cavalry, to find a solution to the vexing problem of increased battlefield mobility. The Cavalry, as described by Colonel Hamilton in 1935, needed a reconnaissance car that could equal the best characteristics of the horse, while the Infantry required a weapons carrier for the heavier arms and their ammunition to replace the mule and cart. Development and testing during the latter half of the 1930s had shown an adequate vehicle did not exist between the motorcycle and sidecar and the ½-ton 4x4 truck. Infantry testing had shown that the latter vehicle provided the most suitable foundation for their needs; however, they needed the best characteristics of the Howie Machine-Gun Carrier incorporated into any solution, and that did not exist. Other branches of the Army, the Field Artillery in particular, needed a vehicle, but were slower than the Infantry and Cavalry to investigate solutions.

As World War II commenced in September 1939 and carried on into 1940, all using arms of the United States Army remained without a vehicle that combined all the requirements and characteristics into one solution needed for so many different using arms.

1940: The Procurement Challenge

Evans and his team had some familiarity with Army purchasing bureaucracy through the failed chassis procurement and Fenn's letter to Lawes demonstrated that he knew that Camp Holabird represented the motor transport center and the post assigned to coordinate the purchase of all vehicles for the Army. Not surprisingly, the red tape of peacetime Quartermaster procurement proved extensive, and the fact that the process entered into in a state of flux in 1940 added to the challenges. Understanding this complexity provides context for action and events in June–July 1940 that culminated in the awarding of the contract to build the first Jeep prototype to American Bantam.

The Quartermaster Corps had the primary group responsibility to purchase items for the Army. During the interwar period this group suffered from the general degradation of capability described in chapter 1. The primary issues within the purchasing process came from conflicting objectives on the method for vehicle procurement compounded by the rules governing government purchasing. These factors not only led to the involvement of the American Bantam Car Company in the development of the requirements for the Jeep prototype, but also as to why they had to compete in a request for proposal to secure the contract.[125]

The overriding objective of Quartermaster vehicle purchasing after World War I revolved around a quest for standardization of models. During the Great War over two hundred different varieties of vehicles had made it to France with the American Expeditionary Force, making the inventorying of spare parts and maintenance a nightmare. The Quartermaster Corps desperately wanted to avoid that scenario in the future. Starting in the late 1920s, and continuing during the 1930s, the Army's purchasing arm, though forbidden by law to purchase finished vehicles according to specific requirements, had instituted a program where they would build a "standard" vehicle by procuring commercially available parts.[126]

The standardization objective stood in direct conflict with the views held by powerful forces in the Army and the automotive industry. These voices contended that the impracticalities of the "standard" vehicle program would entail unacceptable delays during wartime and would not improve maintenance to the extent the program's champions envisioned. Private manufacturers viewed the program as a direct threat to their ability to supply products to the Army. The overriding opinion believed that the Army should not only avoid manufacturing and assembling vehicles, but that it should not even engage in automotive research and development, due to the rapidity of technological change in the industry.[127] These views became encapsulated in regulations promulgated in September 1939.

~ limited the Army to models produced commercially by two or more competing companies,

~ restricted the service to the use of commercially available trucks with few modifications,

~ mandated the use of parts and assemblies from standard production from the automotive industry and,

~ forbid the use of specially designed vehicles and a "standard fleet."[128]

These regulations limited the Army to five chassis sizes ½, 1½, 2½, 4 and 7½-ton models which made vehicle size the only standard item in truck procurement, and note that a ¼-size not specified.[129]

While the Army wrestled with conflicting objectives for vehicle development the overarching rules pertaining to government purchasing also limited the Quartermaster Corps' effectiveness in this area. These laws and regulations directed the awarding of contracts to the lowest responsible bidder, as well as forbade the Quartermaster from providing detailed requirements. Only general specifications such as carrying capacity, speed, or weight allowed and nothing that could lead to standardization. These rules had the good intentions of guarding against favoritism, to allow the Army to benefit from competition between bidders on price, and released the service from keeping up-to-date with vehicle technology advancement. These rules did directly conflict with the Quartermaster's desire for standardization to alleviate maintenance and parts availability in the field.[130]

The unique characteristics involved with vehicle procurement further complicated matters for the Quartermaster. For example, developing specifications for a uniform from one design proved effective because clothing manufacturers, in most cases, could produce similar products, if necessary. For motor vehicles, it proved impossible to create matching models based upon another's design, as the tremendous amount of retooling and machinery changes in relation to the small amount of peacetime purchasing made this option cost-ineffective. The economics, as well as the rules favoring the awarding of contracts to only the successful low price bidder, meant that only that concern could produce the desired vehicle effectively, which negated any chance for standardization.[131]

With the German victories in May–June 1940 the opportunity for change appeared in the procurement area as the Quartermaster sought authority to purchase vehicles through negotiated contract versus competitive bidding. This dynamic would allow for working directly with one manufacturer, significantly speeding up the process and enhancing standardization. Congress passed Public Law 703 on July 1, 1940, which allowed for negotiated contracts, but the Army only slowly adopted the process. Therefore, in June–July 1940 American Bantam, Willys-Overland Motors, Inc. and Ford Motor Company encountered a muddled procurement process which led to numerous twists and turns for the manufacturers.[132]

After the war, the director of the Military Planning Division would comment on the results of this confusing and conflicting situation as follows:

> It has been said too often that the Army started this war with the equipment
> which it had ended World War I. Actually, the situation was much worse. Many

items which had been developed as the result of field experience in the mud and rain of northern France in 1917 and 1918 were "modified" in peacetime to be more suitable for the garrison life at Ft. Benning, Georgia, or Ft. Sam Houston, Texas. Even after the outbreak of the war, the importance of immediately improving existing equipment was not recognized by many … Furthermore, many of the items which are procured by the Quartermaster Corps are of commercial types. In peacetime, research had to be carried out on Ordnance material because there were no commercial items available. On the other hand, it was felt by many that the Quartermaster Corps could and would accept standard commercial designs without difficulty. No single point of view has perhaps done the Army more harm than this one. There are extremely few commercial items which are suitable for military use. The demands which the Army places upon equipment are such that the use of commercial items results in lower efficiency, higher casualties, and incidentally, higher costs. The inadequacies of existing equipment and the dangers implicit in its use were brought out at once in the snow and mud of supposedly subtropical North Africa and in the early campaigns in the Aleutians.[133]

Fortunately for the Army, a "commercial design" for a ¼-ton truck 4x4 light did not exist. This circumstance meant it had to be designed, built and delivered from scratch. The question remained—could this happen in the muddled procurement rules and regulations in place in the summer of 1940?

While many issues impacted the Army procurement process throughout the interwar period, the steps in the procurement process also proved complicated. Ideas for new developments originated from many sources including the using arms and services each of which maintained its own test board (as shown by separate tests by the Infantry and the Cavalry of the Bantam chassis), the engineering branch of the Quartermaster Corps, civilian inventors and direct solicitation by manufacturers (exemplified by Bantam's attempts to interest the Army in a small vehicle throughout the 1930s). In motor vehicle procurement the first action, the development of an overall definition of the desired military requirements came from the using arms (Cavalry, Infantry, Field Artillery, etc.) The General Staff approved these specifications as the representative of the Secretary of War upon which the Quartermaster General commenced a procurement.[134]

The Quartermaster Corps had responsibility for general-purpose vehicles, hauling of cargo, ammunition, personnel, or equipment. The Ordnance department maintained jurisdiction over combat or fighting vehicles such as tanks or armored cars. The QMC divided its vehicles by administrative and tactical, with the former being used for interior lines use, while the latter intended for field conditions and distinguished by having four-wheel-drive. The Jeep prototype procurement represented a tactical vehicle scenario.[135]

With General Staff approval, the project then reviewed and approved by the

Quartermaster Technical Committee (QMTC) which had members from all using arms and services. For vehicles, the Motor Transport subcommittee would have jurisdiction over the procurement and report to the entire QMC Technical Committee. The QMTC was responsible for reconciling differing opinions over the specifications from the using arms (which, not surprisingly, occurred frequently). The QMTC would consolidate, and update the requirements, if necessary, which after approval went again to the General Staff, for the Secretary of War's sign-off.[136]

With general characteristics finalized, the Quartermaster Motor Transport Division, as mentioned, housed at Camp Holabird, Maryland, encapsulated the service branches' wish list into a detailed specification that included every military characteristic desired, which then needed approval by the Assistant Secretary of War to launch the purchase of the vehicle.[137]

1940: The Challenge

Figure 30: A German Panzer Mark IV Ausf C.
Attribution: Bundesarchiv, Bild 183-J08365 / CC-BY-SA

As Hitler's panzers rolled into the Low Countries and Ardennes on May 10, 1940, two major issues confronted the United States military. First, the need for a lightweight, low silhouette, four-wheel-drive vehicle to meet all the using arms mobility needs and, second, a complex procurement process in a state of flux that added increased bureaucracy and time to any purchases made. It was these challenges that the Army would once again traverse, beginning in January 1940, as it sought to solve the problem of replacing the mule and cart for moving troops and light payloads.

PAUL R. BRUNO

Chapter 4: What Do We Want?

In early 1940 the United States Army knew the using arms needed a ¼-ton truck to improve mobility across the service. It would take the efforts of officials at the American Bantam Car Company to get the procurement launched.

February 1940–May 16, 1940—Butler, Pennsylvania, and Washington D.C.

Figure 31: Francis H. Fenn.

The launch included Francis H. Fenn, President and Chairman of the Board. Fenn, a seasoned automotive veteran, would work on the quarter-ton effort from its inception. Bantam's top executive had cut his teeth as an official with the Hupp Motor Car Company, Pontiac, Willys-Overland and Ford before joining the struggling Butler firm in 1937. He took over as the head of the organization in 1939, as mentioned in chapter 3, from Reuben O. Gill.[138] Before becoming a manager he obtained practical manufacturing and automotive experience during his stint at Ford as a managing and production student. In that capacity he had, "studied such matters as the preparation of bills of material, routing, efficiency reports, and the paperwork that goes with production, in addition to the actual processing of components and the assembly of the final vehicle."[139] The ¼-ton project would have a highly knowledgeable and skilled leader heading the business side of the endeavor.

After assuming the role of President of the company, Fenn had attempted to reverse the military's rejection of the Bantam commercial car with no success (chapter 3). Like a lover pursuing their beloved, Bantam's chief would not take no for an answer. Even though the Army had soundly rejected his firm's commercial offering through the Infantry's testing, those working at the Butler firm had concluded that "we could produce a satisfactory vehicle for the Army but it would have to be a special vehicle."[140] He also knew that his company's small car sales had failed and that by the beginning of 1940 bankruptcy once again loomed for the Butler manufacturer. Producing an automobile for the Army represented the only option left to save the company.

The old adage states, "when the going gets tough, the tough get going" and at the beginning of 1940, Fenn initiated the series of events which would improbably lead to the creation of the first Jeep pilot models.

> Early in 1940 Major William H. Ward, Jr. now executive officer of Hunter Field at Savannah, Georgia contacted Assistant Secretary of War Lewis Johnson as a follow-through on correspondence which had taken placed [sic] between the

American Bantam Car Company and the Army for some months... and had a very lengthy discussion with him respecting the possibility of our producing a special car for the Army... Major Ward was connected with the American Bantam Car Company as its general counsel and as a director of the company.

Major Ward reported to me that the Assistant Secretary of War made it very plain to him that while the Army might be interested in a small, lightweight, high-powered vehicle, it would have to be comprised of certain definite military characteristics, such as four-wheel-drive.

That was in January or February 1940. Shortly after that time we employed Harry Payne. Harry Payne was originally employed by us to sell aviation parts. However, in going around the Munitions Building in Washington he reported to me that he had *aroused some interest in a lightweight, high-powered, very small, low-silhouette vehicle* (emphasis added).[141]

The journey of a large procurement mirrors in many respects the trek of a marathoner, and during the 26 miles and 385 yards, or 42.195 kilometers, of the race there are times when only dogged, determined, and persistent effort will keep the runner's legs moving. The almost super-human effort to weed through, and overcome, the Army's bureaucracy to have a project officially created to procure a ¼-ton reconnaissance vehicle would fall to Commander Charles "Harry" Payne.

Payne had experience as an entrepreneur and salesman and possessed an extremely extroverted personality. He began over twenty years of preparation for his moment in the sun in 1940, immediately after the close of World War I, in which he served as a pioneering naval aviator, pilot 483.[142] The history of Payne's activities during the inter-war years reads like a shadowy Hollywood thriller. The product pitchman founded and/or participated in a plethora of businesses, including the Payne Export and Import Company during the 1920s. Under that moniker he personally sold forty-five to fifty planes, along with spare parts, to the Mexican government, as well as selling planes and a tractor to the Peruvian regime.[143]

Also during the 1920s, Payne became the managing director of a firm called the Inter-Allied Aircraft Company. His work with this company would impress upon him the absolute necessity of a small lightweight vehicle that could traverse rough terrain at high speeds.[144] The mission of Inter-Allied included purchasing surplus training aircraft, in particular the Avro, and change over the aircraft to a three-person passenger plane.[145] This side business of training pilots introduced the Commander to the life-or-death need for an all-terrain small vehicle:

Back in 1922 when I was managing director in the Inter-Allied Aircraft Company, we were selling wartime planes, and also instructing students at Roosevelt field. In those days aircraft motors were not very dependable. We had a lot of trouble with motor failure and in teaching men how to fly we had some very unfortunate experiences, a man cracking up—or students, rather—

cracking up two or three miles away from the field, and as a result, a lot of these crashes would catch fire.

Several men were burned up needlessly because the rescue party could not get to them due to the rough terrain of the country. We tried motorcycles and so forth, and they would bog down. Finally, due only to lack of money—and we were pretty well broke in those days—I developed a Ford chassis with an OX-5 engine and a wooden propeller. This would carry 2 men and fire extinguishers. This job weighed around 1200 or 1400 pounds stripped but the wheels and tires were so small that we had difficulty. However, it could be easily manhandled.

This was a very rough rescue car and in 1924 and 1925 I contracted with the Mexican government for several planes, and I built another car which consisted of a Ford Chassis with a Ford engine, and put some over-sized airplane tires on it, two bucket seats, fire extinguishers; and on the right hand we had two jacks and a drum.

To secure—to this drum we attached a cable so that when a plane crashed part of the fuselage could be connected with the wire cable, the rear end of the car jacked up and the wreckage separated so that we could rescue the men who were penned in. The front wheel of the car was anchored to a nearby tree or boulder as the case may be.

About that time I also sold a lot of equipment to the Peruvian Government and built another one of the same type of cars which was used with great success. In those days, as I said before, we lost the lives of many men through fire, and there was no car suitable, and we did not have the money to go into heavy engineering and develop a car that was really needed. However, these cars were a lot better than anything we had, including the motorcycle.[146]

Payne bounced around in numerous ventures from the mid-1920s on, including attempting to pioneer aviation and aircraft insurance as an agent of Payne and Richardson through National Liberty, founding the Aviation Business Bureau Incorporated involved with aviation consulting work and statistics, work on establishing aircraft factories and passenger work, barnstorming and endurance flights, creating the P & E Corporation working on aviation technical advising, and even selling juices for the Bruce's Juice Corporation.[147]

During the early part of 1939 Payne's endeavors brought him into contact with a Major Brownell of the Reconstruction Finance Committee, the agency which had loaned Roy Evans funds to keep Bantam in operation (chapter 2). Brownell introduced the serial entrepreneur to the aforementioned William Ward, American Bantam attorney, and Ward brought Payne to the attention of Frank Fenn.[148]

While Fenn worked on his military small car "Hail Mary pass" in late 1939 he also had another idea to keep the Butler car manufacturer in business. As Payne related, "there was a great demand—yes, there was a great demand about that time for subcontracting from a lot of aviation companies like Douglas, Boeing and so forth. They had men out looking for automotive factories that could build certain aviation parts."[149]

Payne, however, had not forgotten his experience with the small rescue car:

> In the early part of 1940 in my apartment one evening, there was Johnny Moore, who is now acting chief engineer of the Small Airplant Division, Colonel Kutz, who is now Brigadier General Kutz, and I think Commander Hagan of the Navy—I am not sure but there were several others. We got beefing about the war and how soon we were going to get into it, and the question came up about the motorcycle, and how useless it was in cross-country work, especially in muddy weather. These men knew about what you might call my phobia that I had for a small light-weight car, and they suggested the Army might be interested.[150]

The American Bantam President decided in February 1940 to hire Payne to, "try and get them some aviation business because they were more or less at a standstill."[151] In 1940 the United States air arm was still part of the army (the United States created the Air Force in 1947 after World War II). Therefore, Payne's efforts to secure work for the Butler factory would lead him to the Munitions Building to, "start ringing doorbells in the Army."

Payne's initial forays into the labyrinth of the Army's bureaucracy met with little success.

> First, to the Planning Division and met a Colonel Young. He was on the first floor of the Munitions Building. I told him my idea for a small cars [sic]to take the place of the motorcycle. He said he had no authority and he started introducing me to army officers that he thought might be helpful, and I got nowhere in a grand hurry. He (Young) introduced me to some people in the Signal Corps and that was the wrong entrance. They said they had no authority. Finally, I met a dozen different officers probably, whose names I do not recall, and finally I met Lieutenant Colonel Hester, who was in the Quartermaster Department and then assigned to the office of the Secretary of War. Colonel Hester was very sympathetic and, knowing Army routine a lot better than I did, he suggested that I to [sic] go the chief of infantries office (headed by General George A. Lynch).
>
> Lieutenant Colonel Hester introduced me to W. C. Lee, who is the material officer in General Lynch's office, and at the time—the same time, I met Colonel Oseth and a Sergeant by the name of Thomas.[152]

Payne's journey took from February 1940 to mid-May 1940, but his efforts had led him to the exact service arm he needed to find, the Infantry, as well as the next key link in the truck 4x4 light journey, Colonel Ingomar M. Oseth.[153]

Colonel Oseth had served at Fort Benning during the late 1930s at the exact time the Infantry conducted the tests to find a suitable light cross-country vehicle, the results of which had settled upon the ½-ton Marmon-Herrington 4x4 (chapter 3). His duties had required him to develop special knowledge related to cross-country weapons carriers for troops.

> In 1936 and 1937, I was on duty with the 24th Infantry at Fort Benning, Georgia. I had nothing personally or officially to do with the tests conducted at that time. I witnessed them as a spectator. And talked to the test officers, because I was interested. Later, I came into a position where my official duties required that I examine those reports.
>
> I was detailed by the Chief of Infantry to the tank school in 1938 for the one-year course, the nine months course. From there, in June 1939, I went to Washington, to the Chief of Infantries' Office, where I was assigned to the Arms, Equipment and Finance Section, and charged with the development of motor vehicles and signal equipment. Those were my special—that was my special job.
>
> The course itself covered all phases of motors, army motors, including tanks and motor vehicles, motor trucks. Mechanical construction, operation, everything that is necessary for an officer of the line, one of the using services, to know about, including maintenance, and things like that.
>
> As part of that course, I was required to make a research and write a paper on this subject, "Characteristics, Field of Usefulness, and Present Trend of Motorized Cross-Country Carriers for Infantry Weapons and Battlefield Supply." I didn't compose that title myself. It was shoved at me.
>
> I spent several months researching all the records that I could find, foreign publications, especially the Germans, who had German reports, some periodicals, in the German language, and so on, on the general subject of motor vehicles fit for, or suitable for military use. I studied the characteristics and the records of the performance of probably a hundred and fifty vehicles of different types at that time in preparation for this paper.[154]

During the time Oseth worked at Fort Benning, as he stated, he had witnessed the vehicle tests and had familiarity with the type of vehicles and the pros and cons of those means of transport.

> There was an Ordnance track-laying vehicle, as I recall it, built on the chassis of a light tank. There were two commercial track-laying vehicles. Full track, you might call that, full track vehicles. One by Marmon-Herrington and I don't remember who made the other one. They were slightly different in size. There was a small car designed from spare parts found in the junkyard there by Major,

or Captain Howie, which he was at that time, and Sergeant Wiley, made at Fort Benning, called the Howie-Wiley machine-gun carrier. That was in those tests.

There was also tested a Bantam commercial car. I believe, as I recall it, it had a pick-up body. I am not too certain about that. The Marmon-Herrington fourwheel, four-by-four, half-ton, came in while the tests were on, were in progress. It wasn't initially in there. One of those vehicles came to the Port Ordnance Officer at Fort Benning as a utility vehicle. It belonged to the Port Ordnance Officer, and he showed it to the Infantry Board, and it was entered into the test that way.

I witnessed, I think—I know there was an ordinary farm tractor. Large wheel, large rear wheels and two wheels in front. One or more of those were tested at the same time. Also a quarter-ton four by two truck of another make. I observed many of the tests and the results of these tests. I did not see them all, naturally. I had other things to do.[155]

These tests provided the foundation for a general set of military characteristics that eventually coalesced for a lightweight infantry weapons carrier, and the denizen of Fort Benning intimately aware of those requirements, including the need for four-wheel-drive for all battlefield and combat vehicles for the Infantry.[156]

May 17–June 6, 1940—Washington, D.C.

Oseth transferred to the Chief of Infantry's office in Washington D.C in 1939 reporting directly to General Lynch. As part of his official duties, the expert on Infantry trucks represented the Infantry on the Quartermaster Technical Committee and that group's subcommittee on motor transport.[157] That assignment placed him at a key meeting from May 17–20, 1940, at Camp Holabird during which the Army's lack of a suitable means for cross-country movement received lengthy discussion.[158]

That three-day conference at Holabird was for the purpose of considering and revising military characteristics of all motor vehicles, military motor vehicles. And the two that the Infantry were mostly concerned with were the half-ton four by four, which hadn't developed as we wanted it to. It was much heavier and higher, had a higher silhouette. The other was the motorcycle, which was thoroughly unsatisfactory from the modern viewpoint. It had no cross-country ability. We had been trying to get a motor tricycle which has two driven wheels and had much better cross-country ability. Those two projects among others were discussed at great length for three days there at Holabird.[159]

The conclusions reached by the attendees at this gathering found the reduction of the weight and the silhouette of the half-ton 4x4 impractical within the foreseeable future, and

52

that the motor tricycle years away with no prospect of getting it.[160] The Bantam truck and Howie Carrier both deemed unsatisfactory as they, "lacked cross-country ability and sturdiness, the Howie Carrier was deficient in speed, the Bantam was too frail having just about fallen apart with about five thousand miles on it and it got bogged down whenever it got in sand, or mud, or on an upgrade or into a shell hole, or ditch or anything of that nature, in fact, both these contenders lacked all military characteristics."[161] When the conference ended on May 20, 1940, the United States Army had no vehicle to fit into its arsenal between the motorcycle and the ½-ton four by four and no plan on how to procure such a weapon. Then fate once again stepped in on the very day that all seemed lost:

When I (Oseth) returned from the three-day session at Holabird, I had spoken of, as I recall it, it was in the afternoon of the third day, and the Chief Clerk in the office, Sergeant Thompson, told me there was a man there waiting to see me. I then met Mr. Payne, who was sitting in the window, behind my chair, as a matter of fact. That was the first time I met him. He was not introduced to me by anybody. He introduced himself to me.

He was looking, he told me he was looking for Major Howie. Major Howie had been with me as a sort of technical advisor out at the three-day conference at Holabird. Mr. Payne told me he had told–that is, he had been told that Bob Howie could probably be found there. He came to ask me about it. I told him Howie was somewhere in Washington and probably would be in, but I didn't know when. Then the conversation developed between Mr. Payne and myself.

I asked him what particular business he had with Howie. And he told me that he wanted to talk to him about the Howie-Wiley carrier, because he thought the War Department was out to take the vehicle up again. It had been tested and rejected before.

I told him if that was all he wanted to see Howie about, he had been wasting his time, because I was the one making the decisions, subject to being overruled by the Chief of Infantry in respect to what type of vehicle the Infantry would have. And that the Howie-Wiley Carrier was out. I then talked with him, and we had some considerable talk and argument on that.

There was quite a lot of conversation after that, and in the course of that Mr. Payne proposed to me that we accept and test again, retest, the newer model of the Bantam, which he claimed was a great improvement over the one we had tested previously and found deficient. I informed him again that we had thoroughly tested the Bantam and even though it might be slightly improved, it lacked the essential military characteristics that we had definitely adopted and decided upon, and that it would be a waste of time.[162]

The Army's leading vehicle expert then expressed to Payne what he believed a small lightweight vehicle for Infantry use needed.

> I told Mr. Payne, in substance, this, after we had definitely dismissed these other two vehicles, if you will take your Bantam and put a front-wheel drive, a front-wheel driven front axle on it so as to make a four by four, strip the body down to the bare essentials and put power enough in there to keep those wheels turning, we will be willing to talk business with you, because that is what we are looking for. Mr. Payne said it was almost impossible, that there was none in the world that would make axles like that, that there wasn't one in existence, and he didn't know anyone who could make it. That just about terminated that particular conversation for the day.[163]

Payne though discouraged, did not give up. What exactly transpired from May 20, 1940–June 2, 1940, when Oseth submitted a draft of a memo laying out for the first time the general specifications for a ¼-ton four by four truck remains unclear. Payne recollected that he had developed the specifications with another individual in General Lynch's office, Colonel W. C. Lee, and that he had provided the requirements to Lee. Oseth remembered that he, given his extensive knowledge of Infantry vehicles and the needs of that service arm in that area, had presented the characteristics needed to Payne. Given the Bantam representative's gift for self-promotion, as well as his lack of expertise, along with Oseth's character as an officer testifying under oath, the account the Colonel offered represents what most likely transpired.

> Colonel Lee's desk and mine were placed side by side and without any spacing between them, so that I could reach over and touch his shoulder any time. Our offices are very small. We were crowded in there.

> There were no conferences, official conferences, that is, other than possible desultory conversations around the hall between Mr. Payne and Colonel Lee regarding that project or any motor transport project, between the time I first met Mr. Payne (May 20th) and the time when I submitted in rough form to Colonel Lee, the draft of the letter of June 6, 1940. Now I have no knowledge as to what conversations Mr. Payne may have had with Colonel Lee or anyone else outside the office.

> I was the representative of the Chief of Infantry authorized to speak for them and confer about matters of that kind. Mr. Payne addressed himself to me when he had anything to confer about.[164]

The "letter of June 6, 1940" referenced by Colonel Oseth represents the first official document produced in the project that led to the creation of the Jeep. It contained a general list of characteristics of a vehicle that would fill the Infantry's needs between the motorcycle and sidecar and the ½-ton truck. The Infantry officer steadily maintained he had provided the specifications included in that memo to Payne and that he had drafted the document.

Mr. Payne testified at page 370 of the record that in giving specifications to Colonel Lee, he told him that the car would have to have a short wheelbase between 78 and 80 or 81 inches; that it should be narrow gauge, between 47 and 48 inches; that the silhouette was of great importance; it should have 36 inch silhouette was of great importance; it should have 36 inch silhouette to the cowl; that the overall length should be around 126 inches; the ground clearance, 8 ½ inches at the lowest point which is the differential. That the car should have a four-wheel-drive and that it should have a weight of between 1,200 and 1,300 pounds.

(Those are) the characteristics of the one-quarter, 4x4, to which I at that time gave the designation, tentative designation, liaison and reconnaissance car as I recall it. I gave those to Mr. Payne myself. I told him what we wanted. He didn't tell us what the characteristics would be.

The specific dimensions, wheelbase, clearance, things of that kind, did not enter into the question at all. They were details which were determined upon by the Quartermaster General people later on. They were given not given at that stage by Mr. Payne or myself or anybody else.

The characteristics which were given by me to Mr. Payne and later to Colonel Lee was weight not to exceed 1,000 pounds. Silhouette not to exceed 36 inches. Capacity at least two men with a machine gun and 1,000 rounds of ammunition. Drive, an all four, four-wheel-drive; road ability and grade ability equal, at least equal to that of other standard vehicles of the same type.

Those were the characteristics I communicated to Mr. Payne and asked him if he could produce such a vehicle. Those were the characteristics I later communicated to Colonel Lee, in order to get his approval and support, and still later to General Lynch.[165]

While Colonel Oseth drove the development of the general specifications for the quarter ton truck, he did credit Colonel Lee with having an interest in light Infantry vehicles and he worked to gain Lee's support for the ¼-ton project.

Colonel Lee had been for a couple of weeks previous to this carrying around a file of papers describing a Swiss motor car, very light Swiss motor car, called the Bentz car. The file had been sent to him by his friend and mine, Barney Legge, Major Legge, Military Attaché, Switzerland. I had previously examined the specifications of this Bentz car and had decided against it because, for the same reason we decided against the Howie-Wiley Carrier. It didn't have the drive on more than two of the wheels. So when I presented this matter to Colonel Lee, he was intensely interested already in light transportation for the infantry. I remembered I said:

"Colonel, this is right down your alley with your Bentz car project, only it is much better." Then there was some discussion. I think Mr. Payne was there when that conversation took place. I am sure he was. From that time on, Colonel Lee was, if anything more, of an enthusiastic supporter of it that [sic] I was. He followed it, supported me in every possible way and took a sufficient personal interest. So he accompanied me to some of these technical meetings where the characteristics of the jeep were discussed.[166]

The stage now set between Oseth, Payne and Lee to draft a memo officially documenting the general requirements for a quarter ton vehicle for the infantry.

At the time of the conversation with Colonel Lee, when I won him over by telling him it was right down the alley with his Bentz car, I was at that time engaged in drafting this letter (the June 6, 1940, memo) to the Adjutant General. The procedure when a new development was to be initiated was for the Using Service, the Chief of the Using Service branch write a formal letter to The Adjutant General, stating there is a requirement for that equipment and giving the main military characteristics, not in their final form, but the main military characteristics. That is what I did. That was my duty in the office. That was what I did.[167]

To settle the matter Oseth summarized the events of May 20, 1940–June 6, 1940, the latter the date the memo finalized and sent to the Adjutant General. He emphatically reiterated that the general specifications originated with him in conversations with Payne and that General Lynch and Colonel Lee not involved, other than Colonel Lee's cursory interest through his Bentz car project.

General Lynch came into this thing about the 29th or 30th of June (probable misstatement by Oseth, should be May), after Mr. Payne and I had worked out all these characteristics between us, as I have testified before. It is entirely possible, in fact quite probable that General Lynch thought the thing originated when we presented that finished or semi-finished product to him. I am not sure that Colonel Lee wasn't under the impression the first time I called it to his attention that was the origin, the very beginning of this thing, which was definitely not. There had been days and days of consideration and planning before then that neither Col. Lee nor General Lynch knew about personally.[168]

As I testified yesterday, the function of Mr. Payne and the American Bantam Car Company was to tell us whether they could give us what we wanted. We told them I personally gave to Mr. Payne and to Mr. Finn [sic], who occasionally came in with Mr. Payne, the military characteristics that we wanted. The plan, the vehicle in general outline as was designed—I hate to use the first personal pronoun so much—it was designed in my own brain initially.

And Mr. Payne and The American Bantam Company were informed what that picture was. They informed what that picture was. They informed me whether they could produce it or not.[169]

After two weeks of intense discussion Colonel Oseth began preparing the memo around the first of June 1940 following office protocol.

> The system there in the office was anything that has to be worded very carefully, the officer drafting it draws it up in pencil, lead pencil (Oseth). Then it is submitted. After he is satisfied with it, for the time being, it is given to the stenographer, the typist, to make a rough draft. Then the rough draft is the one that forms the subject of conference around, any further conferences among personnel. That was probably the one shown to General Lynch by Colonel Lee, the rough draft, the first typed draft of that draft.[170]

> They approved it (Lynch and Lee). They both approved it as soon as I had the thing drafted. It was after two or three days discussed around the office, and discussed, I think between, perhaps referred to the Quartermaster people, matters of that kind. The thing was typed in final form for the executive signature. He (Lynch) habitually signed papers issuing from the Chief of Infantry's office.[171]

By June 6, 1940, all conferences completed and the memo submitted for signature. The document forwarded to the Chief of Cavalry to begin to gain support from other using arms for this vehicle. In the communication the need for greater mobility stressed, that current offerings too heavy and possessed too high a silhouette for a close combat vehicle, and once again, pointed out that the motorcycle with sidecar not unsuitable for this purpose.[172]

The Chief of Infantry then articulated the first organized requirements for the vehicle as follows:

> Minimum height: 36 inches;
>
> Maximum weight, without pay load: 750–1,000 pounds;
>
> Adequate cross-country ability and grade ability equal to that of standard cargo vehicle;
>
> Caliber .30 machine gun mount either integral with the body of the vehicle or detachable;
>
> Capacity: a crew of at least two men, one machine gun with accessories, and three thousand rounds of ammunition or equivalent weight;
>
> Armored face shield for driver;
>
> Four-wheel drive (except where tricycles are considered);
>
> Ground clearance: maximum possible consistent with desired silhouette.[173]

The memo also indicated that a frame and body designed for amphibious operations desirable if it did not unduly delay procurement of the vehicle and the obtainment of "a sufficient number of vehicles conforming to the above characteristics, to equip an infantry regiment (rifle) with such vehicles in lieu of standard command and reconnaissance trucks for company units with 6 additional for the Infantry Board (or a total of 40) for extended field test in comparison with the present standard vehicles."[174]

Oseth had thrown in the requirement for an "armored face shield for driver" for the specific purpose of keeping the Quartermaster Corps from taking over the procurement, due to a bad experience with obtaining a vehicle based upon the 1938 tests which had identified the Marmon-Herrington half-ton 4x4 as suitable for Infantry weapons carrier purposes (chapter 3).

> I put in there a requirement for face armor. It was, I will admit, sort of a lawyer's trick, because that automatically would take it out of the hands of the Quartermaster General with whom we had been having trouble in development of the motor vehicle and made it an ordnance vehicle. The peculiar rule in effect at that time was if a vehicle had armor, laid a track, was a track-laid vehicle, had some other thing like that on it, the Chief of Ordnance was responsible for its development, if it was of the general purpose type, truck carrying on truck, passenger cars, so on, the Quartermaster had it. I didn't want the Quartermaster General to get a hold of this thing because of this difficulty of putting it out of bid and then getting something we didn't want.[175]

The Infantry Colonel also included in the memo a last recommendation that, "Since the desired type of vehicle is a special one, and since experience has shown the impracticability of securing development of the proper type of vehicle from among present commercial types, it is recommended that the requirements for competitive bidding be waived to the extent necessary to bring about procurement of the best possible design."[176] He described his reasoning as follows:

> Well, we had some sad experiences with the Quartermaster people on this motor procurement matter because in the case of the Marmon-Herrington half ton, 4x4, the law was interpreted by the Quartermaster required they call for bids, and the contract for the vehicle was let to the best bidder. That resulted in the case of the half ton in an unsuitable vehicle. The Quartermaster people, I think Colonel Van Deusen had told me shortly before that, it may have been Colonel Laws [sic], I am not sure, they had told me they were considering, or had gotten authority form the Secretary of War, I am not sure which it was, to waive the requirements for bids, competitive bidding, in certain special cases, if requested by the Using Arms. That was the purpose of putting that in there.[177]

Therefore, due to Oseth's "lawyer's trick" it would fall to the Ordnance Technical Committee to determine the next steps in the development of the truck 4x4 light. Oseth summed up the significance of his June 6, 1940, memo vis-à-vis the specifications laid out:

> Individually, singly, there was nothing new in any of these characteristics. They had never been combined in one vehicle before. That was the only new thing about this vehicle, combining those characteristics in a vehicle that was light enough, small enough for infantry battle-field use.[178]

In one memo Oseth had combined years of research, testing and effort surrounding a light truck for military use into one coherent list of general specifications. In doing so he initiated a series of events over the course of the summer and fall of 1940 that would result in the building of three pilot models that eventually evolved into one of the most iconic vehicles created in military and automotive history, the Jeep.

PAUL R. BRUNO

Chapter 5: A Vehicle Takes Shape

Throughout June 1940, through a series of actions coordinated by the Ordnance Technical Committee the procurement moved forward, but by the end of the month the responsibility for the endeavor would rest squarely in the hands of the very agency Oseth had attempted to avoid, the Quartermaster General. The challenge of developing a detailed set of specifications from which an automotive manufacturer could build a vehicle would rest squarely with that agency of the United States Army.

June 7-18, 1940—Ordnance Technical Committee, Washington, D. C.

Chapter 3 detailed the Cavalry's interest in a small lightweight reconnaissance vehicle as articulated by Lieutenant Hamilton in his 1935 Cavalry Journal article. Oseth's gambit to begin gathering support for the project by transmitting the June 6, 1940, memo through that using arm, paid immediate dividends as the Chief of Calvary responded quickly, writing to the Adjutant General on June 8, 1940, endorsing the endeavor as follows:

> The Chief of Calvary is interested in the possibility of using a light, cheap car for command and reconnaissance purposes in the cavalry. He therefore concurs in the recommendations of the Chief of Infantry in the basic communication and recommends that he be kept informed of the development and that twenty cars, when manufactured, be made available to him for test.[179]

However, the Adjutant General did not break protocol and exclude the official purchasing department of the Army from the project. He forwarded, on June 14, 1940, the Infantry's general specification memo to the Quartermaster General and Chief of Ordnance seeking "comment and recommendation."[180]

During that eight-day period, Payne actively promoted Bantam's interest, as Fenn recalled.

> He (Payne) telephoned me and asked me if we could produce such a car. I told Payne that I thought we could. A few days later (early June 1940) he wrote me and asked me to send him all correspondence between our company and the Army, which I did.

> Approximately fifteen days after that (most likely June 17 or 18, 1940) he called me and said he was bringing to the American Bantam Car Company plant a technical committee of several officers. At that time he did not name the members of the technical committee.[181]

The exact nature of Payne's efforts after he received all correspondence from Fenn remains unclear; however, he must have read in those records of Bantam's efforts with the Quartermaster General during the late 1930s to interest the Army in their products. Bantam's D.C. player likely spoke with representatives of that department, as the Administrative division of the QMC forwarded the Adjutant General's request for comment and recommendation (on the same day the request received, June 14, 1940), to the Commanding Officer of Camp Holabird stating the following:

> In view of the fact that the vehicle is required for command-reconnaissance purposes as well as for combat purposes, it is considered that the chassis development be a responsibility of the Quartermaster Corps. Comment is required as to the practicability of securing a commercial vehicle with all-wheel drive conversion, meeting the vehicle's characteristics set up in the basic communication. *The light passenger car of the American Bantam Company is suggested as a possible solution of the problem* (emphasis added).[182]

American Bantam's long odyssey to interest the Army in their vehicles now became a reality as the Army's chief procuring arm, just six months after that same department had condescendingly brushed off their products, now recommended them![183] By June 15, 1940, the War Department General Staff, Supply Division entered the loop and acting under the authority of the Secretary of War, Brigadier General R. C. Moore, Assistant Chief of Staff who issued orders, labeled "IMMEDIATE ACTION," to the Adjutant General, Quartermaster General, Chief of Ordnance, Chief of Cavalry and Chief of Infantry.

1. In view of the fact that the Chief of Ordnance is being directed, in a separate communication, to give further consideration to the Howie Experimental Weapons Carrier, the attached copy of a letter to this office, regarding the proposed military characteristics of a vehicle for Infantry use (Oseth's June 6, 1940, memo), is forwarded for appropriate action and recommendation through the Ordnance Technical Committee.

2. In this connection it is desired that consideration be given to the possible use of the American Bantam car manufactured by the American Bantam Company, Butler, PA.

3. It is further desired that the subcommittee appointed to investigate this matter, include, in addition to those members of the Ordnance Technical Committee you wish to designate, a representative of each of the following arms and services:

4. Chief of Infantry (Lt. Col. Lee)

5. Chief of Cavalry (Maj. Tompkins)

6. The Quartermaster General (such representatives as he may wish to designate)

7. You are authorized to request travel orders for such members of the Ordnance subcommittee as may be necessary to conduct a thorough investigation into this matter, and to confer with officials of the automobile industry in the development of a vehicle possessing the desired characteristics.

8. Your recommendations are desired at the earliest practicable date.[184]

To add weight to these orders, Moore had forwarded the memo to the Adjutant General and that office, also on June 15, 1940, sent the exact same orders to the Chief of Ordnance and the Quartermaster General under their authority to act on behalf of the Secretary of War. Oseth had placed the Army's key munitions expert squarely in the sights of top brass regarding the development of a light infantry vehicle. With "immediate action" being called for from the highest levels, the Ordnance Chief quickly called for a meeting of his technical committee on June 17, 1940.[185]

The Subcommittee of the Ordnance Technical Committee met on the subject of the development of a light infantry vehicle on June 17, 1940. The exact discussions remain lost to history, but the meeting went decidedly in favor of Bantam's interests as the official minutes recorded.

2. DISCUSSION:

a. From a consideration of the above references (Oseth's June 6, 1940, memo and the Adjutant General's June 15, 1940, orders [mirroring Moore's directives]), the Subcommittee concludes that two types of vehicles are under consideration:

  a. The Light Command and Reconnaissance Car.

  b. The Howie Weapons Carrier.

b. The Light Command and Reconnaissance Car represents a new type of vehicle, the proposed military characteristics of which are stated by the Chief of Infantry in reference b. (June 6, 1940, memo) The Subcommittee feels that these military characteristics are satisfactory, in general, but will give them further study at the conference to be held at the American Bantam Company's plant.

c. The letter of instructions from the Adjutant General to the Chief of Ordnance (reference c.) [June 15, 1940, orders] refers to par. 1 to instructions to the Chief of Ordnance to further consideration of the Howie Weapons Carrier. The Howie Carrier was considered by the Infantry Board (reference a. [1938 report detailed in chapter 4] in 1938. In this reference the Chief of Infantry recommended that no further development be made of the Howie Cart.

    d. In view of the instructions which have been received (O.O. 451/10001, reference c.) it will be necessary to give further consideration to the Howie Weapons Carrier at this time. This vehicle is closely related to the Light Command and Reconnaissance Vehicle discussed above.

    e. In order to obtain full and prompt information concerning the design of both types of vehicles, the Subcommittee will visit the plant of the American Bantam Company, Butler, Pennsylvania, on Wednesday, June 19, 1940. The Subcommittee desires that Major Howie be present at the plant in order that the design of the Howie Weapons Carrier can be considered at the same time.

3. RECOMMENDATIONS:

1. That the Subcommittee visit to the American Bantam Company for conference with the officials and engineers of that Company in regard to the military characteristics and design of:

2. The Light Command and Reconnaissance Car.

3. The Howie Weapons Carrier.

4. That after this visit military characteristics be drawn up for both vehicles, and further recommendations made as to the future development of both vehicles.[186]

They sent these minutes that very day to the Adjutant General who quickly replied on June 18, 1940, that, "the recommendations contained in Paragraph 3, attached Subcommittee Report of the Ordnance Technical Committee, dated June 17, 1940, subject: 'Light Infantry Vehicles—Development Of,' are approved." It was likely that Fenn received Payne's telephone call concerning the subcommittee's visit either on June 17th or 18th, giving him very little time to prepare. The Army would visit Butler, and Bantam would have one opportunity to prove they could get the job done.[187]

June 19-20, 1940—Butler, Pennsylvania

Despite its bankrupt status American Bantam had available a small cadre of "hands on" automotive talent that would comprise the individuals who would actually build their prototype. With the Army heading to Butler, it was time to bring into the effort the first of these individuals, Harold Crist, the Butler automotive manufacturer's factory manager (chapter 2).

Crist served Bantam in that capacity from 1937–May 1, 1942. Before that, his work in the automobile industry dated from the same year World War I began, 1914, and in a twenty-five-year career (up to 1940) he primarily worked as a draftsman, as well as supervision, design work and as a machinist, i.e. he had extensive knowledge of cars from the ground up.[188] Crist's knowledge and experience would come in handy, as Payne put it, to prove, "the theory of the short wheelbase, narrow gauge, lightness, and in fact that it (Bantam chassis) could be made into a four-wheel-drive" and that, "Bantam knew how to engineer a small car." [189]

In the annals of Jeep history, the Army's visit to the Bantam plant represents an indispensable milestone in the creation of that vehicle as it eventually developed over the course of 1940. Frank Fenn provided a detailed description of exactly what transpired during those two critical days.

> On June 19 Mr. George Thompson, the treasurer of the company, and myself met this group at the Pittsburgh Airport and brought them to the plant. The committee consisted of Major Howie, Armored Forces, Colonel Lee, Infantry, Major Tompkins, Cavalry, Lieutenant Colonel Atwood, Ordnance, Mr. Robert Brown, civilian engineer, Quartermaster Corps, and Mr. Beasley, civilian engineer, Ordnance.

> When they arrived at Butler they were introduced to various members of our organization, among them Mr. Crist, the factory manager, Mr. McMillan, purchasing agent, Mr. Croll, secretary, and after a general discussion we got in Mr. Tompkins car and my car and accompanied by two standard Bantam roadsters went to the county fairgrounds.

> When we reached the county fairgrounds we first ran the roadsters around the race track at high speed. Then we took them to the inside of the racetrack, which, like all county fair racetracks, most of them anyway, is full of rubbish and high grass and mud and muck, and the various members of the committee drove the cars at high speed. They performed quite satisfactorily.

> Then we took them down to the far end of the racetrack, which was already steeply banked, went outside and drove them up the steep embankment on the outside of the track. The cars came up to the fence but couldn't go any further because of the fence.

> Then they had some discussions (at the fairgrounds). I mean by that the Army committee group broke up, some of them talked with Mr. Thompson, some with Mr. Crist, and some myself. We came back to the plant and took a trip through the factory.

> After taking a trip through the factory we then took a standard Bantam chassis and

Figure 32: The Bantam Chassis with 4,500 pounds of sandbags—June 19, 1940. Photo taken in Shipping Department at the American Bantam Company Plant. Source: United States National Archives, College Park, Maryland

loaded it with 4500 pounds of sandbags. The chassis did not collapse in any way. A picture of it was taken. And then Mr. Crist and Mr. Beasley and Mr. Brown began to talk about our production facilities, and again they walked through the plant. After, I would say, 45 minutes of that procedure, we then went up to the offices and went into my office and had a general discussion regarding the proposed car that the Army had in mind.

I did not see any papers or any documents or specifications or anything else in the possession of any member of the committee during that discussion. Down at the factory we had more or less decided that it would be necessary for us to add 5 inches to the wheelbase of the car and we made it very clear that in our opinion only a few components of the standard Bantam could be used. Those points were emphasized during the conference in my office.

Colonel Atwood, Colonel Lee, Major Tompkins, Major Howie and Mr. Brown outlined what they expected of this car. They said they wanted a small silhouette because it would be used for reconnaissance purposes and that it would be necessary to drive it up close to enemy positions, probably park it behind low bushes, something of that sort, and the men would get out, take a look around, get out and run, if necessary.

They stressed the desirability of outstanding performance and great power because the car would have to go anywhere. Colonel Tompkins made it clear that as far as cavalry was concerned they wanted an extremely tight radius and expressed the opinion that perhaps we would have to build four-wheel steering jobs also.

We discussed whether any parts of the present Bantam car could be used in the construction of that car. I told them that in my opinion certain body parts, such as the cowl could be used, that the transmission could be used, with small changes, that a great portion of the sheet metal, such as fenders, might be used, the hood, that is, it was possible, if we were successful in keeping the weight low, that we might use standard Bantam axles.

It was definitely understood that it would have to have a four-wheel-drive (eliminating Bantam axles). I (Fenn) called Fred Hall, of the Spicer Manufacturing Company, who were the manufacturers of our regular axles, and told him that we're in a huddle with the Army regarding the production of a special vehicle that must have a four-wheel-drive, and asked him if they had any four-wheel-drive experience.

Mr. Hall told me that they had thoroughly explored the four-wheel-drive field, and that they, with very little difficulty, provided the proper universal joints for the front axle could be obtained, which they thought could be obtained from

Bendix-Weiss or Zephyr, that they could produce the axle.

I told him that time was of the essence and that we would like to talk to him about it immediately and Mr. Hall agreed to come, to arrive at Butler the next day. After calling Mr. Hall we took an ordinary yellow scrap pad, such as this gentleman is using (indicating) and Mr. Beasley and Mr. Brown made a sketch which incorporated their ideas of what this car should likely be like and look like.[190]

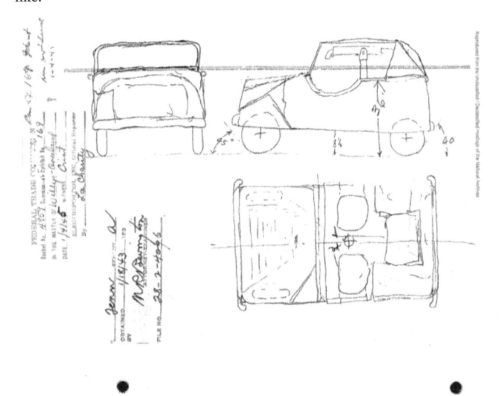

Figure 33: The Beasley-Brown Drawing—June 19, 1940. This is the very first sketch ever made of a Jeep-type vehicle. Source: United States National Archives, College Park, Maryland

The Army and the Butler team had covered a great deal of general ground in just one day. They had identified what would become the key component of the ¼-ton truck 4x4 light, the front axle. During that same day the committee and Bantam officials had also delved into the engineering details of the vehicle taking shape as Fenn described.

Well, I believe you might call it one time because, after all, the whole day was spent in discussing characteristics of the proposed car and the possibility of using any Bantam components, and also using their (Bantam) "know-how" in constructing the proposed vehicle.

Now, there are certain well-established procedures that have been followed in the construction of these light vehicles over a period of years. They naturally wanted to know what our frame construction was. We showed it to them. We pointed out to them the fact that we could not use the present frame. In fact, we stated very promptly that that type of frame would not be sufficiently strong to do the job they wanted.

We discussed transmissions, with the possible change of the second speed and one of the shafts, would be entirely satisfactory. We discussed our axles. It so happened that we had a safety factor of about 150 percent in those axles as far as the commercial Bantam was concerned. There was considerable conjecture as to whether those axles would stand the gaff or not. On the first day we were inclined to believe they might, because of the safety factor involved, take care of the heavier engine.

We discussed our own power plant and we rejected it. We discussed other power plants and I made the statement to Mr. Brown and to the other members of the committee that we weren't concerned about a power plant because there were three or four other engines on the market which we could obtain in reasonable quantities until this entire thing had been entirely worked out that would suit the job.

I made it very plain to Mr. Brown and Mr. Beasley, and to the other members of the committee, that the Bantam Car Company, while it had a complete engine plant, could not attempt to build a special engine unless the quantities involved ran to 25 to 35 thousand, the cost of tooling would make the cost of the car entirely prohibitive.

We discussed body construction and we outlined this, that by widening our roadster cowl we could use it, and that by using our flooring pan and making some adjustments in that, we could use it. At that time members of the committee raised no question as to the type of fenders and we said we thought we, without a question we could use our own fenders.

They explained the standard headlights were used but in addition to standard headlights, blackout lights were used. They also explained about taillights, how the taillight they used was a special taillight, that light, because of possible attacks and strafing from the air, could only show so many feet to the rear, and that the blackout lights could only show so many feet from the front.

We had an idea that we could use our regular 16-by-5-inch tire but they explained that in their opinion the car would have to have more flotation than a 5-inch car (probably meant tire) would provide. On top of that they insisted that the tire be of a standard size which they were using in other vehicles, because they were interested in standardization and could not have a lot of 5-inch tires standing around the place which were useless on any other vehicle.[191]

Army officials and the representatives of the American Bantam Car Company had developed a definitive outline of a vehicle. For the majority of the committee their work ended that first day as Fenn recalled.

> Colonel Atwood, who seemed to have charge of the group, suggested that they all return to Washington with the exception of Mr. Brown and Major Howie and that Mr. Brown and Major Howie and ourselves continue to canvass the situation so that Mr. Brown might bring back with him more conclusive data after conferring with Mr. Hall of Spicer.
>
> The second day Mr. Fred Hall arrived. We told him what we had in mind. By "We", I mean Mr. Brown with a few remarks by Major Howie who was not particularly active that day. Also Mr. Crist and myself. We told Mr. Hall very frankly that in the opinion of everyone the Bantam engine was out, although we were going to explore it and see whether it could possibly be used. But we did express the opinion to Mr. Hall that the Bantam axles could be used. Mr. Hall said that he thought they might if the horsepower and the torque and size of the engine did not exceed a certain size.
>
> We talked about costs. Mr. Hall explained to us that it would be necessary to produce the pilot model actions out of nothing but bare stock and that they would simply have to be organized out in the tool room. We discussed constant velocity joints and Mr. Hall recommended the Bendix-Weiss job. We discussed our transmission, and Mr. Hall agreed with the position that the American Bantam Company had taken the day before that it would be necessary to modify the transmission to a small extent.
>
> We discussed whether Mr. Hall could produce transfer cases and whether such a transfer case could be attached to our present transmission, which Mr. Hall agreed to be done. We made up certain figures as to the cost, the probable cost of the axles. Mr. Hall, with what meager information we had, was compelled to do quite a little guessing, and so stated. However, we did get some figures which Mr. Brown took back with him to Holabird. We started to type those figures about 5:30 in the afternoon and the minute the figures were typed Mr. Crist took Mr. Hall and Major Howie and Mr. Brown to Pittsburgh.
>
> Mr. Brown left us, taking back certain information and drawings which Mr. Crist gave him, which dealt essentially with the commercial Bantam car and left with the understanding that we were to immediately go to work and do our best to get together information and specifications which would be forwarded on to Mr. Brown and that jointly we would develop this unit, using the best knowledge of what the Army wanted and our best knowledge of what we could manufacture.[192]

The Ordnance Technical Subcommittee on light infantry vehicles upon their return to

Washington now had in their possession a more detailed idea of what the ¼-ton truck 4x4 light might consist of, but the Army still needed to develop detailed specifications that a car manufacturer could build from. That document would result from twelve days of frantic effort centered on the very department the Infantry had wanted to avoid, the Office of the Quartermaster General.

June 21- July 2, 1940–Washington D. C. and Camp Holabird, Maryland

The subcommittee on the development of light infantry vehicles met two days after returning from Butler (June 22, 1940) and developed a detailed directive for the next steps of the procurement.

- o The subcommittee and the officials and engineers of the American Bantam Company discussed the possibilities and limitations of the Bantam chassis for use as the basis of the light vehicles under construction;

- o A brief operating test was conducted with several of the Bantam 2-wheeled drive cars on roads and cross-country. Some of this operation was hilly country including grades estimated at 10%. These 2 wheeled drive vehicles performed well with loads of one or two men. The gross load was approximately 1500 pounds;

- o A stripped down chassis weighing 600 lbs. was statistically loaded with 4500 lbs. of sand without damage to the chassis;

- o Discussion of engineering details resulted in tentative decision to require the following:

- o A driving front axle with a 2-speed transfer case including provisions for de-clutching the drive to the front axle. The tread of the axle to be the same, front and rear. Tires 5.50-16 with bullet sealing tubes;

Body of rectangular construction to enclose the wheels, in lieu of mudguards, with bumpers front and rear. All bumpers to be provided with means for attaching tow ropes. Angles of approach and departure at least 45° and 40° respectively. A folding windshield to provide for a maximum height of vehicle not to exceed 36 inches. The top to consist of a single bow at the rear and a quickly removable strip of canvass attached to the rear of the body and top of the windshield. Three bucket type seats, two forward and one centrally located in the rear part of the body;

Provision for mounting a cal. .30 Light Machine Gun on a telescoping pedestal located between the two forward bucket seats and provision for the transportation of 3000 rounds of cal. .30 machine gun ammunition;

Amphibious characteristics to be included if this is practicable;

The following miscellaneous items:

Mount the radiator on its side to reduce silhouette and add a water pump;

Increase engine power at least 10%

Increase fuel capacity to 8 gallons and an auxiliary fuel filter;

Increase the capacity of electrical units and use shunt wound generator with voltage regulator;

Provide a radiator guard;

Provide blackout lighting system;

Oil bath cleaner;

Hydraulic Brakes;

Full-floating axles; and,

Skid shoe under transfer case[193]

The memo then outlined the "draft military characteristics for the Light Reconnaissance and Command Car are stated as follows" (similar with some additions to the June 6, 1940, initial requirements).

- o Weight without payload: Not to exceed 1200 lbs;
- o Height: Not to exceed 36 inches;
- o Four-wheel drive chassis: Wheelbase approximately 75"
- o Angles of approach and departure 45° and 40° respectively;
- o Driver must be able to see the road at a distance of not more than 10 ft. ahead of the front of the car;
- o Armament: One Cal. .30 Light Machine Gun on telescoping pedestal and 3000 rounds of machine gun ammunition;
- o Crew: 3 Men including the driver; and,
- o Performance:
- c. Sustained low speed of 3 m.p.h. and maximum speed of not less than 50 m.p.h. on level hard-surfaced road.
- d. Two-speed transfer case with provision for de-clutching the drive to front axle for good road operation
- e. Maximum practicable ground clearance, but not less than 8 ½"; and

    f. Cross-country performance and grade ability comparable to that of standard multi-wheeled cargo vehicles.[194]

The final recommendations for the committee would form the outline for the procurement.

- That the military characteristics stated in paragraph 2 above be approved;

- That 70 Light Reconnaissance and Command Cars be procured for service test by Infantry, Field Artillery and Cavalry. 40 cars for Infantry – 20 for Cavalry and 10 for Field Artillery;

- That since this vehicle is a commercial wheeled type without armor protection, the Quartermaster General be charged with its development and procurement;

- That this light vehicle development be limited to the Light Reconnaissance and Command Car type, in general accordance with the military characteristics stated in paragraph 2; and,

- That if this vehicle is found satisfactory, consideration be given to its use in place of the motorcycle with sidecar and the tricycle type of vehicle.[195]

This directive officially transferred the effort to the Quartermaster General and brought into the endeavor the next individual of significance to the work, Colonel Edwin S. Van Deusen. A 1917 graduate of Syracuse University with an AB degree in chemistry, minor in mineralogy, and some engineering courses, he joined the Army right after graduation during the mobilization for World War I.[196]

Van Deusen detailed to the Quartermaster Corps in 1920 and served as a commanding officer of operating companies, shops, an instructor at the motor transport school, commander of supply depots, and command of the overhaul and spare parts depot at Sandy Hook, New Jersey. He worked as a senior instructor at the Quartermaster motor transport school; chief of engineering branch at Holabird Quartermaster Depot; from 1937–1940 he attended various Army schools; and from 1939 to 1940 performed planning work pertaining to motor transport matters in the Office of the Quartermaster General.[197]

During the 1930s the Quartermaster Corps monitored developments in the field of light combat vehicles as Van Deusen recalled:

> We kept abreast of all developments, both domestically and in the foreign fields (of light combat vehicles). Our mission was not particularly with relation to combat vehicles. That was the responsibility of the Ordnance Department. We were aware of certain developments that had been undertaken by the Ordnance

Department and we also later—in the later thirties, when we knew about certain developments that had been undertaken at Fort Benning which involved the use of wheel vehicles—also studied the light type of wheel vehicle.

In the late thirties we had tested at Holabird, had worked with a Bantam, an American Bantam, commercial chassis, in developing the capabilities, possibilities of that chassis for use with a project paralleling that inaugurated by Major Howie at Fort Benning in connection with what is known as the Howie carrier.

The Bantam commercial car, as tested at Holabird, proved itself totally incapable as performing or having the stamina required for military service. It was underpowered and was structurally weak for military application. We had a development project on a vehicle in the half-ton class. I think in 1936, the records will show that we procured a group of half-ton four by fours from the Marmon-Herrington Company to fulfill a request from the Infantry for a light-weight weapons carrier type of vehicle. Those vehicles were all-wheel drives and were quite satisfactory.

Previously, the half-ton four by four was very acceptable to the Infantry as produced and tested in the design of the Marmon-Herrington Company. At that time we were entirely following the competitive rule in Procurement under the provisions of revised statute 3709, and other limiting legislative acts, and were not able, under the general policy of procuring motor vehicles, to specify or model or details of construction. The Infantry was so well pleased with the half-ton four by four, as built by the Marmon-Herrington Company, that we were requested to procure larger quantities of a similar type vehicle.

However, the competitive angle of that procurement resulted in the procurement from another manufacturer of a vehicle of the same general type and classification answering generally to the characteristics which were not acceptable, however, to the Infantry. It was a heavier vehicle. It was a much higher silhouette, and, generally not as satisfactory.[198]

Van Deusen had knowledge of the Army's efforts to develop a light vehicle during the 1930s and in 1940 his duties placed him squarely in the path of the ¼-ton 4x4 light procurement. He had attended the pivotal Quartermaster Corps Technical Subcommittee meetings on Motor Transport held from May 17–20, 1940, the very same conference Colonel Oseth had participated in. The procurement officer vividly remembered the Infantry's position.

The need for lighter vehicles was stressed by the Infantry representative, some replacement for the motorcycle and sidecar. We discussed tricycles, which were also involved. The matter was left in abeyance at that time for further investigation of what could be done with the dissatisfaction, expressed by the Infantry, of the half-ton four by four as being produced at that time. We knew we would have to go into some form of investigation regarding the other type of vehicle they wanted.

They (the Infantry) wanted definitely to go back to that type of vehicle (Marmon-Herrington half-ton four by four truck) in a lighter model. They were not satisfied with the truck that was being produced in the half-ton class.[199]

The beginning of Van Deusen's involvement with the ¼-ton truck 4x4 light occurred right around the time Colonel Oseth drafted the critical June 6, 1940, memo, and that connection involved the ever-present Charles Payne.

When, and under what circumstances did you meet Charles H. Payne? Either the last week in May, or the first week in June 1940. I was in the Office of the Motor Transport Service. Col. Johnson was out. I was in charge of the office. I was notified that a gentleman must see the Chief of the Service immediately on a matter of great importance. Mr. Payne was admitted to the office, and I talked with him at my first meeting.

He represented himself as being connected with a high executive position, the American Bantam Car Company of Butler, Pennsylvania. And his expressed purpose of the visit was to sell Bantam cars to the government, feeling that would be something which the American Bantam Car Company could do.

In the original discussion with Mr. Payne, it was pointed out to him that we were using an entire four-wheel-drive, that the Bantam design of commercial chassis was not suitable for our purpose.

I told him (Payne) we were unable to act. Our hands were tied so far as any action toward procuring is concerned. I suggested that requirement for any vehicle of that class would have to be presented to us by the using arms and services. And I also suggested that he might be able to develop some requirement for a vehicle such as the Bantam people were producing by further discussion with the officers of the Chief of Infantry, who were primarily interested in such a type of vehicle.[200]

Payne may have taken his advice, or had already begun working with the Infantry, as previously documented. Nevertheless, within a week after the June 19–20, 1940, Butler conference, the responsibility for the development of specifications to procure a lightweight vehicle for the United States Army would fall squarely on Colonel Van Deusen and the Quartermaster Corps.

Immediately on the return of the Quartermaster Corps, with a representative from Butler (June 21, 1940), we were advised that the project would be transferred to the Quartermaster Corps. I immediately gave a directive to the engineering group at Holabird to start the drafting of specifications based on the general characteristics appearing as part of the committee report of the Butler meeting.

The formal transfer, I believe, occurred about the 27th or 28th of June, 1940, by formal endorsement. But immediately following the committee meeting, we had already started the mechanics of the engineering work that would be required.

For several days I participated directly in the work which was performed in respect to the writing of the specifications. In fact, the specifications were written by our engineers, one of the engineers in my office. I had brought this engineer over to Washington to write these specifications in our office to expedite the publication of them and to permit conferences with the representatives of the using arms and services who were located in Washington, and would thereby be more readily accessible in connection with the writing of those specifications.

Mr. Robert F. Brown was the engineer in charge of the drafting of the specifications and at various times, sometimes alone, singly, sometimes jointly. Then I believe Lt. Col. Lee, Major Oseth, Capt. Tompkins, or Major Tompkins, Capt. Claybrook. They were the principal officers who conferred with us.

Under Mr. Brown's supervision, George Engler prepared the body drawing which was issued as part of the specifications who was an engineer at Holabird, one of our engineers. The body drawing was prepared at Holabird in accordance with certain agreements that had been reached as result of the Butler conference, certain agreements among the army personnel.[201]

Van Deusen's small team, Brown, Engler and one Mr. Dowd had two primary documents to create, the aforementioned detailed specifications and a body drawing which later became specification ES-No. 475 and QM Drawing 08370-Z. A tremendous amount of seat-of-the-pants engineering work went into the development of these two critical requirements documents.

There was no ¼-ton 4x4 truck available at the time. However, after date of their return from Butler and the return of the specifications, since we had one or two Bantam chassis at Holabird, which had been subject to previous testing and since the general characteristics developed at the Butler conference fitted somewhat generally on to a chassis of that size. At Holabird we did make up in a wood body in general as described, as a result of the Butler conferences. And also demonstrated for representatives of the using services who went to

75

Holabird, in that period, performance of that time of a vehicle as represented by the two-wheel drive Bantam chassis. It was hardly a ¼-ton truck. It was a cobbled up sample of what could be made at the time to approximate that type of a vehicle, less the all-wheel drive feature and limited power to that available in the Bantam engine.[202]

The Quartermaster Corps determined early on not to repeat the mistakes that had led to the ½-ton truck debacle by including the using arms at the ground floor of the specifications development as Colonel Oseth recalled.

The first thing that happened after this project was referred back to the Quartermaster General was that Colonel Van Deusen called a meeting of the technical, Quartermaster technical committee on motor transport. He had just succeeded Colonel Johnson as chairman of that Committee. At that meeting we received the report, went over the reports that came back from the Ordnance Department and adopted certain changes that had been suggested, approved certain changes that had been suggested by the Ordnance technical committee.

And as I recall it, one or two further slight modifications that were suggested by the Quartermaster representative, of which Colonel Van Deusen was one, were approved. Then there were two or three meetings of a small committee. The infantry and cavalry were the only two branches interested. The others showed no interest in the thing so the committee meetings were very small. I suppose there were two or three of those meeting in Washington, here, to come to a definite understanding, going a little further, I mean proceeding from the point that this letter (June 6, 1940, memo) brought us to.

Then the next step was that the chairman of the committee and the representatives from Holabird, stated they wanted the committee to go to Holabird and consider on the ground a body type and size and dimensions and all that sort of thing, in connection with the Bantam chassis that they had at the depot, the Quartermaster depot there at Holabird. So a few days afterwards, Colonel Lee and myself and Major Tompkins' office went out there to Holabird and they had this Bantam chassis setup on the concrete floor. They had sketched in chalk on the floor the outlines of what they conceived the body would look like under these characteristics. They had put the front wheels up on a four by four in order to compensate for the difference in height between a normal axle and the power-driven axle that was to go in there. We went over the sketch on the floor and all those various things were changed on the suggestion of various members of the committee.

Then after we agreed on that step, the Quartermaster technicians up there, the engineers, said they would go ahead and make a mock-up which is a wooden model, a cardboard practically, model of the body so we could come out and look at the thing. It was two or three days later they said they would have that thing ready. At the end of that period we went back there. At that time I don't think Colonel Lee accompanied me, although I am not too sure about that. I still don't remember if Mr. Payne was there that particular one. They had this Bantam chassis with this wallboard mockup body on it. There wasn't anything to that body. It was just a rectangular, low body, hollowed out a little, making a little cut there to enable the driver and assistant driver to get in and out without catching a heel in the thing. It was also necessary to put wheel wells or houses, whatever you call them in the body itself, in order to get room enough in the vehicle for any useful purpose. In other words, instead of putting a fender, a mudguard on the outside of the wheel, the mudguard was incorporated right in the body of the vehicle.

They had that wallboard mock-up there and we went over it, suggested changes. Their object was to find out whether the using services represented by myself and Tompkins were satisfied with it, and we finally approved the thing as it was. The next step was to make a wooden body of sufficient strength so we could get in it to sit in it. And as I recall it, that was the first trip out there when we looked at the final effort and tried to take this vehicle up a steep test ramp they had out there, about I don't know what, it must have been about thirty degrees, I guess, or better, the slope of the thing. We loaded both the driver and assistant driver, and I sat in the back of this thing. It got halfway up the hill and wouldn't go any further.[203]

After all the effort expended to develop a working model of the ¼-ton truck 4x4 light the initial test proved a failure and with Colonel Oseth ready to declare defeat, but once again, Charles Payne saved the day.

As I understood it, although I am not sure about that, the original Bantam engine, the four-cylinder, water-cooled engine was in there at that time. As the representative of the majority stockholder, the infantry, I announced I was afraid the thing was washed up, the whole project was washed up, because it didn't have the power. Mr. Payne was there at that time, I remember now, because he spoke up and said, "Don't worry about that. We have already got a larger engine lined up that we can put in there." And so he saved the project from being shipwrecked on that particular rock.

That was in general the procedure, a constant series of visits, by myself and Major Tompkins to Holabird to confer with the engineers, Mr. Brown, being Robert Brown, and Captain Engler and Major Skip Johnson—I don't know his first name—and Colonel Laws [sic] out there at Holabird. Step by step the specifications were being developed by them, and as they came to something which they thought might conflict with our views, on the thing, they asked us to come out and conferred with us personally on it. I, personally, on behalf of the Chief of Infantry Ok'd such parts of the specifications as they were submitted to me. That is the specification part, not the characteristics. It was more detailed specifications they were working on.[204]

By actively including the key using arms in the process the QMC ensured that the specifications eventually drawn up matched what they wanted. The engineers had also included Bantam in the process through both Frank Fenn and Harold Crist.

The Bantam President remembered his role at this time.

I talked to Mr. Brown over the telephone regarding many of the details and many of the conclusions which we had arrived at, at Butler (chapter 4), and he suggested that I come to Holabird and discuss it with him. I went to Holabird and discussed them with Mr. Brown.

At approximately June the 28th…what was the subject matter of the discussion that took place between you and Mr. Brown on that occasion? Placing a minimum cubic displacement on the engine of 85 inches; the use of the Studebaker axle, our transmission and a Spicer transfer case; a discussion on the size of the wheels and the tires and the consequent necessity for having a minimum of 85 cubic inches. I stated to Mr. Brown that we were convinced that the power plant must have a cubic inch displacement of at least 85 inches. Mr. Brown agreed. I stated that as a result of work by Spicer and ourselves we were convinced that, due to the service which they expected of this car, it would be unwise to use our axle, and it would be wise to use a Studebaker axle, although a large sum of money would be involved in tooling. Mr. Brown agreed.

I stated that Zephyr joints were available or that Bendix-Weiss joints were available in limited quantities but they were the best on the market as we thought and recommended, and recommended that joint. I don't remember if Mr. Brown agreed to that or not. I stated that we could use certain of our body parts, such as the cowl, the windshield, brackets, and so on, and Mr. Brown accepted that statement. I stated that it would be necessary for us to revamp any commercial engine then in production that we used in order to get sufficient oil capacity to take care of the sharp angles at which the vehicle would have to operate. Mr. Brown agreed. And I discussed cost of tooling and told him that in my opinion that the extent of tooling would run in the neighborhood of $25,000 and Mr. Brown agreed.

We discussed the flotation of the vehicle, and I took the position that I thought our 5-inch tire would do. Mr. Brown on the other hand reiterated the position of the Army that they would have to use a tire then in production and being used on other vehicles, and I acquiesced. At that time I said it might effect [sic] the size of the engine we would have to use, but there would be no considerable increase in cost. I discussed the facts that we would undoubtedly ask York-Hoover to build the first bodies because they would have to be handmade and we wouldn't attempt to tool our body plant for pilot models. Mr. Brown said he thought it was a good idea, and we discussed such other possibilities as the use of the panel hooks, spare tire, and items of that sort. We took the position that no spare tire was needed. Mr. Brown said that would have to be a matter to be decided later and would appear in the specification under which we would ultimately build.[205]

Crist conferred with Brown by telephone and also visited Holabird on July 1, 1940. The Bantam factory manager discussed primarily the body and axles along with other items and took prints with him to the in-person meeting.[206]

The Army finalized a detailed specification on July 2, 1940. A chalk outline on the floor, a cardboard mock-up, and a wooden mock-up that was thoroughly reviewed by all interested parties resulted in Quartermaster Corps drawing of the vehicle numbered QM 08370-Z. Numerous meetings, consultations and informal discussion resulted in an eleven-page specification given the number ES-No. 475 detailed in Table 1.

Table 1: ¼-Ton Truck 4x4 Light–Specification ES–No. 475 (page 185)

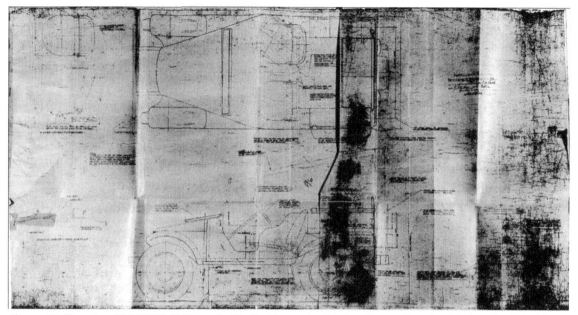

Figure 34: Drawing QM 08370-Z–Note the Similarities to the Beasley–Brown Drawing Made at Butler on June 19, 1940. Source: United States National Archives, College Park, Maryland

In twelve hectic days at the end of June and into the beginning of July 1940 the Quartermaster Corps had put on paper the specifications of a vehicle many in the Army had desired since the end of World War I, and had achieved signoff on the requirements from the key using arms, the Infantry and Cavalry.

As Colonel Oseth succinctly observed, this incredible process done in such a short timeframe represented, "a very fine piece of coordination."[207] The next phase would entail answering the question, "What process would the Army follow to find a manufacturer who could build the vehicle to specifications?"

Chapter 6: Bidding for the First Jeep

The Quartermaster General and prospective bidders would have two critical challenges to overcome in finding a way to obtain the vehicle described in specification ES-No. 475 and QM Drawing 08370-Z; the first, navigating the usual litany of "red tape" that goes along with government procurement, the second, a military establishment caught squarely in the middle of attempting to reorganize its purchasing process from a peacetime paradigm to a wartime footing (see chapter 3). The acquiring of a light vehicle for military use would fall right into the sweet spot of both challenges and the burden to overcome them to win the contract for Bantam would fall squarely on the shoulders of Frank Fenn.

July 3-11, 1940—Washington, D. C.

The Quartermaster Corps under the leadership of Colonel Van Deusen had created a detailed specification and drawing for the proposed car the Infantry and Calvary desired. As stated in chapter 5, the purchasing leader mentioned that the official transfer of the project to QMC auspices occurred on June 27, 1940. The orders accomplishing this action emanated from the highest level, the Chief of Staff. This document summarized the work through the end of June 1940 and would guide the endeavor through its completion:

Figure 35: George C. Marshall—Chief of Staff, U.S. Army, 1 September 1939-18 November 1945

> June 27, 1940–MEMORANDUM FOR THE CHIEF OF STAFF: Subject: Military Characteristics for Light Reconnaissance and Command Car.
>
> The problem presented:
>
> To determine advisability of developing and procuring a Light Reconnaissance and Command Car.
>
> Facts bearing upon the problem:
>
> In letter, dated June 6, 1940, (copy attached, Tab A), the Chief of Infantry recommends development of a light vehicle to be used for reconnaissance and other purposes in the Infantry battalion. He states that the present standard command and reconnaissance car (½-ton) is unsuitable for this purpose because of its weight and relatively high silhouette. Military characteristics for a type of vehicle desired are submitted in his letter.

In a conference with the Chief of Infantry (Lt. Col. Lee), a representative of the American Bantam Company expressed the belief that a vehicle could be developed by his company which would meet the needs of the Infantry. In accordance with verbal directive of the Chief of Staff to give immediate consideration to the possible military use of the Bantam Car, the above letter from the Chief of Infantry was referred to the Chief of Ordnance for action by the Ordnance Technical Committee (Tab B). This action was concurred in by the Quartermaster General in order that both the Bantam car and the Howie Weapons Carrier, an Ordnance development item, could be considered by one technical committee in the final determination of military characteristics of a vehicle to meet the requirements of the Chief of Infantry.

The results of study by a subcommittee of the Ordnance Technical Committee are contained in the attached subcommittee report dated June 22, 1940, (Tab C). The subcommittee concludes that in its present state of development the Howie Weapons Carrier is unsuitable for the purpose proposed by the Chief of Infantry; that after conference with the American Bantam Company it is believed a suitable light vehicle can be developed.

Based on the military characteristics proposed by the Chief of Infantry in his letter of June 6, 1940, and on technical considerations brought out in conference with representatives of the American Bantam Car Company, the subcommittee submits revised military characteristics (par. 2a, page 3 of Tab C). The subcommittee recommends:

That the revised military characteristics for a Light Reconnaissance and Command Car be approved.

That 70 Light Reconnaissance and Command Cars be procured for service test by Infantry, Field Artillery, and Cavalry (40 for Infantry – 20 for Cavalry – and 10 for Field Artillery).

That the Quartermaster General be charged with the development and procurement of this vehicle.

That light vehicle development be limited to the Light Reconnaissance and Command Car type, in general accordance with the military characteristics submitted by the subcommittee.

That if this vehicle is found satisfactory, consideration be given to its use in place of the motorcycle with sidecar and the tricycle type of vehicle.

The above recommendations are concurred in by the Quartermaster General, Chief of Field Artillery, Chief of Infantry and Chief of Cavalry, through representation on the subcommittee of the Ordnance Technical Committee.

The Chief of Infantry (Lt. Col. Lee) informally requests that a quantity of these vehicles be procured immediately in order to give them an extended service test during the August maneuvers. The Chief of Ordnance (Lt. Col. Atwood) informally advices [sic] that officials of the American Bantam Company stated the 70 vehicles desired for service test could be manufactured within eight weeks at a cost of approximately $165,000; that is thereafter this type of vehicle could be supplied at a cost of less than $600 each.

G-4 believes that if a satisfactory vehicle can be developed which will meet the needs of the Infantry, as stated in letter from the Chief of Infantry, dated June 6, 1940, (Tab A), and provide a possible solution to the present unsatisfactory situation with regard to the motorcycle, the expenditure of $165,000 for this purpose is warranted.

The Quartermaster General (Lt. Col. Johnson), Chief of Infantry (Lt. Col. Lee), Chief of Field Artillery (Lt. Col. Beasley) and Chief of Cavalry (Maj. Tompkins) concur in action recommended below.

Action recommended

That the military characteristics for a Light Reconnaissance and Command Car proposed by the subcommittee of the Ordnance Technical Committee in Tab C be approved.

The Secretary of War directs:—

That the attached correspondence, with inclosures [sic], be forwarded to the Quartermaster General (through the Chief of Ordnance) by Immediate Action indorsements [sic] substantially as follows:

Attention is invited to the attached subcommittee report of the Ordnance Technical Committee, dated June 22, 1940, subject: Light Infantry and Cavalry Vehicles – Development of. The Military Characteristics of a Light Reconnaissance and Command car, as recommended in paragraph 2e of this report, are approved. The Quartermaster General is charged with the development and procurement of this vehicle.

As recommended in paragraph 3b of the attached subcommittee report, it is desired that the Quartermaster General immediately initiate development and procurement of seventy (70) Light Reconnaissance and Command Cars in accordance with the approved military characteristics. The expenditure of not to exceed $175,000 from funds allotted the Quartermaster General is authorized for this purpose. When procured, these vehicles will be given an extended service test by the Infantry, Field Artillery and Cavalry; the number of vehicles to be supplied each of these arms for this test to be in accordance with the recommendations contained in paragraph 3b of the attached report. If possible, it is desired that these vehicles be procured in time to be employed in the maneuvers scheduled to be held late this summer.

These vehicles will be tested under the supervision of the Infantry, Field Artillery and Cavalry Boards. The recommendation of these Boards will be coordinated by the Quartermaster Technical Committee, after which final recommendations will be submitted to this office by the Quartermaster General. In the conduct of this test, it is desired that consideration be given to the use of this vehicle in place of the motorcycle with sidecar and the tricycle type of vehicle.

That the Chiefs of Infantry, Field Artillery and Cavalry be furnished copies of Action a.[208]

This memo formally endorsed the Light Reconnaissance and Command Car effort from the highest level in the Army, the Chief of Staff. This document additionally laid out the parameters as follows: time (by August maneuvers); budget ($175,000), resources (Quartermaster General, Infantry, Cavalry and Field Artillery) and quality (the requirement of an extensive service test).

Colonel Oseth, representing the Infantry, realized this directive changed the priority of the project, "After the project was referred to the Quartermaster General's office, it had very powerful support of General Marshall, the Chief of Staff, and his office. I merely mention that because it was a fact that he had set aside $170,000, as I recall it, from some fund, towards this project."[209] In 1940, like today, money talks.

The Quartermaster General needed to decide what process to employ to procure the seventy vehicles, a competitive bid procedure, or a negotiated contract with one vendor. After the Butler conference Fenn believed the QMC would use the latter method, "Mr. Brown left us with the understanding that the two companies (Bantam and Spicer) were to collaborate in the production of this vehicle and as soon as we could arrive at a price we would submit it. There was nothing said about any possibility of anyone else being in the picture." [210]

However, Van Deusen operated under a different set of constraints:

Our procurement policy since 1933 and up until the time we actually were able to break away from the competitive method of procurement depended on the use of manufacturers' proprietary designs, which resulted from their own independent engineering efforts; that is, in motor transport. There was a different policy that has been followed by the Ordnance Department with tanks or with artillery and small arms and ammunition items. We adopted, as a standard, the proprietary design of a manufacturer. We never detailed in our transport vehicles all the factors in the vehicle.[211]

Not very well (ability to procure identical vehicles from different vendors) under the system we were operating under at that time (1940), which was the competitive type of procurement, and, under the policy which I mentioned yesterday, expressed in G. O. 9, War Department, 1933, which forces us to take complete vehicles as such from the producing industry, we would not have been assured of securing the identical vehicle from each of the three manufacturers.

We were, as I explained yesterday, depending on the manufacturers for detailed engineering, and we adapted and accepted the proprietary engineering designs that independent manufacturers developed in so far as the vehicle was concerned as long as it met our characteristics and specifications.

Colonel, what was the effective date of the Act of Congress commonly referred to as the Negotiable Contract Act? (allowing sole sourcing to a vendor without competitive bid) That was the Act of July 1, 1940. That Act was in force at that time, but we had been advised and instructed by the Assistant Secretary of War that the principles of that Act would not be applied to the procurement of motor vehicles which were an article of commercial manufacture.[212]

Despite Fenn's belief, the Quartermaster had a direct order to proceed with the procurement of the Light Reconnaissance and Command Car through a competitive bid process. Specification ES – No. 475 forwarded from Camp Holabird to QMC headquarters on July 3, 1940, one day after their finalization.[213] Officials in Washington, D.C. reviewed the requirements against the June 22, 1940, Ordnance Technical Subcommittee report and differences noted. The assessing officer, a one Mr. Burgan, in a July 5, 1940, memo to the Chief of Motor Transport recommended approval of ES – No. 475 and reported that he had ironed out the discrepancies.

I discussed the apparent differences mentioned above with Mr. Brown, Holabird Quartermaster Depot, on July 2, 1940, and again this morning after checking the specifications, and the differences referred to either have been agreed to by conference at the last meeting at Holabird, or are the best compromise that is possible under the circumstances. For instance skid plate mentioned in D-1, but not specifically called for, and omission of definite grade ability requirements due to lack of data as to weight and the increased amount of power that can be obtained from the modified engine they propose to furnish.[214]

The Adjutant General (also on July 5, 1940) signaled his support of the project endorsing the Chief of Staff's July 27, 1940, directive.[215] On July 9th, Payne, operating under the incorrect assumption of a negotiated contract process, sent a letter to the Quartermaster General detailing a sole source contract based upon ES – No. 475 and QM Drawing 08370-Z quoting a price of $2500.00 per vehicle for a total contract amount of $175,000 and promising delivery between August 20 – 30, 1940, in time for the August maneuvers, as directed by

General Marshall.[216]

The Quartermaster, however, on that same day had inquired of the Infantry about the feasibility of delivery for the August maneuvers. The using arm replied that by the summer remained impracticable and recommended, "October 15, 1940, a satisfactory date for the completion of the delivery of the test lot to the troops."[217] On July 10, 1940, with the die cast for a competitive procurement, the purchasing arm of the Army requested the following of the Assistant Secretary of War:

> g. Approval is requested for 10-day advertisement under Invitation for Bids to be issued by the Holabird Quartermaster Depot for the following:

70 Trucks, Light Reconnaissance and Command Cars, ¼-ton, 4x4, for extended service test by the Infantry, Field Artillery and Cavalry, authorized by the Adjutant General in 4th Indorsement [sic] dated July 5, 1940: Files AG 451(6-15-40)M-D.

> h. In view of the fact that delivery of these vehicles is required by the Infantry within ninety-five (95) days from this date, and considerable engineering development will be required by the successful bidder, the 10-day period for advertising is the maximum which can be used. Since preliminary development of this project has been accomplished with the collaboration of the American Bantam Car Company, Butler, Pa., this firm has offered to produce the vehicles under a negotiated contract at a price considered reasonable for such a development program, but this offer involves tooling costs and acceptance would place the firm at a decided advantage over competitors in possible future procurement of this type of vehicle.

> i. It is believed advisable, therefore, to issue 10-day advertisement for the vehicles in order to permit any other qualified and interested potential producers to submit bids. A longer period is deemed unnecessary, since only one potential bidder besides the American Bantam Car Company is known to this office, and the quantity involved is small.[218]

Eight hundred and fifty (850) copies of the bid documents, under the moniker Invitation for Bids No. 398-41-9 went out from Holabird for forwarding to "prospective bidders" on July 11, 1940. The proposal set the opening date at Monday, July 22, 1940. The package included a standard vendor questionnaire, specification ES-No. 475, QM Drawing 08370-Z and a number of QMC standards pertaining to vehicles.[219]

QMC mailed papers to one hundred and thirty-five members of the automotive industry following a, "policy of circularizing an entire cross-section of the industry in 1939 or previous to that time because of complaint that we had received from various manufacturers in the use of selective lists of manufacturers capable, in our (the QMC) opinion, of manufacturing certain types of vehicles."[220] These vendors included Willys-Overland Motors, Inc. and the Ford Motor Company. Chapter 9 includes details on the former's bid. The following section details Bantam's journey through the bid process.

July 12-21, 1940—Butler, Pennsylvania

The rejection of their offer and the need to participate in a bidding process caught Fenn and Payne off guard. American Bantam in fact did not have an engineering department and would have to immediately create one to compete for the contract. That would bring onto the Bantam team the next key individual to move the effort forward: automotive engineering veteran Karl K. Probst.

The Detroit engineering expert, at sixty and having thirty-seven years of industry experience by 1940, would represent the seasoned veteran of the Bantam team. A mechanical engineering graduate of Ohio State University, he worked for a number of years for various companies, landing in Detroit by 1933. He established a consulting office in that city, and over the next seven years, would work with almost all the firms in the car business including Packard, Ford, Chrysler, and some for General Motors.[221]

Figure 36: Karl K. Probst.

As Probst recounted years later, "1940 was a time to work and pay your bills, not consider jobs with no guaranteed salary." At that time, however, the Germans mounted blistering daily bombing raids against England, which caused Fenn to take the initiative.

He called Arthur Brandt, a General Motors employee (and former President of American Austin) working with the newly formed National Defense Advisory Committee (a body created to begin coordinating efforts between the government and industry for the nascent military buildup) which William Knudsen, the head of General Motors led. Fenn wanted Brandt to convince Probst to come to Butler and work for free (with the provision that if Bantam won the contract he would receive compensation) to design the vehicle for the bid.[222]

Brandt contacted Probst on Saturday, July 13, 1940, but the Detroit automotive designer did not want to drop everything and go to Butler. He told Brandt to have Fenn call him on Monday. Fenn reached the engineer on Monday, July 15th, and after some discussion Probst told the Bantam President to call him when he had the bid specification.[223] Brandt telephoned on Tuesday, and as the Detroit design consultant later recalled, on this call Brandt pulled out the "big guns".

I got a call from Art Brandt in Knudsen's office in Washington. Knudsen knew of my work; years before, I had presented my plans to him for a lightweight GM car. Knudsen was deep in the Army Scout car project.

When Art told him of my attitude, Bill said to tell me that this was important to the country, forget about the salary, to forget about my own office. "We think you can do this job faster than the big companies," Art told me referring to Bantam. "Financing will be available if you produce a vehicle to specs," Art advised me.

"Well, if you put it like that," I replied, "I can't refuse Mr. Knudsen."[224]

Fenn called again on Wednesday, July 17th, after receiving the bid specification. The two executives engaged in a detailed discussion on the challenges inherent in what the Army proposed, but eventually Probst decided to leave for Butler that night. He stopped at Spicer Axle to discuss that critical component with Fred Hall and Robert Lewis, manager of the axle division and chief engineer of the railway and axle division, respectively.[225] Probst recalled:

I discussed with them the requirements of this proposed vehicle. They showed me the four-wheel design, roughed out, using the Bantam axle, which were considerably lighter than were later selected. They had previously done work for Bantam on a vehicle of this type but of somewhat less horsepower, and the specifications which came through called for more horsepower; therefore, the axles and the other work which had been done by Spicer were not applicable, so it was necessary to get heavier axles and transfer cases. We discussed that and got them set and they were started at that interview, at the time I stopped, on Wednesday.[226]

The seasoned automotive designer arrived in Butler on Thursday, July 18th with Bantam's bid proposal due on Monday, July 22nd.[227] Probst introduced to Crist that morning and he conferred with Bantam factory manager, who presented the Detroit engineer with tentative "specs" for the vehicle, and the former Studebaker employee helped Probst develop a vision for the vehicle.[228] They decided 50% of the chassis parts would need to come from already existing components changed to meet the needs of the new vehicle. After consulting the telephone book for possible parts suppliers, and the available blueprints for ideas, the designer began drafting the vehicle at 1:00 PM.[229] Probst worked throughout that day, slept, and then worked a full day on Friday, July 19th to complete his work. A chassis parts list completed overnight and on the 20th estimated costs calculated with the help of Crist. The bid forms completed on Sunday by Fenn and Probst, and the two-headed toward Baltimore for an evening meeting with Payne.[230]

July 21, 1940—Baltimore, Maryland–Late Evening

While reviewing the documents that night, Bantam's Washington D.C. representative initially only found some minor items to correct.

> Well, if I remember, he (Payne) thought the angle of approach we had shown – I believe he wanted that changed, and I believe the size of the gasoline tank in our specifications I believe were a little under. I can't remember exactly what changes we made that night. I think they were minor changes that would conform more to the specs than the ones we had drawn. They were minor changes affecting minor changes in the job and the thought we had not quite met the specs as originally issued and maybe we could do better on a few dimensions and we changed a few figures.[231]

The seasoned automotive expert, testifying in an official court case in 1945, failed to mention that Payne had found a major issue, as Probst explained in a later recollection.

> Going over the bid forms, he came to my weight figure of 1,850 pounds. He exploded, "Don't you fellows know you can't get accepted at that weight? They never expect you to make the weight in the specifications but you've got to bid it at the 1300 pound figure. We'll get it revised after we get the contract."[232]

Probst was flabbergasted at the idea of misrepresenting the weight, knowing full well that it was impossible to meet the 1,300-pound requirement. The designer figured the gig was up. However, Payne stated he would use a contact at Holabird to obtain new blank forms that night and would enlist the hotel manager's stenographer to retype the forms. She arrived at 3:30 AM, retyped all the forms (with a new weight of 1,273 pounds). She finished just in time for Fenn, Probst and Payne to make it to the QMC motor vehicle depot at 8:30 AM on Monday, July 22nd.[233]

July 21, 1940—Bantam's Bid Proposal

The Bantam team took the statement "bidders are cautioned to read carefully all instructions contained herein as well as those in Standard Government Instructions to Bidders (Standard Form No. 22)" to heart and completed their bid forms to the Quartermaster's exacting demands.

The Butler firm's response contained the completed "standard government form of bid" cover page for an invitation for bids No. 398-41-9, and showed a proposal opening date of 10:00 AM EST on July 22, 1940. The form dated July 20, 1940, showed its completion in Butler, Pennsylvania. This entry confirms Probst's account that he finished the documents in Butler. As he related, though, they retyped the questionnaire in Baltimore in the middle of the night to correct the weight requirement.[234] The Bantam team stated:

> In compliance with your invitation for bids to furnish materials and supplies listed on the reverse hereof or on the accompanying schedules, numbered: Sheet No. 1b, and Q.M.C. Tentative Specification ES- No. 475 dated July 2,

1940, the undersigned American Bantam Car Company a corporation organized and existing under the laws of the State of Pennsylvania a partnership consisting of … an individual trading as … of the city of Butler, Pennsylvania hereby proposes to furnish, within the time specified, the materials and supplies at the prices stated opposite the respective items listed on the schedules and agrees upon receipt of written notice of the acceptance of this bid within AT ONCE days (60 days if no shorter period specified) after the date of opening of bids, to execute, if required, the Standard Government Form of Contract (Standard Form No. 32) in accordance with the bid as accepted, and to give bond, if required, with good and sufficient surety or sureties, for the faithful performance of the contract, within 10 days after the prescribed forms are presented for signature.[235]

The upstart small car manufacturer offered a 1% discount and Francis Fenn signed the form as President of the American Bantam Car Company, Butler, Pennsylvania.

In accordance with the bid instructions a schedule included which contained a main bid and two alternative bids as shown in detail in Table 2.

Table 2: Bantam Main Bid and Two Alternative Bids (page 1877)

Shipments

Bantam offered all vehicles F.O.B. (free on board/freight on board) Manufacturer's Plant for shipment on Government Bill of Lading or Driven away by Government personnel. The bidder included stipulations, which marked the company's first recognition of the greatest risk to the work, to wit, the development of a front axle that would meet the military's four-wheel-drive requirement. Further, they recognized their second greatest risk, the incredibly short development time[236]:

> At the present writing no four-wheel-drive equipment in this size is in production. The actual design and layout for this equipment is practically complete however. We will deliver the Pilot model to Holabird forty-nine days from the date of order as this is the best time that can be made because of the necessity of waiting for the new four-wheel-drive axles.[237]

The carefully developed proposal next contained the completed instructions to bidders page, which stated in capital letters at the bottom – DO NOT DETACH THIS SHEET. It obligated the bidder to the stipulations contained on the page. Then Fenn signed a clause that read:

> It is hereby warranted that all unmanufactured articles, materials or supplies furnished under this agreement have been mined or produced in the United States, and that all manufactured articles, materials, or supplies have been

manufactured in the United States from articles, materials, or supplies mined, produced or manufactured in the United States, except as noted below or otherwise indicated herein.[238]

The bankrupt firm in Butler's acceptance of the exacting specifications in section-D and award-winning responses to the questionnaire provided the foundation for the contract. This document also guided the way the team built its pilot model and provided the basis for how the Army tested the vehicle upon delivery as shown in Table 3.

Table 3: Bantam's Response to Army Requirements (page 188)

RFP for Tactical Vehicles

The RFP had described in great detail what the Army required of the vehicle in both performance and parts as laid out in specification ES-No. 475. This document referenced a number of other specifications, as well as laid out extensive service requirements. The overall general requirement, referenced in section C, Service Requirements, as C-1 stated:

> The trucks described in this specification are intended for use as tactical vehicles by the United States Army. They will be required to transport the rated payload, which will consist of personnel and ammunition, at relatively high rates of speed over all types of roads, trails, open and rolling cross country, with the driving wheel tires, at times, equipped with tire chains, under all conditions of weather and terrain. The truck shall be of such a design and construction as to permit of its servicing, adjustment and repair, with the minimum practicable difficulty, time and tool equipment, under difficult field service conditions. The following service and detailed requirements must be fully complied with to insure that the trucks will satisfactorily perform the required functions.[239]

Bantam also completed the one page "Standard Government Form of Bid" as well as the front page of the "Instructions to Bidders" document. The Butler manufacturer completed all the documents and submitted a conceptual drawing of their proposed vehicle the only bidder to do so.[240]

The Butler upstart clearly intended to attempt to meet the Army's desired specification with the exception of the weight requirement.

July 22, 1940—Camp Holabird, Maryland

At Camp Holabird on the morning of July 22, 1940, the American Bantam Car Company had competition. Willys-Overland Motors, Inc. (the phantom "other interested party" referenced in the Quartermaster's July 10, 1940, memo seeking the Adjutant General's permission to proceed with the bid process) had prepared a bid package, though handwritten and represented a time and cost bid only: no plans, weights or specifications.[241] Willys had sent a letter to the Quartermaster Corps on July 20, 1940, stating:

> We have been rather rushed in preparing this bid due to the fact that we did not receive complete information until Wednesday of this week. Therefore if there are any additional facts that we can supply or any questions which you may have concerning our bid I would greatly appreciate if you will call me collect at Willys-Overland Motors, Inc. Toledo, Ohio.[242]

The Toledo manufacturer had a case as the bid came as a complete surprise to them (Chapter 9). Meanwhile Bantam had the advantage of having helped develop the generic requirements and detailed specifications. That Willys entered a bid at all testifies to their desire to compete for this opportunity.

Ford and Crosley would round out the competitors at the depot when Major Lawes called for bids, an unusually low number for a procurement. At the proposal opening time of 10:00 AM, Ford and Crosley declined to submit arguing the impossibility of building the prototype in forty-nine days, Willys offered their package and Fenn, Payne and Probst tendered their proposal.[243]

As Probst later described:

> On that sweltering July 22, 1940, we waited only thirty minutes for the decision. I thought I was sweating it out but discovered later that the temperature hit 101 degrees that day and two people died of the heat.

> Major Lawes, the purchasing and contracting officer for Holabird, called us into his office at 10:30 with the Willys people. He started by saying, "Willys has the low bid," and paused. The bottom dropped out of me. Frank turned white. Payne cracked his knuckles. "However," Major Lawes continued, "our requirements are forty-nine days delivery for the pilot car. Bantam has bid forty-nine days; Willys has bid seventy-five days. The contract will be awarded to the company that commits to our delivery requirement – Bantam."

> Dismissing the Willys group, Lawes said to us, "We know you have no engineering department left. Probst will have to find one quickly. It will take ten to eighteen days to process the contract through the various departments. But from then on, you must, under penalty, deliver in forty-nine calendar days; seven weeks, no more."[244]

Lawes then laid out the salient details for building the pilot model.

    j.   Bantam had to create engineering resources immediately;

> k. Two weeks to complete the award and then Evans' and Fenn's team would have seven weeks, forty-nine days, to deliver the prototype; and
>
> l. If the vehicle survived the testing phase the firm would receive an order for the seventy vehicles for field testing.[245]

At this juncture the active role for Commander Charles H. Payne ended. He had accomplished his mission, begun in February 1940, to interest the United States Army in a lightweight vehicle and have the American Bantam Car Company build it. Colonel Oseth recognized the former naval aviator's contribution.

> Well, Mr. Payne, as a representative of the Bantam Company, furnished the opportunity that we (the Infantry) had been looking for to have an infantry battlefield vehicle manufactured and designed. He did extremely valuable work as a high-pressure salesman, and he was a good one in lining up, in removing objections within the War Department itself.
>
> There are a great many things that stand in the way of a project of this kind when it is initiated. There is a natural conservatism sometimes, here and there, on the part of individuals. Mr. Payne worked continuously. He was practically ubiquitous in getting in touch with these people that objected, either having them overruled by the next higher person, or removing their objection. His contribution was that of a salesman and promoter, who furnished us with the opportunity which we hadn't previously, of getting what we wanted in a battlefield vehicle.[246]

Bantam won the RFP process, and while the Quartermaster Corps drafted a contract based upon the RFP and Bantam's response, the team in Butler began preparations to build their prototype.

PAUL R. BRUNO

Chapter 7: Building the First Jeep

While the Bantam team returned to Butler after the bid award to prepare to attempt the seemingly impossible, the Army's bureaucracy churned out the last of the appropriate paperwork. The frantic attempt to make history in 49 days began on August 5, 1940.

July 23-August 5, 1940—Washington, D.C.

The Army quickly completed a technical analysis of the winning bid. Table 4 contains the key findings of the review.

Table 4: Technical Analysis of Bids Submitted (page 192)

Bid Endorsement

Official endorsement of the technical analysis came on July 25, 1940:

1. Award under invitation for bids No. 398-41-9 will be made to the American Bantam Car Co., Butler, Pa., as follows:

    Item No. 1.a. (Alternate) —For sixty-two (62) Trucks, Light Reconnaissance and Command Car 4 X 4, at a unit cost of $2419.50, less 1%-10 days, plus $8.06 per truck for furnishing one (1) spare wheel, tire and tube; Total Net Cost: $148,763.11.

    Item No. 1.b. (Alternate of Item No. 1.a.) – For eight (8) Trucks, Light Reconnaissance and Command Car, 4 X 4, at a unit cost of $2823.00 less 1%-10 days, plus $8.06 per truck for furnishing one (1) spare wheel, tire and tube; Total Net Cost: $22,422.64.

    Total net value of award—70 Trucks: $171,185.75.

2. Recommendation of your depot contained in the Technical Analysis of Bids are concurred in, except that the offer made by the American Bantam Car Company under exception noted in Par. F-34. D. 2 (spare tire location), should be accepted, and complete compliance with the requirement of Par. D-5. should be required.

3. Necessary funds, Tr-Authorities and route orders will be furnished under separate cover at an early date.[247]

Contract

The Army sent official notification of the award to Bantam by telegram on the same day (July 25, 1940) that they accepted the Butler manufacturer's bid.[248] The contract was dated August 1, 1940, and finalized on August 5, 1940. This document provided the final information the squad in Butler would have to build the pilot and included some changes and additional information as reported in the technical analysis.

The agreement first specified the number of vehicles ordered as well as their cost as follows:

ITEM NO. 1.a: 62 Each TRUCKS, MOTOR, GASOLINE, LIGHT RECONNAISSANCE and COMMAND CAR (FOUR WHEELS-FOUR WHEEL DRIVE), in accordance with Q.M.C. Tentative Specification ES-No. 475, dated July 2, 1940. To be equipped with FULL-FLOATING TYPE REAR AXLE:

Unit Cost	$2,415.50
Gross Cost of Item 1.a	$149,761.00
Less discount of 1% for payment in 10 days	1,497.61
Net Cost	$148,263.39
Plus $8.06 net per truck for one (1) spare wheel tire & tube	499.72
TOTAL NET COST OF Item 1.a	$148,763.11

ITEM NO. 1.b: 8 Each TRUCKS, MOTOR, GASOLINE, LIGHT RECONNAISSANCE and COMMAND CAR (FOUR WHEELS—FOUR WHEEL DRIVE), in accordance with Q.M.C. Tentative Specification ES-No. 475, dated July 2, 1940. To be equipped with FULL-FLOATING TYPE REAR AXLE and FOUR WHEEL STEERING MECHANISM:

Unit Cost	$2,823.00
Gross Cost of Item 1.b.	$22,584.00
Less discount of 1% for payment in 10 days	$225.84
Net Cost	$22,358.16
Plus $8.06 net per truck for one (1) spare wheel tire & tube	$64.48
TOTAL NET COST OF Item 1.b.	$22,422.64
TOTAL GROSS COST	$173,070.56
TOTAL NET COST [249]	$171,185.75

The amount of the arrangement just under the $175,000 that the Army had budgeted to procure the vehicles. The Quartermaster Corps between July 22, 1940, and August 1, 1940, had completed a more thorough analysis of Bantam's bid and included twenty-four additional stipulations, requirements, and requests for information in the contract.

Table 5: Contract—Additional Requirements (page 193)

The final section of the deal would detail the overall requirements including the stipulation that would make history: delivery of the pilot model in just forty-nine (49) days.

> As set forth in your bid you agree to complete deliveries as follows: Pilot Model within forty-nine (49) days, that is on or before September 20, 1940; Sixty-one (61) vehicles under Item 1.a. to be delivered twenty-six (26) days after delivery and approval of Pilot Model; an additional two (2) weeks will be granted for delivery of the eight (8) vehicles under Item 1.b. To enable this office to have an inspector at your plant when these vehicles are ready for shipment it is requested that you notify this office at least five (5) days in advance of the date same will be ready for Government inspection. War Department Registration Numbers will be furnished as soon as they become available to this office.[250]

Forty-nine days from the contract date of August 1, 1940, ended on September 20, 1940. It took a little more time to iron out the details and the Quartermaster set the clock ticking on August 5, 1940. September 23, 1940, no later than 5:00 PM, became the deadline to supply the Bantam pilot model to Camp Holabird.

June 22-August 5, 1940—Butler, PA

Figure 37: Pilot Chassis Rail—September 3, 1940. Photo Courtesy of Robert Brandon, Butler, PA

As mentioned in chapter 6, Fenn believed in June 1940 that Bantam would receive the work to attempt to build the new vehicle through a negotiated contract. Having no idea when the Army would award the contract for the vehicle or their expected delivery date for the trucks, the Bantam President did not delay in beginning preparations.

> I told them (Bantam personnel) to immediately get to work and compile all possible data with the view to assisting drawing specifications on the proposed vehicle. We had several draftsman and detailers, and I didn't feel that the thing was far enough along to warrant us in employing any engineers on the job.

> During the first and second days that the members of the technical committee were there they laid down certain performance characteristics that the car should have, so we went to work to see how many Bantam components could be used to meet those performance characteristics. We were constantly in touch with Mr. Hall and we immediately began to call in manufacturers of small engines, such as Hercules and Continental. Hercules were very much on the

ball and were in our plant quite frequently. In fact, they were in there two and three days at a time.

Now, they had one particular engine that if you were to look at it you would say, "Well, it is that engine." The bore was different in respect to several sizes which would give the engine a greater cubic displacement and consequently more power. As we were shooting for weight, however, we were not quite satisfied with the weight of the Hercules engine, and we asked Continental to come in. Continental came in, and we found we could get more horsepower with less weight by making certain changes, such as changing the Bell housing.

Another thing that was very important was the fact that Hercules were reluctant to make any changes in their standard engine and Continental were willing to make the changes. For example, it was brought out during the conference between ourselves and the technical committee that this car would

have to operate at impossible angles, that is, it might be tilted up 15 to 20 degrees on one side, and such as that, and it might have to climb grades as steep as 60-degree grades. That would necessarily mean that in order for the engine to have a proper supply of oil that we would have to have a deeper oil pan; and Hercules weren't particularly anxious to go along with the changes in their standard engine that would be necessary to meet those requirements.

Figure 38: Chassis Coming Together—September 5, 1940.
Photo Courtesy of Robert Brandon, Butler, PA

So we began to swing to Continental, because of their willingness to make those changes, and the lighter weight, although at the time the tender of bid was made (July 22, 1940) we had not reached a conclusion as to whether we would use Hercules or Continental. From the standpoint of clearance the Hercules engine offered some advantages. We had not reached a decision as to whether those advantages outweighed the advantages offered by Continental.

We had numerous telephone conversations with Mr. Hall and after the Spicer Manufacturing Company, who, after all, are specialists in the building of differentials and propeller shafts, items like transfer cases, after they had completely explored the thing they advised against the use of the Bantam axle.

Then followed a lot of shuffling around to see what axle could be used. They were in production of the Studebaker Champion axles, and it was decided that we would use that axle. Then came the problem of the frame, and weight of the frame, and the type of construction, and we decided the frame should be a box-type frame, which was not in use in the automotive industry, either the truck industry or the car industry, at that time. That meant additional weight. As a result of our work the box type frame was adapted and the whole construction of the car had to be canvassed.[251]

Figure 39: Ralph Turner Examining the Engine. Photo Courtesy of Robert Brandon, Butler, PA

By the time of the award of the contract on August 5, 1940, Bantam had decided on the box-type frame; aero plane-type shock absorbers; the modified Studebaker axle with their transmission with certain changes in it and a transfer case to be built by Spicer; that the body could not be made to conform to the originally expressed desire for a 36-inch silhouette, and the silhouette at least 40 inches; the radiator and carburetor to use; the use of stock lighting ignition, and that the engine would have at least 85 cubic inches capacity.[252] Fenn also remembered that:

> Pending the outcome of the bid he (Crist) started procedures for securing material from which to fabricate many car and chassis parts in advance of engineering. He also selected two other men to assist him in the actual construction of the first vehicle or prototype. Others were selected to provide backup assistance and supply to the three doing the physical creating.[253]

After the award of the bid to Bantam on July 22, 1940, Probst went to work building the engineering capacity not needed just one month earlier.

Figure 40: Body Tube and Rail Assembly—September 4, 1940. Photo Courtesy of Robert Brandon, Butler, PA

> "Bantam had no engineers at that time and it was necessary for me (Probst) to go to Detroit and find some engineers to do this job. It took me about a week to line up three or four men with any experience. I think I got them back to Butler about the first of August, the engineers, and I believe the award came in the 4th or 5th of August, the official date."[254]

The Bantam team had wisely used the six weeks from the time the Army committee left on June 21 to the award of the contract; however, as the dog days of the summer of 1940 wore on, the forty-nine-day deadline still seemed impossible.

The Butler automotive manufacturer had two experienced hands in Probst and Crist to guide the engineering and hands-on building of the pilot model. However, the Bantam factory manager would also need other experienced staff to pull off the almost unfeasible feat of building the vehicle from the ground up. Fenn's right-hand man wanted to keep the core team small and he knew exactly who he needed to round out his group.

August 6-September 17, 1940—Butler, PA

Chester Hempfling, born, raised and graduated high school in Butler, and went to work at the Armco Steel mill until 1929. He joined the predecessor to the American Bantam Car Company, American Austin, in 1930, and remained gainfully employed by both establishments for the next eighteen years. He represented another "can-do, jack-of-all-trades" automotive man as shown by his imaginative solution to directly delivering a vehicle to a customer during his time with American Austin:

Figure 41: Chassis Drive Train Under Construction. Photo Courtesy of Robert Brandon, Butler, PA

> We lined up the service car and the one to be delivered and attached a tow bar. Next we would tie-in the ignition of the new car to a toggle switch in the service car. I adjusted the throttle screw of the towed car so that the engine would be running about 30–35 mph, shut off the engine and set the car in high gear. To start off, I would tow the rear car, then cut in the ignition of it with the toggle switch. It would jerk a little, then settle down and off we would go. At a hill which might slow the Austin down, with that car pushing and no one in it, I'd go up the hill at 35–40 mph! At traffic lights I would shut off the rear car and control the front one. Once, in Pittsburgh, I was too busy in traffic controlling the front car to shut the back car off and it jack-knifed and pushed me sideways up on the pavement. There was a lot of power in the hook-up![255]

Figure 42: Chester Hempfling with the tin snips the German metal smith used to cut the rounded hood on the pilot model. Photo Courtesy of Robert Brandon, Butler, PA

Hempfling would form one half of a dynamic duo that contributed greatly to the successful completion of the Bantam pilot model. Crist also hired another experienced individual in Butler native Ralph Turner. During his high school years he worked in a watch repair shop and after graduating in 1928 he sold Hudson automobiles. He lost that job at the depths of the Great Depression and fell back on his timepiece experience finding work at the Elgin Watch Company factory in Elgin, Illinois. He returned to Butler eight years later to take over the watch repair shop after the death of the man who had employed him during his youth. At this establishment, Crist made the acquaintance of this mechanically gifted individual. The Bantam factory manager talked him into joining the American Bantam Car Company and made him general foreman of the production line. In this capacity, destiny would tap his shoulder and thus make him a key individual in the building of Bantam's Light Reconnaissance and Command Car prototype.[256]

The improbable had met the impossible and Karl Probst, Harold Crist, Chester Hempfling and Ralph Turner had their work cut out for them. While all had vast amounts of hands-on automotive experience none had ever attempted something of this magnitude, building a revolutionary new vehicle with strict requirements, in the seemingly unimaginable time of forty-nine days. The doubters were many, including the legion of experts in Detroit, who betted 5–1 against Bantam.[257]

Probst laid out the general game plan for completing the vehicle in forty-nine days.

> We can find the engine; I'm thinking of a commercial engine (A Hercules was specified first, then a Continental) I've used before. I know the clutch and transmission we'll buy, the Spicer transfer case and, of course, the axles from Studebaker. To make that ridiculous forty-nine days, we've got to lay our hands on every possible part that's already available in production today.[258]

Probst knew he had a top-notch leader in Harold Crist: "On Thursday the 17th (of July) I met with Frank Fenn and his factory manager, Harold Crist. Crist was a human dynamo. He and his four key men (Hempfling and Turner the most important) could produce tools and parts—some with no drawings. We needed that ability for sure."[259] The prototype's building would be a design, build, design, build iterative process with rework the norm.

> As with any completely new prototype, everything had to be made by hand. Even stock items, such as brakes and steering gear, required alterations. The shaping and fitting of sheet metal was accomplished by trial and error. Hundreds of parts, including jigs and fixtures, were fabricated from rough sketches. There had been no time for the preparation of detailed drawings.[260]

Figure 43: Transmission and Transfer Case. Photo Courtesy of Robert Brandon, Butler, PA

The team's responsibilities broke down as follows:

Crist was the boss. Turner was responsible for the chassis and the engine. I

(Hempfling) was responsible for fabricating the sheet metal parts. I would like to say at this time that Ralph and I were "mechanics" not engineers. Engineers are college graduates who do drawings, and the drawings are sent to the workshop for production. Most engineers have no idea of how to work the machines used in production. We mechanics hand made the parts. They were then laid out on a block and pictures were taken. They were then sent to the drafting department and blueprints were then made. The blueprints were made after the part was made.[261]

One writer characterized in glowing terms how this group of intrepid, talented individuals found themselves thrust into the center of history.

Gathered at American Bantam's Butler factory, north of Pittsburgh, was a group of ingenious seat-of-the-pants engineers, craftsmen, and inspired mechanics so typical of the early days of the automotive industry. One of them was Harold Crist, who had been an engineer in the heyday of the Stutz Motor Co. of Indianapolis, builders of the legendary, cutting-edge Stutz racing cars. Crist focused on the contract bid with two Butler-area natives, Ralph Turner and Chester Hempfling, both imaginative, resourceful, and highly skilled hands-on craftsmen/mechanics.[262]

Ralph Turner described the overall process of how the first Jeep came to life:

I had the job of cutting the metal, and then putting it together. I can remember Crist sitting by the hour on a nail keg changing the design a little here and there as we finalized the first prototype.

I first went to Armco Steel which was located next door to the Bantam plant to get steel cut in the shape that we wanted to make the frame. I took it back to Bantam, and made a "box frame." A box frame is light and strong because it has the ability to twist and give without breaking. We then cut the sheet metal to shape, and formed the body of the Bantam. Crist wanted a curved and rounded hood. No one knew how to make a rounded hood, so Crist hired a German metalsmith to do the job. The man took an acetylene torch and a series of hammers, and pounded a perfectly rounded hood. The engine was provided by the Continental Engine Company of Butler (45HP). The differential came from the Spicer Company of Toledo, Ohio. I had to take each axle and cut it down to size. We had Ross steering, Stromberg carburetors, Harrison radiators, etc. All companies buy common components from specialty companies.

The next step was to make a transmission with a transfer case. I went down to a local junk yard and acquired two Chevy transmissions. I then cut the sides out of them and welded them together. I had to totally rework the insides to get the desired result. I had to re-drill some of the holes, line up the shafts, and, re-gear the transfer case, and make it work.

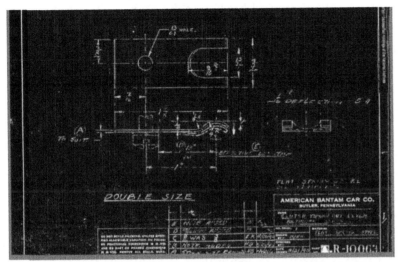

Figure 44: The Clutch Throw Out Lever Original Blueprint for the Bantam pilot model. Source—United States National Archives, College Park, Maryland

I remember once that Crist and Probst got into an argument about the front engine mount. Probst wanted a straight mount coming up from the frame- Crist knew from practical experience that the mount had to be angled to accommodate the torque of the engine. Crist won the argument and the Bantam was built with a front motor mount that set at an angle.[263]

The men worked tirelessly day after day seven days a week. He (Crist) was known as a "go-getter" and now he proved the phrase aptly applied. As he and his small group worked unremittingly day and night selecting components, assembling, adapting and adjusting parts, solving problems and ever racing time to complete the job within specified bid time limitations... the impossible was accomplished. Each morning the chief draftsman of the Bantam Company (Probst) had checked the progress of Harold and his crew, made sketches of the items successfully installed the day and night previously, and added them to the list of builders materials. The end result was a vehicle which incorporated, in all major areas, those ideas which later proved to be so fundamentally correct as to be used in that order even today some forty-odd years later.[264]

Crist, Probst, Hempfling, and I (Turner) worked almost 24 hours a day during these 49 days. Sometimes, the project would be on schedule, and I would go home to get some sleep. No sooner would I get to sleep than Crist would call and say "Come on back Ralph; We have a new problem." I never thought that men could get so tired and still work.[265]

Crist worked us day and night. He wouldn't let us leave. Ralph and I (Hempfling) slept many nights in the upstairs girl's restroom ... A German metalsmith used an acetylene torch and a set of hammers to form the rounded hood. I still have the tin snips that the German "special ordered" to cut the sheet metal.[266]

You can only put just so many men on a job like this, so working around the clock became more of rule for us all than an exception.[267]

Late into the night, seven days a week, Crist and his key technicians – Chester Hempfling and Ralph Turner – worked with tireless determination. Evans visited the experimental shop whenever possible, often rolling up his sleeves and lending an extra pair of hands.[268]

Under Crist's watchful eye, Turner and Hempfling fabricated some of the parts on the Butler factory floor and purchased others from the richly laden shelf of automotive products available in the American industry – axles from Spicer, a radiator from Harrison, a Continental four-cylinder engine, a Stromberg carburetor. Turner got steel from the neighboring Armco steel plant and personally welded and fabricated the sturdy box frame for the vehicle. At a Butler junkyard he bought two Chevrolet transmissions that he cut, welded together, modified, geared, and mated to a transfer case to provide four-wheel-drive. In a way, Crist's team worked backwards, fashioning the vehicle almost ex nihilo, without a set of blueprints. Bantam draftsmen converted what they built into drawings.[269]

The team operated by the seat of their pants, but their hard work and years of hands-on automotive experience began paying off. However, even with all their extraordinary effort and expertise, the work progressed slowly and a major item (the front axle) remained unresolved as the dog days of August ended and the cool nights of September ticked by.

The two key issues that the team needed to overcome revolved around the front axle and the vehicle's weight. Early on Bantam decided to ignore the weight requirement and build the vehicle to specifications.

Figure 45: Chassis Assembly as of September 10, 1940. Photo Courtesy of Robert Brandon, Butler, PA

"Karl," he (Fenn) screamed, "Are you ready for the kicker? Do you know what it's supposed to weigh? Thirteen hundred pounds! That's what our twenty horsepower job was supposed to weigh. And it's got to be delivered in forty-nine days under penalty!"

With the patience of an older person Probst waited before addressing the issues:

When he calmed down a bit, I replied, "We can produce drawings faster than our competitors (allaying the forty-nine day fear). Of course we can't make the weight, but neither can anyone else."[270]

This left resolving the front axle situation, identified as the critical component from the very beginning of the project, based upon the fact Fenn had called Fred Hall of Spicer to Butler on June 20, 1940, (chapter 5). Probst related how he and Fenn determined the Army's specification had made Bantam's axle unusable for the prototype, which led to the choice of adapting the Studebaker axle.

> Wednesday, July 17th: Fenn called shouting so loudly that he almost didn't need long distance. "We have the formal bids. Somebody made just one little change. They raised the horsepower from the Bantam's twenty to forty! Karl, you know what that means. Our transmission won't take it; our axles won't take it; frame, suspension. We'll have to jack up the horn button so you can design a new car under it."[271]

Probst and Fenn did not fold their cards at the first sign of trouble. They brainstormed a possible solution on the spot, a characteristic the Bantam team would exhibit time and again.

> "Well", Frank said, "start now for Spicer (a specialty axle supplier which ironically had built axles for American Austin).[272] We'll have to get heavier axles; also the two-speed transfer case. Can you get here by nine Thursday morning?" I said I could by driving at night. I had made up my mind.

> In my '38 Buick Special coupe, I headed toward Telegraph Road to Toledo. At Spicer, I met with Bob Lewis, who had to give up any plans to convert the Bantam axle. Spicer made another axle, however, which was used by the Studebaker Champion, a 2,100-pound car with 65 hp; we decided to use that. We did some work on the transfer case and by three o'clock, I was driving east to Cleveland and then towards Butler, putting pieces together in my mind as I drove.[273]

Figure 46: Body Added Sometime After September 10, 1940.
Photo Courtesy of Robert Brandon, Butler, PA

Probst and Fenn had laid the groundwork for mitigating this key risk, but could Spicer deliver?

Fred Hall and Robert Lewis unwittingly became involved in the maelstrom of the light reconnaissance and command car project due to one single factor: Spicer Manufacturing represented the only firm in the United States that could produce the axle, which transmits power from the rear of the transmission to the wheel. The Army required it, and the military, as well as American Bantam, knew that only Spicer could manufacture the axle that would make the critical four-wheel-drive function.[274] That capacity, combined with a powerful engine, would make the new vehicle truly special.

Fred Hall had worked at Spicer as the manager of the axle division since 1929 and Robert Lewis worked alongside him as chief engineer of the railway and axle division. These two men represented the preeminent axle experts in the world at that time. Lewis provided a detailed account of the background of the axle that was eventually developed for the Light Reconnaissance and Command Car.[275]

> The history of the axle design and development goes back to our original basic patent on axles in 1933 and '35; all axles we manufacture are based on these original patents. In December 1939 we started the particular design for a four-wheel-drive half-ton truck for the United States Army for Camp Holabird. Those designs were continued on until about the middle of 1940, and drawings submitted to Major William B. Johnson, and also, conferences were held with Major Johnson and Captain Newell. This design, although larger, was almost identical to present (1944) Jeep axles.
>
> June the 19th, 1940, I was in conference with Major Johnson and Captain Newell at Holabird when Mr. Hall was called to Butler in connection with a small Jeep. Hall was there to help in crystallizing the ideas as to what could be done, and the axles and transfer cases is one of the main units, and Hall was there to represent what could be done along that line. On Mr. Hall's return from Butler he brought back a tentative car specification of a small four by four car, using a small engine of 35-foot-pounds torque, which he obtained according to his notes given to me, from Bob Brown at the conference in Butler, Pennsylvania.
>
> June the 28th, 1940, we started our first sketches of the four-wheel-drive car, four-wheel-drive axles for that car on our small model 10 axle, which was the original model axle used on the original Bantam car. These designs were carried along until we got word that they were stepping up the engine size to 65-foot-pounds, which came out in the new Federal specifications. We received that on July 15, 1940, which has already been covered by Mr. Hall. On July 16, 1940, we started the same design carried along to the larger size axle, which was our Model 23 axle, and these drawings were submitted to American Bantam.
>
> On July 19, 1940, and July 23rd, we made sketches showing the proposed gear and shaft locations. On July 24th, 1940, we received the first Bantam print of the chassis layout showing the axle carrier on the right-hand side. On July 29, 1940, we sent Bantam preliminary prints of our layout, axle layouts. On August the 7th, the Spicer final drawing of the experimental axle on the first job that was built.
>
> August the 9th, 1940, additional car specifications were received. On August 12, 1940, we released the first drawings for the material to be made for the very

first axle. On August 20, 1940, we received a Bantam print of the body layout showing the axle carrier on the left hand side, and also a print of the drawing on the front axle assembly. On September 18, 1940, we finished assembling the first axles and shipped it to the American Bantam Company.[276]

By modifying the Studebaker axle that Fenn, Probst and Spicer had determined could do the job, and through a Herculean effort that Lewis downplayed, the two axle engineers supplied the key component five days before the due date for delivery to Holabird. The timely delivery of this key part made an on-time completion of the Bantam prototype possible.

September 18–22, 1940—Butler, PA

As the days grew colder, the leaves began to turn autumn colors and with time running out the combination of preparation, hard work, and talent finally began to come together.

Sunday, September 15th (8 days before the deadline) was the day the sun shone on Bantam. Bob Lewis at Spicer came through with our axles and we could see the last of our potential bottlenecks. I wired our ten major suppliers, "On Sunday, September 22nd, you will have up to one hour with our car and a driver to discover any required changes and adjustments …" late the following Saturday (September 21, 1940), it all came together. We filled the tank with

Figure 47: Bantam #1—The Very First Jeep—Minutes After Assembly Completed on September 21, 1940. Crist is driving, Bob Brown is in the passenger seat, Probst leans against the spare tire at far left.
Photo Courtesy of Robert Brandon, Butler, PA

gas for the first time and rolled the car out. It had been forty-seven days since we'd started with what seemed like nothing more than a horn button. "Get a Kodak," somebody shouted and we crowded into and around the car, all sixteen of us, nearly all the people who had worked so hard to get the job done. In the snapshot, I'm leaning on the spare tire.[277]

After they took the photograph the team still had the first of many issues to resolve and that included what to call the new vehicle. After some discussion, they agreed upon "Bantam Reconnaissance Car", and thus gave birth to the BRC.[278]

The pilot model now existed, but the journey remained far from over. The team had just one day to assess the vehicle and work out any issues they could before delivering the pilot model to Camp Holabird, 400 miles away, no later than 5:00 PM on September 23rd. For a revolutionary new vehicle that would face, as Probst described, "the most grueling proving test imaginable," one or two days of check out amounts in practical terms to no time at all.

Probst described what happened during the first day of testing, late on Saturday, September 21, 1940. Without knowing it Harold Crist would have the honor of being the first person to drive a Jeep.

> Without any preliminaries, we started it up. Crist and I drove out of town looking for the steepest hill we could find. "Lucky we're in Pennsylvania rather than flat Detroit," I told Crist. We sighted a hill, must have been forty-five percent. No road, of course, because cars don't go up forty-five percent inclines. I cut in the four-wheel-drive and we crested the hill with power to spare. "Whatever it is," I told Crist, "it's a performer."[279]

The following day, Sunday, September 22, 1940, would prove hectic for the Bantam team as they crammed in as much testing as possible.

> Sunday was a ninety-degree day in Butler, Pennsylvania. Everybody drove the car. It did not overheat, but I told Crist, "To hold down the weight, I put in the smallest radiator I figured would work. We'll take the slightly larger one with us to Holabird to be sure it doesn't overheat on the long hills." We also selected heavier springs as spares and decided we could improve the angle of the steering arm. The suppliers came up with their adjustments, but on the whole, the way we built it was the way we took it to Holabird. Sunday was a great night to sleep.

> Further testing by ten suppliers on the 22nd was concluded without incident. By the end of the day the odometer indicated 150 miles, scarcely enough to warm up the oil, much less reveal any shortcomings in the design, but no time remained to find out if it would stand up under prolonged abuse. That night some minor changes were made to improve the steering and brake system, and

a final coat of olive drab paint was applied.[280]

The application of the paint to the vehicle completed the work and only the final delivery to Holabird remained.

Figure 48: A Quick Test Spin Around the Factory.
Photo Courtesy of Robert Brandon, Butler, PA

September 23, 1940—Camp Holabird, Maryland

Monday, September 23, 1940, dawned, the 49th day, and the time had come for the team to deliver their "miracle of the 49 days at Bantam" to Maryland.[281]

The honor of driving the Bantam Reconnaissance Car to Camp Holabird would go to Ralph Turner. Fenn, Crist and Probst followed the former watch repairman in the Bantam factory manager's car.[282] Probst described events as follows:

> Before eight o'clock on Monday morning, we were on the road to Maryland. We drove slowly at first, telling ourselves it was important to break the vehicle in. But as we wound through the hills of Pennsylvania, the five o'clock deadline we had worked toward these seven weeks seemed to come closer. To make Holabird come closer too, we were soon pushing the car to the limit, and it really was fun. At 4:30 we drove through the gates of Holabird. It was the forty-ninth day.[283]

A group of soldiers, officers and civilians waiting to see if Bantam would deliver met the Butler team as they delivered their vehicle. About 100 individuals, including the Ford, G.M.C. and Chrysler test crews, converged on the strange little car. They had seen many experimental vehicles of every shape and description, but the BRC represented something uniquely different, even for Holabird. With a tread of only 47 ½ inches and a wheelbase of 79 inches, it looked more like a fugitive from a rich kid's playroom than a combat car.[284]

Probst recalled the on the spot initial test of the vehicle.

> We made a demonstration at Holabird on the field there and climbed the sixty-percent grade, and Major Lawes, who, I believe, was head of Holabird at that time, asked permission to drive it. He took it out for about twenty minutes and went out around and down in the holes and every place, and then he came back

and asked for the man who had produced the vehicle and Mr. Fenn introduced me, and also Mr. Harold Crist, as the factory manager.

Major Lawes said he had tested Army vehicles for almost twenty years and he said he could tell in twenty minutes whether a vehicle was good or not. He said he thought this vehicle was going to be absolutely outstanding.[285]

The intrepid "band of brothers" of the American Bantam car company had done it! In a period of eleven weeks, beginning in July 1940, this group of never-say-die individuals had designed, bid and then built a revolutionary new vehicle that would, in the prophetic words of Major Lawes "be absolutely outstanding." However, before Bantam's creation could step into destiny, the BRC would have to pass the rigorous tests the Army had planned for it.

Review—Parts Analysis

The request for proposal had required that "all unmanufactured articles, materials or supplies furnished under this agreement have been mined or produced in the United States."[286] Table 6 presents a sampling of the parts included in the first seventy BRC's built.

Table 6: Parts: ¼-Ton, 4x4 Truck ("Jeep") (page 195)

Chapter 8: Testing and Accepting the BRC

The journey to Holabird completed on time with great pride of accomplishment, Bantam and the BRC still had far to travel. The next step in the continuing saga would consist of the Army's aggressive tests to prove the vehicle's worthiness.

September 24-October 29, 1940—Testing

The intrepid Ralph Turner serviced the pilot model throughout the testing period and he stayed on post twenty-four hours a day seven days a week from the time of the delivery of the vehicle to when he drove it back to Butler after the completed evaluation.[287]

E Company 23rd Quartermasters under the direction of Captain Eugene Mosley, chief of the test section, would evaluate the vehicle. Sergeant Lawrence H. Ross served as a test driver and team leader for six of the thirty-five men assigned to this unit.[288] Turner worked closely with both these individuals. Moreover, the former watch repairman, who had helped hand-build the BRC, proved indispensable. He made sure the new vehicle would successfully traverse the myriad of difficult tests the Army had planned for Bantam's creation.

Sergeant Ross described the general testing practices and the overall evaluation process for the BRC.

Figure 49: Troops Testing the Bantam Pilot. Source—United States National Archives, College Park, Maryland

Pilot models that came from different factories were to be tested. We had six drivers and myself, seven men. We drove according to the schedule that was put out in the different places in camp on the test course on the highway cross country, through mud holes, in general tried to tear up the truck.[289]

I think it (the BRC) came in September, the latter part of September, and we drove it every day for about five or six days, I believe, and then we had a breakdown. It was laid up for a couple of days for parts and then we started back driving it again. I drove it approximately eight hours a day. We worked Sundays, Saturdays, and other days, every other day for eight weeks.[290]

The Army wasted no time putting the latest vehicle in their arsenal through its paces after its delivery on Monday, September 23, 1940.

On the following day, the 24th, they demonstrated the BRC for the procurement heads of the Army and Marine Corps, who had come up from Washington. The weather turned foul and cold; and it rained constantly. Capt. Eugene Mosley, chief of testing section, shuttled the brass around the test track until early afternoon.

> The Holabird proving grounds featured a mud pit called "the hell hole," an artificial bog about 300 feet in diameter and several feet deep in the middle. Only large six-wheel-drive trucks and tanks had succeeded in traversing the treacherous quagmire. The Washington people wanted to see how long the Bantam would last in the muck.

> Mosley backed far enough away for a running start and was on the point of assaulting the pit when several high-ranking observers motioned him to wait. The captain was riding alone and the officers insisted the test be made with a full crew aboard. In the absence of volunteers, the officers themselves climbed in and Mosley stomped on the throttle. Half-way across, the Bantam was hopelessly swamped, its carburetor choked with mud and water. The marooned passengers could do nothing but sit in the drizzling rain and contemplate the wisdom of their decision. Possibly the idea of installing a canvas top occurred at that this time.

> Lawes summoned a six-wheeled rig and the gumbo-plastered Bantam and its occupants, wetter and wiser, were hauled to solid ground. While the mud was being cleaned from the carburetor, Probst remarked that he thought the car could push through the muck if Mosley skirted the center and went in no deeper than two feet. After all, it had to have air, and beyond that depth the Bantam was practically submerged. This time Mosley coaxed the car all the way across. The observers nodded their unanimous approval.[291]

There remained a final issue to resolve and that centered on the BRC's weight, the same concern that had bedeviled the Bantam team since the vehicle's design. Probst recalled this critical turning-point moment in Jeep history.

> It was now time for top-level appraisal. We drove out to a restricted area. After all the good things were said about its gutsiness and go, one of the generals rubbed his chins and asked, "What does it weigh?"

> "It weighs 1800 pounds now," Payne replied very quickly, "But Probst believes he can cut 350 pounds in production." As chief engineer for Bantam, I was on the spot.

> "Perhaps Commander Payne has misunderstood me," I said, looking straight at the general. "Less fuel, oil and water, about 100 pounds, this vehicle weighs 1840 pounds. We'll probably have to add thirty to fifty pounds to strengthen weaknesses that will show up in our tests. In time, with new designs of parts not

now in production, it may be possible to get you a vehicle of 1300 to 1400 pounds." (Maybe that's why I'm not known as a company man.)

Standing there I knew the question of approving the Bantam Reconnaissance Car was in the balance.

The Cavalry general helped to decide it. "If two men can take it out of a ditch, we need it." He was about six-foot-three and weighed 250 pounds. In his shiny boots, he walked to the Bantam; grunting, heavy leather belts creaking, by himself, he lifted the rear. He nodded approval.

Bob Brown – chief civilian automotive engineer for the Army – also helped decide it. "Today we've seen the remarkable performance of this unit. To ask Probst to cut the weight like that may make it far too weak to take the punishment it is going to receive. Don't cut the weight." Under the circumstances, approval of the car at its weight had to be one of those "great decisions."[292]

With one lift from a general, and one affirmation from Robert Brown, who had attended that already long ago June meeting which birthed the BRC—they settled the issue of the vehicle's weight. The customer could now see what the BRC could do and on-the-spot reevaluated this critical requirement. While not the most scientific approach, the lift test won the day.

An official report of further tests on September 25, 1940, went favorably.

Memorandum for The Chief of Staff:

Subject: Demonstration of Light Weapons Carrier

> m. On Wednesday, September 25, 1940, Lt. Col. Earl S. Hoag, of this Division, together with officers from interested arms and services, witnessed a demonstration of the light reconnaissance and weapons carrier vehicle built by the Bantam Company, at Camp Holabird. This is the first item on a production order of 70 vehicles ordered by the Army.

> n. The vehicle is powered by a 113 cu. in. displacement engine, is 4-wheel drive, has six forward speeds, a maximum speed of approximately 65 miles per hour, an overall height of 40", and will carry 4 people. A towing device is installed, and it is contemplated the vehicle can be used as prime mover for the 37 mm. gun.

> o. In the demonstration yesterday, it appeared to have ample power for mobility provided conditions were such as to provide traction for the

wheels, and it appears to be able to do everything previously contemplated for the motor tricycle, if not more.

p. Representatives of the Bantam Company (Mr. Fenn, President) stated that present production capac-ity, with slight additional tooling, is 20 cars per day. He also stated that given 45 days additional tooling production could be established at the rate of 50 cars per day and that the unit cost in quantity orders should be around $600.00 each.

Figure 50: Bantam Pulling a 37mm Howitzer the exact weapons carrier role the Infantry had so long searched for in a lightweight vehicle. Source: United States National Archives, College Park, Maryland

q. The plans are being made to demon-strate the car in Washington, probably on Sunday, September 29. Define information as to the exact place and time will be furnished later.[293]

After the first two days of grueling but successful tests, still the intrepid Bantam submission had a difficult path ahead. The question on everyone's mind remained how long before Lawes, Mosley, and their crews could destroy this upstart truck?

The testing section officially received the Bantam BRC on September 27th. In the weeks ahead it would undergo an unmerciful pounding at the hands of Capt. Mosley and his drivers. Their mission—which seldom ever failed—entailed breaking prototypes as soon as they could. The Bantam underwent testing that included driving full tilt over log roads and plowed fields, through sapling forests and across sand traps calculated to tear the heart out of a vehicle. Mosley tried every trick in the manual and devised a few of his own for good measure. Sooner or later, something had to crack.

On one occasion Mosley thought he could fracture the frame or tear the body loose if he drove the Bantam off the end of a four-foot freight loading platform. He tried it time and again at speeds of ten, twenty and thirty miles per hour. Nothing failed. Mosley would have gone off at forty, but his back ached from the bone-rattling jouncing. Lawes told him to give it up and try something else.

Another time the Bantam was being demonstrated before Army engineers at

Fort Belvoir, Virginia. A 75mm field piece had been attached and Mosley began towing the heavy weapon across the parade grounds. He had gone about 100 yards when he realized that observers, who were watching from a distance, were shouting frantically. The gun crew had neglected to lock up the recoil sprig and it had plowed a deep furrow across the field. Clearly, the Bantam had tractor-like pulling power.

Once, on the way to Butler for a factory inspection, the Bantam was forced off the road and slammed into a drainage ditch, nearly turning over. With the help of two motorists, Mosley and a corporal were able to extricate the battered vehicle. A hasty inspection revealed that a front-wheel had been knocked out of alignment, otherwise the car was reasonably intact. Despite violent wobbling of the wheel, the Bantam finished the trip under its own power.

Finally, on October 16th, Mosley succeeded in putting the Bantam temporarily out of service. After twenty days of continuous abuse, the body was beginning to sag in the middle. Both frame side-members had cracked under the severe strain. By this time, however, the vehicle had proved itself to the Army's satisfaction. [294]

Crist supported Turner's 24-hours a day seven days a week assignment by visiting the base three to four days every week.[295] During one of his visits, on October 4, 1940, he witnessed a public relations demonstration of the BRC for top military brass, D.C. officials, reporters, and photojournalists, which showed just what Bantam's creation could do.

Figure 51: The Bantam Proving Sergeant Ross Correct—it could do anything. Source: United States National Archives, College Park, Maryland

Well, the fact is the photographers, I was present at this demonstration and that particular day we had such a rough test on another car Captain Mosley drove up to me and told me, he says, 'Crist, you don't have to take this treatment of your car if you do not want to, if you say so we will stop it,' and I says, 'You give her the works, we want to find out what she will do, and if she fails in these tests we will correct the condition.'

And he very courteously thanked me and he said, 'That is the spirit,' and then he gave the fellows a very severe demonstration, his driving ability was very good, and then when he was making one of these runs through the mud and jumping out of one of the holes there, which represented a shell crater, the news photographer said, 'Do it over,' and he said, 'give it a little more speed,' and this Sergeant Ross, he came forward, in the company of his commander, and put up a very stiff argument with the news man, and during this argument with the news reporter, the photographer, said he did not believe the car was any good and it was a little more than this man Ross could stand so he immediately exploded and said that the Jeep could do anything.[296]

Turner demonstrated his usual "jack of all trades" skills to fix the oil pan after the Army had ripped a hole in it. He realized then that the part hung too low to the ground and put a skid plate under it. During the rugged tests the one-piece windshield broke. A new two-piece part (a divided windshield) was shipped down from Butler and installed by the Butler firm's general foreman of the production line. The chassis also broke late in the testing (as related above, around October 16, 1940). As Ross recalled, "I do not know every darn thing that broke. There were a lot of breakdowns but I know a lot of things that broke." Turner fixed them all. Clearly his destiny encompassed acting as the first Jeep mechanic. He serviced the pilot model through the successful completion of some of the most rugged treatment any vehicle has ever endured.[297]

Before they learned if their pilot model had indeed passed the Army's trials, Bantam would have to wait until the reports on the testing were completed and reviewed. The placement of the order for the next 70 vehicles as stipulated in their contract with the military would confirm acceptance.

TEST REPORTS

The final reports on the test, as detailed in Table 7, were contained in three separate documents, Inspection Report on Pilot model ¼-Ton, 4x4 (Bantam) Chassis Light Reconnaissance and Command Car (October 23, 1940), Test Report on Bantam, ¼-Ton, 4x4, Pilot model Contract No. W-398-QM-8269 (Invitation for Bids 398-41-9) American Bantam Car Company (October 23, 1940), and Final Inspection Report on Pilot model ¼-Ton, 4x4 (Bantam) Chassis Light Reconnaissance and Command Car (October 28, 1940).

Table 7: Inspection Report on Pilot model ¼-Ton, 4x4 (Bantam) Chassis (page 197)

The Severest Tests

The BRC underwent the severest tests the Army could devise, and while numerous failures, corrections and comments resulted from the trials, the BRC had held up remarkably well considering its status as an experimental vehicle built in an incredibly short time. The critical issue of weight, a challenge from the initial specification, proved Probst right all along. A vehicle with the specifications the Army desired for a weight of 1,300 pounds always remained infeasible. The military realized this during the course of the test and as outlined in Par. D-1, most likely reluctantly accepted a more realistic weight requirement of 2,000 pounds. Bantam could otherwise address the majority of the rest of the findings before building the next sixty-nine BRC's.

Nothing in the first inspection report disqualified the car from passing. However, two more reviews remained, the official "test report," and the final inspection report on Par. D-25 referenced above. If the prototype passed these two final hurdles the Bantam team would officially have met the requirements specified.

Table 8: Test Report on Bantam, ¼-Ton, 4x4, Pilot Model (page 200)

The most sophisticated vehicles testers in the United States had driven the BRC the equivalent of across the country, in the toughest conditions they could conceive, and the pilot model had stood up remarkably well. Just one more obstacle remained to overcome, the inspection on the chassis mentioned in Par. D-25 of the initial inspection report.

Table 9: Final Inspection Report on Pilot model ¼-Ton, 4x4 (Bantam) Chassis (page 202)

It would remain for the committee responsible for the procurement, the Transport Subcommittee of the Quartermaster Corps Technical Committee to make the final determination. That committee met on October 18, 1940, before the official completion of the field inspection reports or the test report on the Bantam pilot model. Given that the evaluation had gone so well the committee felt a recommendation possible on the BRC. Thus, in one of the greatest understatements in history, the Army approved Bantam's vehicle:

> The pilot model has been examined by the interested arms except for Armored Forces and is being tested at the Holabird Quartermaster Depot. The Commanding Officer of the Depot has informally reported that the test is practically completed *and the vehicle found satisfactory (emphasis added)*, subject to modifications found necessary as a result of the test.[298]

Bantam's vehicle so perfectly met the Army's requirements, and had met every testing challenge, that the BRC received the Army's stamp of approval even before the official issuance of the test reports!

Bantam's victory would prove short-lived as their bid competitor, Willys-Overland Motors, Inc. had embarked on their own truck ¼-ton 4x4 light journey and their story unfolds next, while soon thereafter came the unexpected late entrance of a third heavyweight contender.

PAUL R. BRUNO

Chapter 9: Willys-Overland Motors, Inc.

Willys-Overland entered the Army's light vehicle saga early on. They presented the lowest bid in July 1940 but failed on the mandatory delivery date. Once they lost the bidding round, their evocation of the ¼-ton 4x4 light truck meandered up and down through troubled waters only eventually to reach a very hard-fought goal.

1873-1940—Company History

Figure 52: John North Willys c. 1917.

Tracing the events antecedent to those of 1940 illuminates the emergence of the second major competitor in the Army's quarter-ton vehicle journey. It goes back to the latter half of the 19th century to the history of one man, John North Willys. He was born on October 25, 1873, in Canandaigua, New York, a small town located in the Finger Lakes region of New York State. During his formative years in the 1880s, young John exhibited an aptitude for business. For example, at fifteen, he bought into a laundry business which he sold at a profit a year later. This would mark the first of numerous business adventures for the entrepreneur from Canandaigua.[299]

Willys would begin college in 1891 with the intent of becoming a lawyer; however, fate intervened when his father died mid-way through his undergraduate years and he returned home to help support his family.[300] One of his greatest skills, salesmanship, emerged after returning home as Willys engaged in the sales and service of bicycles for the remainder of the decade and built a flourishing business, something he would soon accomplish in the automotive world.[301]

The upstate New York businessman observed his first automobile in 1899 and the entrepreneur knew a winner when he saw it. He quickly bought a car and added selling them to his already robust bicycle business. Initial sales proved dismal and Willys had trouble finding a reliable vendor so he set out to sole source his supplier. He settled upon a vehicle called the Overland, manufactured by Standard Wheel, a well-known and respected company, in Terre Haute, Indiana. He completed a sole-source deal with the Hoosier state firm in 1904.[302]

Figure 53: John North Willys c. 1927. Courtesy of the Patrick Foster Historical Collection.

Figure 54: 1904 Overland Model 15. Courtesy of the Patrick Foster Historical Collection.

The Overland experienced serious issues soon after Willys bought in. Standard Wheel lost interest in the vehicle, and bankruptcy loomed by 1906. Only the intervention of the Overland's creator, Claude Cox, and the owner of a buggy company, David Parry, saved the car. In that same year, the duo formed a new company to sell the vehicle christened Overland Auto Company.[303]

The reprieve didn't last the year and Willys, who had bankrolled the firm with $10,000 to ensure his supply, became aware of trouble in November 1906. He travelled to Overland headquarters in Indianapolis, arriving on a Saturday, to find the entity in total financial and operational disarray. The type-A personality arranged for financing, by the very next Monday, to rescue the firm. He remained the early automotive manufacturer's main dealer through 1909 when he decided to buy the company outright and renamed it the Willys-Overland Corporation.[304]

Figure 55: 1911 Overland Roadster. Courtesy of the Patrick Foster Historical Collection.

The new organization experienced great success, in large part due to its owner's sales and business skills, as well as his work ethic: 7 days a week, 12–16 hours per day schedule. The second decade of the 20th century saw Willys-Overland rise to the number two slot in car manufacturing; however, storm winds buffeted the company in the last year of the decade through mistiming of war production, labor unrest and overextension through the purchasing of various entities. When a recession developed in 1920 the automotive pioneer's company proved ill-prepared to weather it.[305]

With enormous debt burdening the firm, Willys' creditors lost faith in its namesake and brought in Walter P. Chrysler to rescue the enterprise at the exorbitant salary of a million dollars a year for two years. The two years, 1921-1922, proved difficult for John Willys; however, by the second year of the decade, the interloper had left and saw the man from Canandaigua back in control. The Toledo manufacturer (having centered operations there in the prior decade) saw solid sales, profitability and well-received products for the remainder of the 1920s.[306]

Figure 56: 1914 Overland Model 79C Coupe. Courtesy of the Patrick Foster Historical Collection.

The election of Herbert Hoover as President in 1928 impacted Willys-Overland Motors directly. Shortly after assuming office in 1929, the 31st chief executive offered Willys' namesake an ambassadorship to Poland and he accepted. After selling his stock he moved to Europe just as the Great Depression took hold in the United States and around the world. The same economic calamity that claimed American Austin brought the

Figure 58: 1921 Overland Roadster. Courtesy of the Patrick Foster Historical Collection.

once-mighty firm to its knees, losing 35 million dollars between 1929 and 1932, and

Figure 57: 1927 Willys Whippett. Courtesy of the Patrick Foster Historical Collection.

falling into receivership in early 1933. The intrepid salesman from the Finger Lakes returned in 1932 to rescue his company, but three years of tireless effort bore little fruit and wrecked his health. John North Willys died on August 26, 1935, without knowing if his beloved organization would survive.[307]

Before Willys passed away, he had directed his attorney, George Ritter, to devise a plan to bring the firm out of receivership. The lawyer had done so and had received the company's

Figure 59: Ward Murphey Canaday.

founder's approval before his death to implement the proposal. Assuming the Presidency of the company after Willys passed, Ward Canaday began executing the strategy. As part of Ritter's plan, the new chief executive renamed the automotive manufacturer to Willys-Overland Motors, Inc.[308]

The latter half of the 1930s saw some restoration in the newly minted organization's fortunes except for the "recession inside the Depression" year of 1938. The company focused on improving its outdated engine, naming it the Go-Devil, an investment that would prove critical in events soon to follow at the dawn of the next decade. A new President arrived in 1939, Joseph W. Frazer, and he brought with him a reputation as a doer and an outstanding sales executive. Canaday became Chairman of the Board, and while still losing money in 1939, the outlook for 1940 appeared promising. Sales rebounding and increasing business from the War Department made the prospects for a complete recovery appear bright.[309]

Figure 60: 1937 Willys Sedan. Courtesy of the Patrick Foster Historical Collection.

September 1939-March 1940—Initial ¼-Ton Truck Actions: Toledo, Ohio, and Fort Benning, Georgia

The outbreak of war in Europe at the beginning of September 1939 provided Willys-Overland with an opportunity for even more work with the Federal Government, which included the production of vehicles. The Toledo firm's officials related the genesis of their involvement with the truck ¼-ton 4x4 light project in a letter to the Federal Trade Commission in 1943:

> During the fall of 1939, Ward M. Canaday, Chairman of the Board of the Willys-Overland Motors, Inc. and Col. E. J. W. Proffitt, Aide to General Drum, in New York City, discussed the subject of a light car capable of great flexibility, with speed in maneuvering and carrying protective and offensive weapons. Col. Proffitt at Mr. Canaday's suggestion discussed the matter with Major Daniel Wallingford with a view to the development of a sketch.
>
> Further discussions were held between Mr. Canaday and Army officers during the War Department's showing of their war needs at the Aberdeen Proving Grounds during the third week of October 1939.
>
> In Washington between that time and December 22nd, preliminary ideas for a "mosquito" car were discussed with Col. Rutherfore, Chief of Planning Section of the General Staff and sketches embodying the same were made.
>
> From these discussions Willys-Overland Motors, Inc. formulated fairly definite general ideas as to the needs of the Army for this vehicle which have since proved to be sound.
>
> About the same time, in the fall of 1939, the Bantam Company approached the problem from a different point of view. They had conceived a substitution for the motorcycle with sidecar, a protected messenger service for the infantry and cavalry of light and speedy general qualifications, but with three-man load, rather than that of a sturdy and powerful reconnaissance car.[310]

As with the Army and Bantam, it would take several key individuals to make Willys-Overland's ambition to build a vehicle for the military into a reality. The first two to come on board, Eugene M. Rice and Delmar G. Roos, held the positions of government sales force representative and Vice President of Engineering respectively. Prior to joining the Toledo manufacturer, Rice headed up fleet sales for Chrysler and due to that work had visited Holabird many times since 1929 and knew that all Army vehicle developments went through the Maryland depot.[311]

Delmar Roos began his tenure at Willys in February 1938 and by the age of fifty-two in 1940 had spent decades in the automotive industry. He represented the heart and soul of

Figure 61: Delmar Roos.
Courtesy of the Patrick
Foster Historical
Collection.

Willys' efforts to create a quarter-ton truck and became involved with the project at the next major event in the Willys story, a meeting at Fort Benning, Georgia, in March 1940. Before relating those events, given Roos' legendary involvement with Willys' pilot and subsequent models MA and MB, a detailed recounting of his career experience will provide insight into the individual whose extensive expertise went into those vehicles.[312] Roos related his career experience as follows:

Primary school in New York City, Pratte Institute High School, and graduated from the Manual Training High School of Brooklyn, Cornell University, Ithaca, New York, with a degree of M.E. and E.E. specialized in electrical engineering.

I went to the General Electric Company, turbine research department, and worked under Dr. Sanford A. Morse, the inventor of the supercharger, and did work at that time on what was the forerunner of the modern supercharger; namely, the centrifugal compressor and turbines.

I left the General Electric Company approximately the beginning of 1912 and went to the Locomobile Company of America, at Bridgeport, Connecticut, as laboratory assistant.

I stayed with the Locomobile Company and rose, first, to the position of chief engineer-research engineer and then assistant chief engineer, and stayed with them through World War I, at which time I had charge of design of the Riker Truck, the Locomobile cars which were built for General Pershing's personal use, and assisted as a member of a special committee to design the Mark VIII tank, which was then the biggest tank produced in World War I.

After the war was over Locomobile Company passed into the hands of a new group reorganized under the name of Hares Motors, Incorporated, and I left Locomobile at that time and went to Europe in a consulting capacity for a firm in New York known as Gaston, Williams and Wigmore to investigate the condition of post-war industry as far as automotive products were concerned in Europe. Gaston, Williams and Wigmore went the way of most of those war babies, and I returned to the United States and went with the Marmon Motor Car Company of Indianapolis as chief engineer, and there brought out the first small Marmon straight 8 overhead valve engine, which was later known as their model 75.

I was at the Marmon Company when I received an invitation to join forces with Studebaker Corporation, and I went to the Studebaker Corporation in the fall of 1926 with the nominal title of assistant chief engineer, there was no chief, and after a period of 6 months' trial I was made chief engineer, which position

I held, and was later raised to the position of vice-president in charge of engineering when the Company reorganized under receivership. I stayed with Studebaker where I was responsible for all the cars and trucks; the design of all the cars and trucks that were brought out between the periods of 1926 and the time when I left them in January 1937.

In January, 1937, I had the joint position of being consulting engineer for Studebaker and also consulting engineer for Sir William Rootes of the firm Rootes Securities, England, and I went to England as an employee of Sir William Rootes, at the same time being in the employ of Studebaker as consulting engineer.

It was obvious in the spring of 1938 that war was coming, and I had my family in England, and decided although Rootes Securities wanted me to stay in England, that I would bring my family back to the United States, and I opened negotiations across the water with Willys-Overland, and came back to the United States in the spring of 1938, and as vice-president in charge of Willys engineering of the Willys-Overland Motor Car Company, and have held that position to the present time (1944).[313]

Roos' wealth of knowledge, obtained over a long and varied career, would prove invaluable to Willys' efforts. In particular, he had experience with small vehicles, and in another ironic twist of fate, with light cars in England, bringing an English connection to Willys' efforts, mirroring Bantam's English roots. When asked at the FTC trial if he had any experience in designing and building small cars Roos related that:

Well, the Marmon overhead valve straight eight would be considered a light car. It was one of the lightest of its day.

At Studebaker we brought out first a car known as the Erskine, which was judged by the then standards a light car, and later the Rockne, which would also be the light car class. That means a car in the neighborhood of 2500 or 2600 pounds.

When I went to England much of my attention and my talents were employed in revamping the Hillman 14 horse-power car and the Minx ten horsepower car, both of which typified that class of cars common on the continent and in England as the light car. They weigh generally 2500 pounds and have small engines because of the tax which is placed on cars based on engine displacement or bore. So most of my work over there was devoted to studying not only the cars in England, but I went several times to the continent, both Germany and France, and studied the production of such cars as the Opel, the light Mercedes, the Renault, and other small continental cars.

I was very much interested in these because I felt that sooner or later economic situation in the United States was going to force America into the production of something approximating that type of car. And my reason for selecting Willys-Overland Company to come to, although it was not in a particularly happy state of business prosperity at that time, was that it was the only car in the United States being manufactured at that time that represented in my mind what would be called a truly light car that might be made into something in the future.[314]

With the initial discussions completed toward the end of 1939, it would take a letter from the head of the Harrington-Marmon company to Roos to initiate the next step in Willys' early involvement with the truck 4x4 light.

In February 1940, Mr. D. G. Roos, Vice President in Charge of Engineering of Willys-Overland Motors, Inc. received a letter from Col. Harrington of the Harrington-Marmon Company at Indianapolis stating that General Walter C. Short, Commandant at Ft. Benning, Ga., was interested in a small, motorized machine gun carrier that Major Robert Howie, on General Short's Infantry Board had developed, and that the General would like to have Col. Harrington and someone that he would suggest come down to inspect the vehicle with the idea of perfecting it.

On March 15, 1940, on arrangement through Colonel Harrington, Mr. J. W. Frazer, President of Willys-Overland Motors, Inc. and Mr. Roos, went to Fort Benning and met General Short and Major Howie and saw the proposed vehicle. The vehicle which Major Howie had was a small light vehicle weighing approximately 1,200 or 1,300# and to carry a payload of 600#. Mr. Roos, an automotive engineer in high standing and with more than twenty-five years' experience, discussed engineering details in full with General Short and Major Howie. General Short stated that he would endeavor to get an appropriation of $10,000 to develop one of these vehicles and that he would advise Willys-Overland as soon as he obtained the appropriation. General Short requested Mr. Roos to call the British Commission because Mr. Roos had acted as a consulting engineer in England. Mr. Roos communicated with Colonel R. Earle of the British Commission in New York.[315]

Figure 62: General Walter Short.

Unfortunately for General Short, he would later command the Army's Hawaiian Department responsible for the island's aerial and ground defenses. He would hold that position when the attack on Pearl Harbor occurred, which led to the abrupt end of an otherwise distinguished career, his story lending another historical twist to the

Jeep saga. Joseph W. Frazer, the President and General Manager of Willys-Overland from 1939 to September 30, 1943, had overall management responsibility for Willys' quarter ton truck initiative which led to his accompanying Roos to Georgia.[317]

> Early in the year 1940, Mr. Roos came in my office and said he had had a telephone call from his old friend Arthur Harrington, Colonel Harrington, so-called, stating that there was a small vehicle being built for the Army by the Quartermaster Corps, in which he felt we would be interested because he thought it would fit our engine, and certain other units, mechanical units of our automobile, and lend itself to manufacture in our plants, and that vehicle was going to be discussed at Fort Benning by a group of officers, including General Short who was then in charge of Fort Benning. Mr. Roos and I decided we would go down to look at this vehicle, which we did in March, I believe, '40. It wasn't anything like the four-wheel-drive reconnaissance car that afterwards came to life and became known throughout the country as the Jeep, but it got us interested. Apparently, the Army became interested in it, and I think it was in July that same year we were asked to bid, and shown some blueprints of about what they wanted.[318]

Frazer described the vehicle and the status of the efforts after the meeting:

> So-called Howie "belly-buster", we called it. It was a car you had to lie on your stomach to control, and the idea was to build a car that could carry two doughboys and a machine gun, and as General Short explained to me, that four doughboys could carry across any stream, and I think it was to General Short or one of the officers that we suggested they might build a car that would carry the four doughboys across any stream that four doughboys could carry this thing across.

Figure 63: Joseph Frazer 1942. Courtesy of the Patrick Foster Historical Collection.

> General Short said he was trying to get an appropriation-and this sounds ridiculous when you look at our National debt now-for ten thousand dollars, and he didn't know whether he could get that much to try and experiment with such a car, and we told him that if he got his ten thousand dollars to look us up, but in the meantime we began thinking about it, and I am not sure whether Mr. Roos or his department did any actual drawing or work on it at that time or not, but we had it very definitely in mind, and were watching for development on it.[319]

Roos recollected this trip in a similar vein:

> My interest was first aroused by a letter from Col. Harrington, who told me there was a development at Fort Benning that might interest us; it was too small

to interest them, and to get in touch with General Short. There was some correspondence between General Short and myself, which led to the trip by Mr. Frazer and I down to Fort Benning on or about the 15th of March 1940.

And at that time we saw demonstrated the so-called machine gun carrier, motorized machine gun carrier, that we were told was the development of Major Howie and his associates at Fort Benning. They took us out to the field and they ran the vehicle around with two men in it. We have a file with photographs of that vehicle. And they discussed the possibility of our undertaking to manufacture pilot models for them, and they told us they were trying to get an appropriation of $10,000.00 from the Government to cover the manufacture of one or more pilot models.

We told them we would be very much interested in making pilot models if there was any interest shown on the part of the government and an appropriation was made. We sat down for lunch and discussed the construction of the vehicle in considerable detail and showed them where they could make several improvements. The question of whether or not it could drive with four wheels or not was discussed and dismissed by Col. Howie, and we agreed to that because if we wanted to keep the weight down possibly driving on four wheels would make it unnecessarily heavy.[320]

Roos did take General Short's suggestion to contact the British Commission.

I want to New York, at the suggestion of General Short, and got in touch with the British Commission, because I had a letter from General Short saying the British Commission had seen the vehicle demonstrated and appeared interested. So I went there and discussed the matter with Captain Earl, who said he would have to take it up with principals in England, and they, in turn, would have to negotiate through the Army and General Short and Major Howie.

We went about getting prices of supply for units that might be used in such a vehicle and had quite a lot of discussions in our engineering department regarding the specifications; we didn't start any serious layout work because in April, Col. Harrington called me over the phone and told me he was positive a specification was coming out on a 4 by 4 car lighter than any Army vehicle that had been built yet, but it would fit our engine and to wait and keep quiet and keep our eyes open; that a specification was coming out. That later proved to be true.[321]

How Colonel Harrington had any inclination in April 1940 that a specification "was coming out" for a 4x4 car constitutes a mystery. Remarkable in that Payne did not begin American Bantam's collaboration with Colonel Oseth until May. Their cooperation led to the June 6, 1940, general specifications memo. It is interesting to note that Major Howie and the Howie carrier (chapter 3) provided a link in Willys' early efforts as well as Bantam's as Payne sought out Howie in May 1940, but instead met Colonel Oseth, and Howie participated at the Butler meeting of June 19, 1940.

From April-July 1940 Willys-Overland Motors, Inc. did not have any involvement with events surrounding the development of a quarter-ton truck for the United States Army.

July 13-21, 1940—Toledo, Ohio

Roos had received wise counsel for Willys to "keep their eyes open". Unfortunately for them, Payne's, Oseth's, Bantam's and The Quartermaster's work on the general and specific requirements from May-July 1940 did not come to their attention. Therefore, it came as a complete surprise when Willys received the invitation to bid on the truck ¼-ton 4x4 light on July 13, 1940.[322]

The primary responsibility for developing Willys' bid fell to Roos. He recalled their efforts to prepare a response.

> The next thing, we got an invitation to bid, on July 11th, I think it was. [It was actually the 13th.–ed.] The invitation to bid, we have here as a matter of record. The minute we got that invitation to bid, we went to work making general layouts and a study. We only had a few days to make it in and we elected at that time, although the bid called for a vehicle of 1300 pounds and a vehicle with an engine of 85-foot torque to carry 625-pound load, we studied that specification and came to the conclusion that it was impossible for us to meet the specification as written, so we sat around the table and prepared designs and a bid and elected to write a specification around Willys four-cylinder engine, which we did.[323]

> We made some layouts on the drafting board to get a general idea of how we were going to set our engine in a frame and dispose of our various parts such as the differential and transfer case and axles, and generally plot out the vehicle, and draw up a list of the various units and estimate, as nearly as we could, their weight, and get some figures together as nearly as we could on costs, and generally plan what might be called a design campaign. We couldn't actually execute in that time anything that would be called finished design, but we got together what would be called in an engineering department a general worksheet, or program, which we would use as a battle order if we got the contract, and had to go ahead and design the vehicle. Later on we used that outline and actually did build a vehicle from it, and we have a copy of that outline that was issued to the various department heads in the drafting room to

follow, so that most of that time was spent in what might be called a preliminary survey in laying out a plan for design, getting sources of supply lined up, and generally making a survey of the situation as to how we would go about building the 70 jobs if we got them.[324]

As was the case with Bantam, Roos immediately realized that the weight requirement represented a major issue.

> You decided it was impossible to build the vehicle which the Army had specified at that 1300-pound weight, is that right?
>
> That was our opinion, yes.
>
> And so you took exception to the weight provision, did you?
>
> Yes, our bid took exception to the weight.
>
> What weight did you decide you could build a vehicle with, with those specifications?
>
> We didn't decide. If you look at our bid, in the exceptions we made a statement it would not weigh less than 1650 pounds, and that was a good guess, if you want to put it that way. We felt positive we couldn't meet that specification or go under that weight, but we didn't know how much over it we would have to go. So we purposely, put that exception to the specification in, because we wanted to open the question of weight to discussion.[325]

Unlike Bantam, who at best fudged their weight number, Willys more forthrightly dealt with the impossible condition stating that they could not meet the requirement. Their bid included the following details on weight:

> The truck shall have a nineteen hundred (1900) pound gross weight allowance to provide at least a six hundred and twenty-five (625) pound payload carrying capacity, and where a requirement in this specification stipulates that the truck shall be fully equipped and loaded it shall be loaded to result in the total gross weight of nineteen hundred (1900) pounds. The payload includes the driver. Gross weight distribution shall minimize the possibility of tire overloading.[326]

Willys also included in section F-1b of the bid that the vehicle would weigh 1,700 pounds and noted in an "Exceptions to Specifications Requirements that, "Amendment No. 1 requires a maximum of 1300 pounds dry chassis weight, our weight will be not less than 1650 pounds dry weight with complete body and equipment specified."[327]

Willys chose to use their Go-Devil engine in the bid, and eventually their pilot model, which represented the second major design decision for the firm. Roos described their initial reasoning.

The next was a problem whether or not we ought to build the vehicle around our engine, which we had in production, and which was tooled. An examination of the specifications would disclose that while specifications gave minimum requirements, that they were written around a vehicle, certainly, that was not intended to use the Willys-Overland engine. The minimum displacement and the torque requested in the specifications, and the weight, all indicated a very, very much lighter vehicle than you would put an engine in of the size and horsepower of the Willys engine. But a conference was held, and it was decided that we would start and lay out a design around the Willys-Overland engine.[328]

Willys' intrepid head of Engineering provided further insight into the crucial engine question.

Aside from the question that you were tooled up for that engine, what was the controlling idea or ideas of using it?

Figure 64: Go Devil Four. Courtesy of the Patrick Foster Historical Collection.

The important one was the reason stated that we were tooled up; next, that the engine had undergone several years of intensive development and was an excellent engine, and since it was built in our plant and…rather, assembled and tested in our plant, we had good control of the quality of the production. And the next important consideration was that I had never seen a vehicle criticized for having too much power and I knew that if we could get this vehicle accepted with that engine and get the weight down to approximately the figure asked for by the Government that we would have a vehicle with a great range of performance, lot of surplus power.

I knew from previous experience in the first World War that vehicles would be used for a lot of things after they went into production such as towing and dragging loads that had not been intended; and I also knew that in every case where you designed a vehicle for specific use and a specific load, they always exceeded those loads. That's been true in the trucking industry, and it is just as true in the Army, even more so. And I felt that we were definitely doing a wise thing in pinning our faith to a bigger engine than our competitors, if you please. I think myself that decision was made because I thought it would put us in a position of advantage from the point of view of performance.[329]

As Engineering worked out the details for the bid, Mr. Frazer noted that he had protested that the time frame to prepare a bid, and the schedule to deliver the pilot model, as unreasonable (chapter 6).[330]

While Bantam agreed to the forty-nine-day delivery date because they had nothing to lose if they failed, Willys specified as accurate a delivery time as possible. The decisions made while preparing the bid regarding the length of delivery time, building the vehicle around their engine, and weight would have immediate consequences (delivery time) and cascaded deeply down into their efforts (engine, weight).

Eugene M. Rice acted as the liaison between Willys' bid developers and the Quartermaster Corps. In the preparation process he had, "helped check the figures, and cost, and see that all the departments of the Company had the necessary requirements in. There were several things besides trucks on an Army bid, which covers manuals, and certain specifications we have to comply with that I helped coordinate, and then I was there when the bid was opened."[331]

Willys' non-involvement in the development of the general or specific requirements for the vehicle gave Bantam a significant advantage in developing their proposal. Yet the Toledo car builder demonstrated significant resourcefulness and dedication to complete the bid form and submit it on time for the opening on July 22, 1940. Table 10 has a complete listing of Willys' response to the Army's requirements (page 204).

July 22-24, 1940—Camp Holabird, Maryland

As detailed in Chapter 6, only Willys and Bantam submitted bids for the proposed vehicle. Major Lawes began the decision meeting by stating that the former Overland Auto Company had the low bid. Payne had assumed that despite their low bid, the Willys rejection related to it being overweight. However, they lost because of the $5.00 per day penalty for late delivery by bidding a 75-day time frame. Contrast that to Bantam, who agreed to the forty-nine days the Army required.[332] As related in Chapter 6, Rice left the bid room, but it did not mean that the Toledo firm would just walk away from the opportunity. Willys' official narrative of events described their actions after losing the bid.

> On July 22nd, 1940, Willys-Overland Motors, Inc. filed a bid pursuant to this request, taking exception to the design which had been submitted. This bid called for a vehicle designed around the Willys motor. The vehicle weight more than 2400#. The high power of the Willys motor required a sturdier frame. Willys-Overland Motors, Inc. believed that its motor was required for the work proposed to be done and this has since proven to be the case. This vehicle, without the power and sturdiness of the Willys motor, would not have met the test nor would it have been as successful as it has been as an Army vehicle.
>
> On July 22nd, 1940, Mr. Frazer telephoned Colonel H. J. Lawes, Commandant at Camp Holabird Quartermaster Depot regarding the time involved and Col. Lawes stated to Mr. Frazer that Willys-Overland's price of $2,150.00 was lower than the other bidder (Bantam); that Willys-Overland had specified 120 days

delivery and Bantam had specified 75 days; that there was a penalty of $5.00 per day which made Willys-Overland's bid higher than Bantam. The axles were to be purchased from Spicer Manufacturing Company by both Bantam and Willys-Overland and each was promised 90 days delivery. Willys-Overland Motors, Inc. would not promise to make deliveries in 75 days when it knew it could not obtain the material in time. Notwithstanding this, the order was placed with Bantam because Willys-Overland would not agree to fix a delivery date which, under the circumstances, was impossible. Col. Lawes then suggested that Willys-Overland build and submit a pilot or sample model at its own expense, which the Army would test to determine the possibility of Willys-Overland securing an order on this type of vehicle. Willys-Overland agreed with Col. Lawes to proceed on the assurance from Col. Lawes that weight would not matter if the vehicle would perform and stood up. Up to this time such a vehicle had not been built by any manufacturer. About August 15, 1940, Willys-Overland immediately began the building of a sample vehicle.[333]

The discrepancy in delivery times between 120, 75 and 49 days arises if you factor in time for the Army to process the contract as related in Lawes' comments and as remembered by Probst. After that administrative period, however, when the contract recipient began the pilot build, they would have forty-nine days to construct and deliver it. Regardless of the actual timeframes, Willys had gone on record that they could not meet the delivery time and it had cost them the first opportunity to build the vehicle for the Army.

While Willys' official version of events states rather casually how they obtained permission to build a pilot model, the details to get to that point, to say the least, did not constitute a straight line. Rice recalled he telephoned Frazer on July 22nd. He told him they had lost the bid on the delivery time element. Within a few days he learned they actually had the low bid sans the penalty.[334] Frazer recalled how he had learned of the loss.

> I don't recall, but I think there was someone from Willys-Overland, probably Mr. Rice, I don't recall who, but I know I protested the time element, and the time given for delivery, 75 days, and Colonel Lawes told me, as I recollect, that our price was low but that our time required was too great, and there was a penalty on days when you were supposed to deliver that you hadn't delivered, and that would bring our price higher; in other words, they couldn't give us the bid because of our time limit. I conferred with Mr. Roos and we found it would be impossible to meet the time limit for delivery, and we did not agree to meet the 75 days.[335]

It appears that Rice, very soon after July 22nd, succeeded in initiating events that would lead to Willys receiving the go-ahead to build a pilot model at their own expense.

> I went to talk to Colonel Ingram and Colonel Johnson relative to the fact that

we would like to make a courtesy model truck.

Well, you suggested that idea to them?

I didn't suggest it. They are the boys that brought it up.

We were low and they wanted to talk about our making a courtesy model, which was common practice with the army in those days; several truck manufacturers made courtesy models. Dodge made three or four. It was the practice of the Quartermasters, because they didn't have much money for developments, to ask the manufacturer to make a courtesy model for trucks along the ideas they had. I don't know whether Colonel Lawes or one of the engineers suggested to me that they were after ideas, and they would like to have us make a courtesy model. As a result of that, Roos and Frazer both came to Holabird to discuss it. I was there, and we went away with the statement of Colonel Lawes that we would make it at our own expense, at least a courtesy model, so-called, and bring it to Holabird for their test; they came shortly after the 22nd.[336]

Rice mentioned Colonel Ingram, in 1940 the Procurement Officer at Camp Holabird. For the Army he oversaw all purchasing and contracting related to motor-wheeled transportation, their tools, equipment, and supplies. Therefore in 1940 Ingram held a rank superior to Lawes, who at that time had only risen to the level of Major.[337] He also identified Colonel J. H. Johnson, the chief of the Motor Transport Division for the Quartermaster Corp in 1940.[338] We first met Major Lawes in 1939 (chapter 3) when he rejected Bantam's commercial vehicles for Army use. The discrepancy in rank arises because Lawes was promoted to Colonel sometime between 1940 and the time individuals testified in the court case in the mid-1940s.

Frazer did not specifically remember going to Holabird to discuss the matter with Colonel Lawes. Roos' recollection of events shows the Toledo firm closing the deal with Lawes to build a pilot model at their own expense, as Rice had negotiated with Colonels Ingram and Johnson.

When we put the bid in, we lost the contract for the seventy vehicles. The reason for losing that, I think, is a matter of record. Mr. Frazer and I went down to Holabird to call on Col. Lawes to see if there was anything we could do to get "in" on this situation. We felt it was vital to our interests, if a vehicle of this kind was going to be built, we had the facilities to build it, we wanted a chance, and we called on Col. Lawes and asked if there was anything we could do. He said, "Yes, you can build a pilot model at your own expense and we would like to have as many people as possible build pilot models. The idea is new and we want as many engineering solutions to the problem as we can get." I am not quoting his exact words, but in substance that is what he said. We said, "How about the question of weight?" He said, "Don't worry about the question of weight now." We said, "Our engine is much bigger than our competitor's engine and that puts us under a handicap." He said, "No, the vehicle is a little heavy, but we don't know the final weight that will be decided upon yet, but submit a pilot model for testing, because we want as many types of designs as we can get in interpretation of this specification."[339]

Roos returned to Toledo and went before the board of directors of the company. He asked for an appropriation to build two vehicles: a four-wheel steer, four-wheel-drive; and a two-wheel steer, two-wheel-drive. Thus with those two vehicles Willys would provide their interpretation, as near as possible, to the Army's specifications.[340]

Willys' Vice President in Charge of Engineering had information that Bantam did not. Neither Fenn, Crist, nor Probst testified that they were given leeway on the weight as they built their pilot model. In fact, the weight issue for Bantam did not reach the beginning of a resolution until after the testing of their pilot vehicle. It came about when the Cavalry general, in his shiny boots, sloshed through the mud pit, lifted the tail end of the BRC, and gave his approval (chapter 8). Notwithstanding Bantam's route, Roos and Willys struggled with the weight of their pilot model throughout its development, testing and beyond.

Frazer recalled closing the deal.

> After we lost the order for the 70 we asked Colonel Lawes if we couldn't build a vehicle at our own expense, and let him test it, and he said he would test such a vehicle, give a fair test with the others if we would build it. And we built not only one, but two at an expense, if I remember, of $35,000. It was our contention that the vehicle needed more power and more weight in certain parts to give it strength, than the specifications of the Army called for, and that is why we wanted to build our own vehicle with our own engine, because we felt confident that it would out-perform the light vehicles.[341]

If Roos' and Frazer's testimony accurately reflects events, it appears that Willys received an opportunity to build their pilot model, on the side so to speak. Without any input from any other using arms, it was entirely at the behest of Ingram, Johnson and Lawes—all Quartermaster officers. Oseth testified about it.

> The knowledge I had concerning the Willys-Overland participation in this thing was imparted to me for the first time by Col. Lawes at Holabird on the day the first pilot model of the quarter-ton 4 by 4 was shown to us out there, which was about the first of October, as I recall it.[342]

The QM would also not notify Bantam of this arrangement which came to light to them in October 1940. The assertion of having manufacturers build courtesy pilot models as a common practice appears reasonable given the financial impacts of the Depression. However, did this typically happen after a contract award to another firm to build a particular vehicle and for this information to be withheld from the key using arm, Infantry, and most likely by extension all other branches, and the main competitor? Did the Quartermaster Corps create an alternative to hedge their bets given the revolutionary nature of the project, the tremendous need for such a vehicle, Bantam's well known financial issues, and the belief by most that the Butler firm could not meet the forty-nine-day deadline? Whatever their reasoning, this "side deal" does seem rather unusual.

Regardless of the merits of the arrangements, Willys stayed in the running. Now they just had to build the two pilot models as soon as possible.

PAUL R. BRUNO

Chapter 10: Willys Builds Pilots While Ford Emerges

With the "award" of permission for Willys to build their pilot models now in hand, Roos and his engineering team began to build them to the Army's exacting standards. However, they stood firm on one key exception, which became a significant development in the history of the Jeep. Roos' work for Willys on these builds required three of his top lieutenants to play crucial roles.

Meanwhile, even though the BRC tested brilliantly and Willys made its progress, around October-November 1940, behemoth player, Ford Motor Company, made its large presence known in the quest for a suitable replacement for the horse and mule, and the motorcycle with sidecar. Game on.

July–November 1940—Toledo, Ohio

Figure 65: Willys HQ 1927. Courtesy of the Patrick Foster Historical Collection.

The VP of Engineering's top lieutenants, Donald Stone, Henry McCaslin and Philip Johnson made huge contributions to the work to build Willys' pilot models. McCaslin, Roos' chief assistant, helped with the July 22nd bid meeting with Spicer representatives on July 17th and on that same date furnished the Toledo axle manufacturer with prints related to their proposal.[343] While others most likely helped as needed, Roos, Stone, McCaslin and Johnson constituted the core team for Willys to build their pilot models, just as Probst, Crist, Hempfling and Turner did for the BRC.

Donald Stone, a mechanical engineer by trade, in 1940 held the position of Director of Research for Willys-Overland Motors, Inc. reporting directly to Roos.[344] He graduated from Michigan State College with a Bachelor of Science degree in mechanical engineering in 1913 and worked in the automotive business for his entire career after graduation.[345] He served in the Army during World War I, in the Ordnance Department on special duty in the Motor Transport Corp. in charge of motor cars and trucks. In a quirk of history his unit went to Vladivostok, Russia (not France!) partaking in the little known American Expeditionary Force sent to Siberia in 1918 after the Russian Revolution. Only about 8,000 troops took part in that adventure (against hundreds of thousands serving in Europe) so to have a veteran of that force working on the truck ¼-ton 4x4 light project indeed marks a historical anomaly.[346]

Stone worked for Buick prior to joining Willys-Overland in 1937, taught night school, and had a membership with the Society of Automotive Engineers. His primary duty included supervising the building and testing of motor equipment for the company. In this capacity, Stone directly oversaw the building of Willys-Overland's pilot models.[347]

Henry McCaslin, Chief Engineer for Willys-Overland in 1940, had attended the University of Nebraska, graduating in 1917 and began working in automotive engineering in 1921 after serving in World War I. He signed on with the Stewart Motor Car Company for about a year and a half, spent a short time with Goodyear Tire & Rubber, and then went with the Oakland Motor Car Company before joining Willys-Overland in 1930. He left Willys in 1933, but returned in 1939 and served as Roos' assistant of engineering from that time forward. In that capacity the responsibility for all the designs for the Willys pilot models fell to him.[348]

Phillip Johnson possessed almost 20 years' experience by 1940 and served as the Toledo car company's experimental production engineer. His duties included responsibility for the entire Experimental Division which built all sample vehicles based upon drawings supplied by Roos and McCaslin's division. His area made all the components by hand and those included sheet metal parts, as well as the necessary patterns for castings the machine parts. In essence, with the exception of items purchased from experienced suppliers, such as axles, Johnson's area made the entire vehicle.[349]

The decision came down early that instead of building two pilot models simultaneously, Willys would concentrate first on the two-wheel-steer upon which it had bid. However, this model, which would include four-wheel-drive as the original bid vehicle, only had a two wheel-steer, two-wheel-drive configuration. Roos described the initial efforts in building the selected pilot model.

> On July 20th, 1940, our general layout was completed, July 20, 1940. That was the one we started our layout work on after our bid was in. On July 22nd our production chassis layout was started. The frame assembly layout was started on the same day, July 22nd. On July 23rd, further detail specifications were given to the Spicer Manufacturing Corporation on the axles and transfer case. We had had some verbal communications with them, because we knew, after we made a survey of the specifications, we would not be able to use our own axle, and I knew Spicer had a Studebaker axle that could be modified to fit in this picture.[350]

Although Willys' initial efforts at laying out and designing a vehicle met with a positive response, their momentum would quickly run up against Roos' team's greatest challenge, the problems caused by designing the vehicle around the Go-Devil engine.

> The first and fundamental difference which forced us to completely depart from anything Bantam had was the use of our engine. That immediately presented a much more severe engineering problem, because our engine is

higher by nearly four and a half inches; it is wider, longer and heavier. So we started out with a Government limitation as to the tread, wheel base and a Government specification as to how we had to seat the personnel in the car, and the dimensions of the body. We started out with an engine that weighed eighty pounds more. That meant we had to have a totally different cooling system. We also had facing us this problem: It was up to me to use as much as I possibly could of the material or the engineering practice that we had used in the Willys-Overland commercial vehicles with our own money and it was up to us to make a decision and if we made a wrong decision, we were out.[351]

Roos further explained that to work out these issues would lengthen the time it took to draft designs that provide the guidance required to build the vehicle.

As I told you at the beginning, in designing our vehicle around our engine we had an extremely difficult engineering problem. I thought I explained to you why, and that meant that a great deal of time had to elapse that was spent on the drafting board, making layouts, and rechecking layouts to see how we could sandwich our engine in within the limits of the specifications and clear the axle, and then how we could make the axles, and a great deal of time was spent in solving the problems of how we were going to mount the right front spring differential, because when we did that we changed the axle carrier so that Spicer had to conduct a special investigation to see if that axle carrier would fit in their jigs and fixtures, which they had on the line, which would take the Bantam and Ford carrier.[352]

While Bantam used a seat of the pants method to assemble their pilot model, Willys utilized a structured approach, which usually leads to fewer issues down the line, but can cause delays early on. McCaslin's engineering division needed to complete the general, chassis and frame layouts and this took time. In addition, numerous plans needed to be created so that all the component parts would fit. They made a draft of a design for a construction-body. It brought them within the confines specified for component parts in the design layouts and allowed the Experimental Division to make vellum drawings for the construction of parts for the vehicle.[353]

Working out these issues would take until August 15, 1940. After that Johnson's department, using the vellum drawings as input, would build, similar to the Quartermaster when developing the specific requirements, a wooden mock-up to move the pilot build to the next step[354]

We then started building up this wood-mock-up around these specifications handed me by the engineering division in order to interpret the limitations that they had to operate under, such as vision, height from the road, length, width, and so forth, also the seating arrangement. We never built a complete mock-up, we only built enough of it to answer certain questions we had regarding vision of the road, seating arrangement. It was not a complete mock-up in the sense of the word, it was just a shell. It didn't have the actual floor in it, nor did we have back panels. We did represent the cowl and body side panels to locate the seat. After we were satisfied with its general dimensions arrived upon with this wooden mock-up, we proceeded with the building of the actual metal parts for the pilot vehicle, the actual work on the metal parts was in the early part of September, I believe the beginning of the second week of September.[355]

With the information from the mock-up the team built a body chassis by the first week of October.[356] However, while the Research Division worked out the kinks in the body, Engineering began ordering, immediately after the solving of the layout issues, the parts to build the pilot. Similar to Bantam, Willys, due to the time pressures involved, would use numerous off-the-shelf components in their vehicle. Table 11 (page 208) provides detail on the many key parts that the Toledo car builder had to obtain to assemble their truck.

The Willys team assembled their vehicle using some of their own parts, in particular the engine. Roos provided a timeline for the construction of the pilot model through the receipt of the major items purchased. This information details the major points of development for the vehicle.

On August 13, 1940, Mr. W. K. Creson of the Ross Gear and Tool Company picked up a print of our layout 10277, which was the general outline of the car showing the steering gear installation.

On August 21, 1940, orders were placed with the Spicer Manufacturing Corporation for two sets of front and rear axles and two complete transfer cases.

On August 28, 1940, work was started in the Willys-Overland Research Body Division building up the two sample bodies for the original quarter-ton four-by-four.

On September 5, 1940, side rail outlined detail drawings were finished for the making of hand forms.

On September 11, 1940, we placed an order with Jamestown Metal Equipment Company for two sample radiators in accordance with our layout L-10291. These radiators were shipped on October 1, 1940.

On September 17, 1940, our order 37969 was forwarded to the Truscon Steel Company for the building of two sample frames and necessary hand forms for the frames.

On October 10, 1940, we were advised by Truscon that one frame was shipped on this date. On October 17, 1940, the frame was received in our research department.

On October 19, 1940, one set of front and rear axles and transfer case were received from the Spicer Manufacturing Corporation. On October 25, 1940, the second set of front and rear axles and transfer case were received from Spicer Manufacturing Corporation.

On November 4, 1940, the first pilot model of the Willys-Overland quarter four-by-four was finished. On November 11, 1940, the first pilot model of the Willys-Overland quarter four-by-four was started to Holabird for test.[357]

Figure 66: Willys-Overland First Pilot Model 1940. Courtesy of the Patrick Foster Historical Collection.

Willys stated in their chronology of events that the axle delivery schedule contributed greatly to their inability to meet the Army's build deadline date in their July 22nd bid. As with Bantam, the axles represented a key unknown and risk for building their pilot models.[358]

Roos described the initial interactions with Spicer.

And on July 17, 1940, a conference was held between the representatives of the Spicer Manufacturing Company and myself and the engineers on the staff. And at that time we gave out as much general information for the front and rear axle, and transfer case as was possible. At the same time a general discussion was held covering other units, such as the transmission, clutch, propeller shafts, and other units that we proposed to use, and their availability, particularly of the units made by Spicer which were the transfer cases and the propeller shafts, and axles, and the possibility of using an axle that was in the process of production at Spicer for Studebaker and was considered and decided on.

We had to tell Spicer what the torque and horsepower of the engine was. And we had to give them approximately an idea of what the wheelbase and tread might be, and only the spring centers, and that was about all we could give them at the time.[359]

Later on, as Willys' pilot model took shape, Roos and his team would provide Spicer with drawings showing the exact center distances of the springs, the width of the chair, the layout of the steering gear, and information as to the wheels, brakes and axle ratio that they proposed to use. They also provided details on the backspace of the transmission, the arrangement of the bow circle on it, and the approximate location of the centerline of the forward and rear propeller shaft, the latter essential in building a transfer case for the new vehicle.[360]

As with Bantam, Fred Hall provided details of how Spicer supplied their axles to Willys.

> Well, on July 17, Mr. Roos asked for a conference regarding this job, as they had received a request for bid from the government, and Mr. Lewis and myself went over to their plant and discussed what was necessary to bring out a job for them. Further specifications were received from Mr. Roos on July 23; as they were able to develop this job we worked right closely with them, being naturally about a mile away from their plant, so we could run back and forth as needed. The first conference was naturally rather preliminary.
>
> On August 5 I had a letter from Mr. Roos asking a quotation on two sample sets, and on August 15 I made such a quotation, and on August 21 received the order for the samples. One sample was furnished on October 19, 1940, and one on October 25, 1940.[361]

Robert Lewis also provided further clarification on the axle development for Willys.

> On the Willys, July 17, 1940, our first conference in connection with the proposed axle designs with Mr. Roos and Mr. McCaslin, car specifications given to me at that time with a gross weight of 2100 pounds, engine torque of 100 feet pounds. July the 17th 1940, we also received the letter with the enclosed prints that were noted in Mr. Ritter's reading of that letter. 7/19/40, I prepared a performance curve giving comparison of engine and car speeds, working out the axle ratio that would be better adapted to attain certain performance, and gave that to Mr. Roos. Willys Print L-10277 on the chassis was received on August 21, 1940. August 22, 1940, the Spicer drawings were started for the experimental, the first experimental axles. September the 6th, 1940, the first Spicer drawings were released for the experimental axle to have the material made up. On October the Third, 1940, the final prints for the experimental axles were sent to Willys.[362]

Figure 67: Willys Pilot Model with Delmar Roos. Courtesy of the Patrick Foster Historical Collection.

Roos stated that "I have always found the Spicer people pretty closed-mouthed about what they are doing for any competitor." Officially the Toledo axle manufacturer did not let either Bantam or Willys know about the work for the other; however, Willys and Bantam most likely found out about Spicer's efforts through unofficial channels.[363]

Spicer had landed in the middle of a duel between two highly competitive manufacturers locked in a high-stakes, time-pressured competition. However, these firms embarked on two very different trajectories that, although similarities existed in the axle designs, major differences did develop. This led Spicer to build two revolutionary new four-wheel drive axles simultaneously! Roos provided details on the dissimilarities between the two.

> When you placed the order did you ask for a duplicate of the four-wheel-drive assembly which was being made for Bantam?

> I certainly did not, because it wouldn't have fitted under our job.

> Why, on account of the differences in the engine?

> That is what led up to it, but specifically because, first, as I explained to you before, the differential is on the opposite side of the axle; second, the front spring, right front spring, is mounted on the differential which makes the front differential case a totally different case than either Spicer or Ford; third, that the tread of the axles was different, which changed completely the length of the axle tubes and the universal joint and driveshaft in the front, and the drive shaft in the rear; and, fourth, because we used a different system of steering on our front axle than either Ford or Bantam.[364]

Roos most likely meant Bantam rather than Spicer in his second bullet point. Hall would also explain differences between the Bantam and Willys axles.

> Well, basically, the carrier, which is the heart and soul of the axle, is the same carrier that we furnished to Studebaker for a number of years prior to the Bantam or Willys job. The knuckle, universal joint part which permits steering and driving forces to go through it, were basically similar. The tread, which is the distance between the tires, was different. The spring centers were different. The carrier is offset from the center of the vehicle in the front in order to get the driver propeller shaft by the flywheel, and in one case it is offset on the one side for Willys, and on the other side for Bantam. That is because of the basic difference in the motor. The difference in the spring center is basically due to the different chassis design, and the tread had to be widened to bring out the wider frame that was used on the Willys. Besides that, the steering of the Willys was different. The Bantam job had a single tie rod. Willys had two tie rods, in an attempt to bring the tie rod up out of the danger of hitting on obstructions in the road.[365]

Lewis provided the coup-de-grace testament to the differences in the axles developed for Bantam and Willys.

> The Willys carrier, which is the center unit of the axle, is offset to the right hand side of the axle. The Bantam carrier is offset to the left. The Willys tread

is 48 ¼ inches, which is the distance between the center lines of the wheels, and the Bantam is 47 ½. The result of changing this offset condition and also the tread resulted in several changes in the parts themselves. The carrier design is of such a nature that in going to the offset on the one side we had to put the spring pad as part of the carrier, where with the other design axle this is not necessary and was not done.

The Willys design with the carrier offset to the right necessitated putting the spring pad or the spring support as an integral unit with the carrier itself and supported by the carrier, which required a special design of carrier, which in itself did not make it interchangeable with any other carrier we had. Now, on the steering tie rods, Willys used the double type of tie rod construction, where Bantam used the single type of tie rod construction. Spring centers also were different, Willys being 27 ½ and Bantam 25. This also made it necessary to make special parts for the two jobs in the housing tubes. Brakes: Willys were using the Bendix brakes and Bantam were using the Wagner brakes. There is quite of bit of difference in the constructions of the two brakes. One is what we call the double anchor, the other the single anchor construction, and there were a few differences in small items which, although small, were very important in regard to performance, and that is the caster angles used and the maximum steering angle adjustments.

The caster angle is the position which – looking at the side of the car is the position in which the axle leans toward the front of the car like this (indicating), of the King pin which is the steering pin by which the car is steered, and that is to correct a condition of tire wear and also control, and especially at fairly high speeds, and to give you that performance that you get there, and that does vary and is made to suit the particular application to the car. It is interesting, all three jobs were set at a different caster angle. I think that covers the main differences.[366]

In the summer of 1940, Spicer worked on different experimental four-wheel-drive axles for two different manufacturers both developing a revolutionary new vehicle under tremendous time pressure. Given the fact that Spicer had a head start (beginning in June) for Bantam, they delivered for the Butler firm just in time to meet their 49-day deadline (chapter 7). Given the challenges for the Willys axles, due to using their more powerful engine, the delivery of the Toledo manufacturer's parts by the end of October represents another tremendous feat of engineering. Hall's, Lewis' and the Spicer team's contribution to the development of the first pilot models proved critical and earns them a special place in Jeep history.

Figure 68: Willys Pilot Model Demonstration.

Besides the axle, the engine proved the most critical component in the Willys prototype. Stone and his team had originally designed and built the engine, but Roos also had a history with this particular component, that began almost immediately after he arrived at the firm and he possessed detailed knowledge of its performance. Given that the Go-Devil was the heart and soul of all the Willys models, pilot, MA and MB, Roos provided details on the evolution of those components.

> When you came to Willys-Overland, Mr. Roos, did you find there in production an engine which was at least the prototype of the little engine that has gone into the quarter-ton, four by four trucks made by Willys-Overland for the Army?
>
> Yes. I found a four-cylinder engine in production and tooled, not too well tooled, and I faced the problem of either deciding to build and design – or design and build a new engine, or to see what I could do with the engine that Willys had.
>
> The Company didn't possess sufficient funds to go through a complete new program of retooling an engine, so the inevitable choice was forced on me to take the engine in production and preserving as far as possible all the major tooling on the engine to see what could be done to improve that engine.
>
> We started in December of 1938 to work on that engine. I will jump ahead for a moment and say that engine now being built and used in the Jeep has every single dimension and important center distance but one, just the same as it was when I arrived from England and found the engine in production. That one change of center distance of importance was the center stud on the cylinder head which I had to move to prevent gaskets from blowing out, put it in a better position.[367]

Willys new Vice President of Engineering questioned his research department on the engine's performance and found it rated at 45 horsepower, would run at full speed for 100 hours at 2800 revolutions per minute. That proved unacceptable to the boss recently returned from England who wanted to know how far it would run at 3,400 revolutions per minute.[368]

> We put an engine on the stand and limbered it up and run it 3,400 revolutions per minute for 22 minutes. The pistons scored, the bearings burned out, and the engine generally gave a very bad account of itself. Today that same engine with a change of one center distance, but numerous detailed changes had given us a high as 65 horsepower in the passenger car, and any single Jeep engine can be taken off the production line and put on the dynomometer, and we do this regularly about every two weeks and run at 4,400 revolutions per minute, wide open throttle, for 100 hours without a failure. And that is as good a standard of performance and quality and ability to take it as any engine that I know of in the automobile industry.[369]

Roos did not provide any more details on how his team transformed the Go-Devil from a 3,400 revolutions per minute, 22-minute failure to a 4,400, 100-hour super engine. However, he did explain the alterations made to the enhanced version to fit it into the pilot model and subsequent Jeep versions.

The fundamental changes won't take to long to discuss. We changed from cast iron pistons to tin plated overground aluminum pistons. We changed the piston rings to a combination of rings which controlled the oil and not pump oil. I brought the water jackets on the cylinder block which formerly stopped halfway up the length of the block, and brought them all the way down to the bottom of the cylinder bore.

The camshaft design was defective. It was neither right as to the timing for power nor was it right as to the design of the cam for proper operation of the inlet and exhaust valves continuously at high speed without the valves burning or giving trouble. So we redesigned the camshaft to give more power and to permit us to operate the valves at very wide clearances on the tappets and still be silent.

We raised the compression of the engine from approximately 5.9 to one to, first 6.2 and then to six and a half to one, where it is now. We redesigned the ports and enlarged the manifold and worked on the carburetor. And the effect of these changes was to develop more power, and we finally got the engine up in the passenger car to 65 horsepower. We cut it down purposely on the Jeep to 60.

This increase in power and increase in speed required the structure of the engine be looked into because increasing power and higher speeds there were failures occurred in the structure. We added counterweighted crankshafts, and we strengthened the crankcase because the bearing loads of course became excessive when we ran the engine up to these higher speeds, and the counterweighting took care of the excessive oil-bearing pressure, and the structure of the crankcase being reinforced took care of the stresses. We did some work on the lubricating system in order to make the engine to function as far as lubrication is concerned satisfactorily all the way up to 4800 RPM, and we have run the engine for as high as several hours at 4800 RPM.[370]

The last piece of the Willys pilot model puzzle revolved around the other parts used in its construction. As with Bantam, the Toledo manufacturer used numerous standard off-the-shelf components with Table 11 (page 227) detailing the major items, when ordered, and when received. Both McCaslin and Stone would describe in detail from whom, and what changes the Toledo manufacturer made, if any, to numerous detailed connecting parts for the vehicle demonstrating that some parts fitted without change and others needed alterations by the Toledo manufacturer to work in the pilot model.[371] Roos, as related below, provided the definitive answers as to the information his team provided to each vendor for the key parts listed in Table 11 (page 227) which completes the final insights as to the intricate engineering that went into the Willys pilot model.

Figure 69: U.S. Army Takes a Ride in the Willys-Overland First Pilot Model.

In the case of the front axles and rear axles, we had to supply them with the information as to what axle ratio we finally decided on, based on the weight of the vehicle, and torque of the engine, and the transmission ratio. We had to furnish them with the center distance of the spring pads, and the width of the spring leaves. We had to furnish them with information in the form of specifications of the brakes that were to be used on the axle, and arrange with the brake manufacturer to furnish us, and for us to furnish them, details of the brake backing plates. We had to furnish them with a diagramatic layout of the front steer and set up, how we wanted to arrange our steering tie rods and steering drag link. We had to furnish them with information as to what wheels were to be used, and what the bolt circles of those wheels were, and we had to give them an approximate figure on the load that was to be carried on the axle pads.

In the transfer case we had – before we could get anywhere with the transfer case, we had to agree with the vendor, who furnishes us our transmissions on the particular transmission we were going to use, and get them to furnish us a layout of that transmission which we checked and lay into our general vehicle layout, and when we saw that to fit and we could arrange our frame and parts so that it fit, then we had to furnish that layout to the Spicer Manufacturing Company together with the general chassis layout showing where our propeller shafts approximately would go, and Spicer had to go to work and develop the design of a transfer case to fit those particular specifications and with the ratios in the transmission or the transfer case we wanted. In this case, those ratios were specified by the Government.

In the case of the sealed beam headlamps, there already was a standard headlamp used on the motorcycles of the size which we finally used on the quarter four by four truck, and the only problem we had there was to furnish the lamp manufacturer with a general layout showing where the lamp was to be located and he, in turn, furnished us with an outline drawing of the lamp and the sockets and attachments, so that we could fix our fender. So that we could arrange the fender construction for the lamp and suitable brackets.

The same thing is true of the combination blackout tail and blackout start lamp. Those lamps were Government standard lamps that had already been standardized by the Quartermaster Corps, and the only information we needed there was outline drawings, official drawings, that we knew were the correct drawings of the official lamps. The same is true of the reflectors.

The starting motor was our standard starting motor that had been used on the Willys engine before, with the exception that there was no relay—yes, there was a relay on the pilot model. The relay was not standard on our starting motor, but a relay was furnished on the pilot model. Gasoline strainer was also a commercial article that had been at that time not yet definitely standardized, but it was the commercial article and the vendor furnished us with the outline drawings on that strainer.

As far as the steering wheel, we had to specify to the wheel manufacturer the diameter of the wheel that we wanted and give him the drawings of the top of the steering column showing the taper that was to be used and the keyways. And I am not sure but I think he had a standard wheel which we adopted that already had molds for. The blackout switch was a standard article furnished by Delco Remy. So was the blackout knob.

The transmission assembly was based on a standard transmission which we had used and was manufactured by Warner Gear and was made to take what we call an overdrive. The reason we selected that particular transmission was that in making the rear end of the transmission so that it would take the overdrive, they had provided for a much larger base circle of bolts that you could apply to the same transmission when it was used without overdrive. And we felt that since our transfer cases were quite large and offset, that it was very desirable to have a large bolt circle. We agreed with the manufacturer of the transmission on that particular arrangement. They made a layout for us. We checked the layout into our chassis layout and then gave a copy of that transmission case layout to the Spicer Manufacturing Company. In the meantime, the transmission manufacturer only required from us the information that that layout was okay, and then they went ahead with the manufacture of the sample transmission.

The ratios had been previously agreed upon and were the standard ratios they had heretofore furnished for our commercial vehicles. And we also made an agreement with them that that transmission would not have helical gears on the first speed and reverse as had been customary before. The reason for that was that they didn't have enough facilities in the way of gear cutting machinery and machinery for cutting helical splines so that we went ahead with the transmission with straight gear teeth on the reverse and first speed.

Cylinder head outlet was merely our standard cylinder head with the casting on the cylinder head modified for thermostat, and the outlet changed in direction, so that it would accommodate this radiator layout which we were just looking at.

In connection with the windshield assemblies, I am not sure how much data we furnished the windshield manufacturer. I think we furnished him the data as to the cowl outline that the windshield was to fit on. We had to do that to give him accurate data, the dimension of the windshield and the location of the point at which we wanted to hinge and the expanse of glass in the windshield, and agreed on the materials that were to be used.

The steering gear assembly, we furnished the steering gear manufacturer with the general layout. And from that he made a detailed drawing of the steering gear to fit in that layout. And from that he furnished us two sample steering gears. The steering gears were modifications of the Ross Cam and Lever type gear we had been using in production on our commercial and passenger car vehicles.

On the front springs we furnished the manufacturer with a rate of the springs; that is, the deflection of the springs, the load the spring was to carry, the detail as to the location of the center bolt of the spring, and the type of shackle we were going to use with the spring which determined the size of the spring eye. And the spring manufacturer, in turn, therefrom designed and submitted a spring to us. We also told him how many clips we wanted on the spring, and the same is also true of the rear spring.

The radiator assemblies, we took the purveyor of our radiators and discussed the problem with them and they had already had a great deal of experience making radiators for cooling this particular motor. And they submitted to us their recommendation for that portion of the radiator which is known as the radiator core, and around that was laid out the rest of the bonnet and the grid, and the radiator manufacturer furnished us with an outline drawing of the way he proposed to make the radiator, showing the top tank, the core, the bottom tank, and the water outlets; and we, in turn, took that layout and put it in our general layout and checked the arrangement on the water outlets and their location, the location of the shroud, and when that was properly checked, sent back to the radiator manufacturer and okayed for his final go-ahead.

The two air cleaner assemblies that we used were also standard air cleaner assemblies, and the only item there was a detailed arrangement of the bracket on the air cleaner assembly so that it could be fastened to the dash of the vehicle; from the very beginning our three vehicles all had the air cleaner mounted on the body of the vehicle and not on the engine because we didn't believe that it should be mounted on the engine.

Inasmuch as in all these cases that I have cited for every one of these items, we were all cut in time every way we could, and in many cases this information was sometimes transferred by telephone, giving dimensions over the telephone in order to save time, but in the end they were always confirmed with a layout on such an important assembly as the radiator.[372]

Figure 70: Willys-Overland First Pilot Model 1940.

The Willys pilot model demonstrated an amazing example of visionary engineering applied to a new and unique problem. Only final assembly and delivery stood between Roos and his team's completed vehicle.

November 1940—Toledo, Ohio and Camp Holabird, Maryland

Willys fought the good fight and with all parts in by the end of October the final assembly of the truck commenced and completed on November 4, 1940. After a week of tests conducted on-site in Toledo, supervised by Donald Kenower, road test supervisor of research, he and Irvine G. Hausmann, general foreman of the research department, delivered the vehicle to Camp Holabird, with little fanfare, on November 13, 1940.[373]

The Toledo manufacturer's pilot build team represented a group of tremendously talented, hard-working, indomitable spirits who faced challenge after challenge, but for whom failure did not constitute an option. Roos' team used a proven engineering approach, as much systematic design as time allowed, worked closely with vendors, and made the tough calls on the key issues of weight and the engine. This allowed Willys to furnish, at their own expense, a pilot model to rival the Bantam. The Army had successfully acquired their desired "another engineering solution to the problem."

Willys delivered the second pilot model, which incorporated the four-wheel steering feature, on December 13, 1940.[374] However, the focus of the events that follow in the fall of 1940 and winter of 1940-1941 revolved around the earlier delivered two-wheel steer vehicle.

Willys and Bantam had delivered their pilot models thus destroying any illusions of the sole-source position Bantam thought they might have had. Moreover, looming on the horizon and moving fast, the 800-ton gorilla—the Ford Motor Company of Dearborn, Michigan.

1903–1940: Ford Motor Company

Figure 71: 1910 Model T Ford.

The history of the legendary Ford Motor Company comprises a narrative too lengthy for the scope of this work. However, a brief relating of key events from the firm's founding to 1940 will provide background for their participation in the events of the ¼-ton truck procurement in the fateful first year of the fourth decade of the twentieth century.

Henry Ford built his first experimental vehicle in a workshop behind his home in Detroit in 1896. He founded Ford Motor Company in 1903 and introduced the legendary Model T in 1908. Due to the high demand for this car the Dearborn manufacturer developed new methods of mass production and the firm quickly grew into a major national and international corporation.[375]

Ford specialized in the Model T and produced that car until 1928 when the Model A replaced it. In 1922 the firm acquired the Lincoln Motor Car Company to produce luxury vehicles and expanded to the Ford V-8 (the favorite car of the criminal Clyde Darrow of Bonnie and Clyde infamy) in 1932. In 1938 they introduced a medium-priced car with their first Mercury.[376]

By 1940 Ford represented one of the most successful and profitable companies in the world and those who knew this included the Army's Quartermaster Corps.

October–November 1940—Dearborn, Michigan

By early fall of 1940 the Army had the Bantam Reconnaissance Car performing well in testing at Camp Holabird and Willys diligently continuing work on their pilot model. At that time the Quartermaster Corp expanded the field by, not surprisingly, bringing in the Ford Motor Company as the final player in the drama. At the beginning of October the QMC reached out to the Dearborn manufacturer and requested a meeting to discuss their building a pilot model ¼-ton truck 4x4 light. This happened on October 4, 1940, ironically the same day Bantam submitted a bid for 500 additional BRC's (chapter 11).[377] Clarence Kramer, assistant body-engineer, recalled the events.

I would say the first contact I had with this quarter-ton four-by-four reconnaissance car was at Holabird, Maryland, and we were called down there to look over drawings of a proposed vehicle and the Quartermaster Corps had on the board in their drafting room.

We were called in with Mr. Brown and Colonel Lawes, brought over to the drawing board where this vehicle was being drawn to look over the silhouette and general outline of the car, and at that time we noted certain items on their drawing which we thought would be detrimental to our designing and so we made certain suggestions at that time.[378]

Kramer went on to state that he also saw a Bantam drawing of the same car, either at that meeting or soon thereafter, and that the concessions, "were agreed to in general because they did not know, nor did we know exactly how we would accomplish what we were trying to accomplish."[379] The body engineer would contribute to building the third pilot model, but Dale Roeder, a fifteen year Ford veteran in charge of truck engineering, would oversee much of the car's development.[380] A graduate of Ohio Northern University with a Bachelor of Science in Mechanical Engineering and an Iowa State College alumni with a Master of Science in Automotive Engineering he started as a draftsman, working on designs and drawings for the Model T, and then the Model A, and assumed the role of head of truck engineering in 1929.[381]

Roeder described events following the fateful October 4th meeting. He explained that "the engineering work was started immediately after a visit by one of our former associates on October 4th to Holabird, and immediately upon his return we started engineering designs for a quarter-ton four-by-four vehicle."[382] He then related how they tackled the now familiar issue of weight.

The original order for seventy jobs or the original specifications for the seventy vehicles to our knowledge called for a chassis weight of less than 1300 pounds and that weight, after our analysis of such a vehicle, indicated that it was too low, the general specification as set up couldn't be built into that weight limitation. So when we started in on our engineering in October, and it was agreed by Holabird that we would waive the weight limitation they said they would set up, or they proposed another figure which was much higher than the one set up in the specifications which were given.

There were other deviations from the specifications because the Quartermaster wanted to get as many of the ideas worked into the vehicle which would cover the general specifications which were submitted, and as we would come across certain problems which indicated that we should deviate from the specifications, contacts were made with Holabird and certain items of the specifications would be waived.[383]

The Head of Truck Engineering stated that design started around October 15th and the Ford team went through a very similar journey as Bantam and Willys to create their pilot model.

> One of the first things we did was to take our four-cylinder motor and see what the possibilities were of working that into the dimensions as either set in the specifications, (I am not sure that those are in the specifications) or dimensions that were procured from Holabird, and see whether or not we could work our engine into the limiting dimensions as set up by the Quartermaster Corps. We were advised by Holabird that the Spicer Company had axles. We contacted them. We reviewed the adaptabilities of our so-called Model A transmission to an engine which was brought along at a much later date than the Model A car. We contacted Spicer also regarding the transfer case, and, of course, as you start any design, the layouts were started on a large draft, and dimensions set up and established on the chassis and turned over to the body department so they could proceed with body clearances for the chassis which we had started to lay out.[384]

Roeder described how they used wood for models to simulate parts, the building of a frame and axles to scale, and to determine clearances for drive shafts and steering linkages. It all happened in an effort to coordinate parts, "one with another, to determine whether or not our design is sound."[385] After the wood models verified the clearances, the team completed detailed drawings, "from which parts were ordered."[386]

While the remaining work most likely contained many challenges, the Ford engineer did not describe them. In a most likely grand understatement, he confirmed that "a pilot model was built and submitted to Holabird."[387] The vehicle obtained the moniker, GP-No. 1, also known as the Pygmy, and it arrived at the QMC's Maryland depot on November 23, 1940. The field thus completed for ¼-ton truck 4x4 light contenders, the story turns to stormy events unfolding in that early fall which would directly impact all three competitors in the months ahead.

Figure 72: 1941 Ford GP. 277,000 units were manufactured by Ford for the War.

PAUL R. BRUNO

Chapter 11: Competition

War raged on in Europe and Asia, yet Roosevelt studiously kept America out of the conflict. Despite that, he slowly increased the United States' support for the Allies, especially through the Lend-Lease Act passed in March 1941. The three ¼-ton truck manufacturers fought for their places in the procurement and beyond into the hallowed halls of world history. In a stunning setback, Bantam did not even know they had competition.

October–December 1940—Camp Holabird, Maryland, Washington, D.C., Butler, PA, Toledo, OH, and Dearborn, MI

The Army did not have a definitive path forward for the procurement beyond the 70 ordered from Bantam at the beginning of October 1940. Yet even before Ford joined the fray, the initial step to proceed commenced, an inquiry of Bantam for procuring 500 additional BRC's.

Figure 73: Lt. Gen. Edmund B. Gregory. The Quartermaster General During World War II.

At this juncture Colonel Ingram became the key individual coordinating the Quartermaster's efforts, acting ultimately on behalf of the Quartermaster General, Major General Edmund B. Gregory. In a letter dated October 4, 1940, Fenn wrote Holabird's purchasing and contract officer that "confirming Mr. Payne's conversation with you this afternoon, we are pleased to quote you the following figures."[388] Bantam estimated the unit cost at $1,173.00 per unit, with caveats that larger orders would see that price significantly reduced, and production could commence the first week of January 1941, sooner if the Quartermaster brought pressure on Spicer to tool up more quickly.[389] Ingram remembered the letter and testified that Payne had received direction from the QMC for a quotation, authorized by headquarters, specifically Colonel Johnson.[390]

On October 8, 1940, Ingram received a requested quote from Rice for 500 vehicles at a unit price of $1,581.38 per car (exactly when the request for quote came from Quartermaster Corps is not mentioned in the records) with delivery starting sixteen weeks after order release and suggesting a "contemplated negotiated contract."[391] Ingram explained the broadening of the field, even though Willys had not delivered a pilot model.

> By the time that the invitation was issued, it was becoming evident that the Army was going to need a considerable quantity of quarter-ton 4x4 trucks, and the Army deemed it advisable to get more than 1 manufacturer acquainted with

the method of building it so that we would not have all of our eggs in one basket, and then too, the Willys-Overland and the Ford Motor Company and the American Bantam were all at that time urging us to give them an opportunity to bid.

You used the expression a moment ago, "It was becoming evident that the Army would need a large quantity of these vehicles." Upon what basis was your statement a moment ago made, that is, that it became evident that the Army would need a large number of these vehicles?

There was a great deal of pressure being brought on the Quartermaster Corps at that time to get a small vehicle with four-wheel-drive. Everyone who saw the pilot model – I say everyone – everyone with whom I came in contact who saw the pilot model, were tremendously enthusiastic about it and could see a great use for such a vehicle in the Armed forces. And it is upon that basis that I made the statement.[392]

Ingram specified that by the Army, he really meant the Quartermaster Corps; however, all key branches of the QMC consulted on the matter and consensus was reached on the decision.[393] The Quartermaster Colonel also reached out to the newly included Ford for pricing and the Dearborn firm replied on October 16, 1940, "In response to your recent request we submit herewith a quotation of $1180.00 each f.o.b Dearborn, Mich., for 500 Light Reconnaissance and Command Cars (4-wheel drive, 2-wheel steer) conforming to specifications accompanying Invitation 398-41-9, dated July 11, 1940.[394]

By mid-October 1940 the Army had quotations for 500 vehicles from all three vendors. Willys had an appreciably higher quote than its competitors, but Ingram showed largess to the Toledo manufacturer as recorded in a letter from Rice dated October 18, 1940.[395]

After talking to you Wednesday concerning our price compared to Bantam […] And since hearing that Ford had put in prices that are based upon additional lots of the ½-ton 4x4s, as quoted you in our letter of 10/8 I asked our factory to get out their sharpest pencil and gamble on a volume basis, anticipating our being able to fill your requirements, along with Ford and Bantam. They have accordingly just given me revised figures, based on specification the same as those on our bid of 10/8 […] This means an average cost, per vehicle on the first 1,000 units of $1046.50 net f.o.b. plus axle tool amortization.[396]

Given the informal nature of this process, Ingram may have not violated any rules or regulations in securing a second quote from Willys; however, on the second attempt the Toledo manufacturer had the lowest figure!

Ingram stated that:

[…]subsequent to the receipt of this Rice come to my office and I probably told him his prices were high and that if he wanted to get in on this business, he had better have the company sharpen their pencils.

Did you tell him what the price was?

I do not believe I did. That was not my regular practice, certainly.[397]

Despite Ingram's recollection, the whole matter leaves open the questions of exactly what information he did share and would Bantam or Ford have received the same consideration? At a minimum it demonstrates further courtesy shown to Willys to keep them in the procurement.

Figure 74: Secretary of War Henry L. Stimson.

While the quotes came in, Bantam now became aware they had competition in an arena, from their perspective, belonged to them alone. The Butler car company wrote a letter to the top level, Secretary of War Henry L. Stimson, to protest developments as Payne explained, "because the specifications of this car had been originated in General Lynch's office with Colonel Lee and myself and the American Bantam Car Company and built the Pilot Model and at this time, that I wrote this letter, Willys, Ford and nobody else had even delivered a pilot model and I resented giving somebody, who had never built a pilot model, an order for cars without the proper test."[398]

Payne wrote the senior cabinet official that "we were surprised to learn that Overland and Ford Companies were also being considered in the order for this Bantam product."[399] The Butler car company's assistant to the President explained in great detail the events of the procurement up to that time and included an impassioned defense of Bantam's development of the BRC and its ability to produce all the vehicles the Army would need for the foreseeable future.[400]

He closed the letter stating, "All facts in this letter can be verified. After serious study of all these statements, I am sure you will agree with us that the contemplated splitting of orders on the product which is our individual achievement should be reconsidered. Our honest endeavors and contribution to our Government's National Defense Program surely merits the consideration we request."[401] What actions Stimson took vis-à-vis this letter remain unknown; however, Payne's Hail Mary pass to preserve Bantam's sole possession of the Army's ¼-ton 4x4 light market eventually proved futile.

While Payne's letter may or may not have had an impact on the Secretary of War it most assuredly did downstream, especially in the Quartermaster Corps. Gregory and Brigadier General J. E. Barzynski, of his staff, summoned him to a meeting and Gregory's assistant chastised Bantam's representative for, "going out of channels, going over my head, and I don't like it."[402] Duly humbled, Bantam's Assistant to the President told him he, "didn't do it intentionally and he would rather—he would write a letter of explanation."[403] Regardless of

Payne's mea culpa these events marked a turning point in the Butler car manufacturer's relationship with the QMG and QMC that deteriorated from then on.

Payne also testified that in early November 1940 one Colonel Dow made a statement to him that he didn't think the Bantam plant had the facilities for turning out 1500 cars in 3 to 4 months, which he had heard from someone else, which marks the first official rendering of QM doubts about the Butler car company's viability as a vendor. Although Payne penned a missive to Barzynski, "explaining to him and correcting false rumors that had been circulated about the Bantam plant" his efforts did not dispel the Quartermaster's concerns which would become more fully voiced after the Adjutant's General award of 1,500 vehicles to Bantam in late October 1940.[404]

Figure 75: Brigadier General J. E. Barzynski, while a West Point Cadet in early 1900s.

The next actor in the evolving procurement drama, the Quartermaster Corps Technical Committee, would discuss the matter of the quarter-ton 4x4 Light Reconnaissance and Command Trucks, on October 18, 1940. The committee formalized the 500 from each manufacturer path because Spicer, as the sole manufacturer of the key axle component, needed an order of at least 1,500 to adequately tool, and, "to allot the entire fifteen (1,500) hundred vehicles to one manufacturer will limit the Army to the development of a single type of vehicle which may not be the most satisfactory of the three types offered. To secure five hundred (500) from each of the three manufacturers will extend the field of development and should not delay the production of the total quantity of fifteen hundred (1,500) vehicles."[405]

The committee recommended immediately extending the program for development and service test from 70 to 1,570 vehicles, negotiated contracts for 500 units from each of the three competitors at a unit cost not to exceed $1,250.00, should a manufacturer fail to meet the price limitation then the order would be divided equally among those that meet the price and notification to Spicer, "of the War Department's intention to contract for fifteen hundred (1,500) vehicles and guarantee them an outlet for fifteen hundred (1,500) sets of axles and transfer cases."[406]

Van Deusen, present at the meeting, explained the committee's reasoning.

> I know the purpose behind this recommendation. This was a new type of vehicle, and giving of quantity orders to each of three manufacturers was intended to produce for testing purposes three different proprietary interpretations in design of our specifications and characterizations in order that in case the vehicle finally was adopted as a standard piece of equipment for the army, the design finally adopted as standard meeting the better features of any of the vehicles procured.[407]

The QM had a path forward, but their decision would meet with resistance from the three key using arms in the procurement, Field Artillery, Cavalry and Infantry. The Chief of Field Artillery wrote a non-concurrence memo stating he objected to awarding contracts to vendors who had not produced a suitable pilot model and if 1,500 vehicles were needed the entire order should go to American Bantam as the sole producer of a pilot model.[408] On the same day the Cavalry provided only "special concurrence" noting that, "contract to Ford and Willys-Overland only be negotiated <u>after</u> the tests of the pilot models and approval by the using arms," and only Bantam receive an order of 500.[409]

Infantry provided the most thorough and detailed objections to the committee's recommendations, written by none other than Colonel Oseth, the driving force behind the June 6, 1940, memo, to the Quartermaster General himself. These included:

- 1,500 insufficient for Infantry's demands,
- unnecessary delay,
- splitting the order will not extend the field of development,
- lack of pilot models from Ford and Willys-Overland,
- QM practice of no negotiated contracts without a pilot model,
- expanding the field inconsistent with fair play and the initiative and cooperation shown by Bantam,
- lack of time limit on procurement, and,
- including multiple vendors delayed the motor tricycle endeavor.[410]

The disgruntled using arm recommended that:

- Infantry receive 1,500 vehicles and other using arms an appropriate number for their needs,
- the unit cost per vehicle not exceed $1,000; Bantam receive the entire order, and,
- no contracts for other vendors until suitable pilot models delivered and tested to the same degree as the BRC.

The Chief of Infantry unleashed his ire personally on the Quartermaster General by having Oseth include the following:

P.S.: The Chief of Infantry has specially directed me to invite attention to recent report of the A.C. of S., W.P.D., Brigadier General George V. Strong, which it is recommended that the using service rather than a supply agency must have the final determination of types and specifications of equipment to be used by that service. The proposed action for procurement of vehicles not tested or approved by the using arm is in violation of this principle.[411]

Figure 76: Emory Sherwood Adams at the start of his assignment as Adjutant General, 1938.

Infantry's and the other using arms' objections apparently fell on deaf ears as the Quartermaster moved forward with the 500 hundred from three manufacturer's decision with the sending of a report to the Adjutant General Office (AGO) on October 22, 1940, detailing the procurement and seeking approval of funds. The QM did cover all bases by including a copy of Payne's October 14, 1940, letter.[412]

In a stunning turn of events the AGO responded to the QMG on October 29, 1940, authorizing, by negotiated contract, the procurement of 1,500 vehicles from American Bantam and that, "future procurement of vehicles of this type for extended service test will be based upon prior approval and acceptance of a pilot model. By order of the Secretary of War:"[413]

In one fell swoop the Secretary of War dramatically altered the course of the ¼-ton 4x4 light project and had undone months of work by the QM to broaden the field of vendors! Instead of 500 each from Bantam, Willys and Ford, the entire 1,500 order would go to Bantam, leaving both Willys and Ford frozen out until they produced satisfactory pilot models, which at that time represented a complete unknown to both firms. The command from the Secretary of War placed the Butler manufacturer in a strong position. However, the directive by the Adjutant General (AG) unleashed a maelstrom that would play out at the highest levels of the United States Army in early November 1940.

Officials at the Quartermaster Corp. reacted by sending a three-page response to the AG on November 1, 1940, signed by Gregory himself. His document proved significantly critical to the tumultuous events that followed, as well as provides insight into the mindset of the Army's procurement arm on the unfolding situation. Thus, it necessitates including it in its entirety:

1. Reconsideration of the action directed in paragraph 3, 1st Ind. is requested based upon the following.

a. The fact that information about the action directed was conveyed to Mr. Charles H. Payne, Assistant to the President and Washington Sales Representative of the American Bantam Car Company in time for him to convey this information to the Holabird Quartermaster Depot and to the representatives there of the Ford Motor Company and the Willys-Overland Motors, Incorporated, on Friday, October 25th, although the Quartermaster General's office did not receive official notification until October 30th has adversely affected vendor relations which are important to the proper procurement of motor vehicles.

b. The original proposal to extend the project for development and service test from 70 to 1570 and to divide the order for 1500 additional trucks between two or three companies was a carefully considered plan initiated by the office of the Quartermaster General, so as to insure the proper engineering development, and, in addition, the development of adequate productive facilities to produce this type of car in the quantities that may be needed, and such a carefully considered program should not be upset unless there are extremely serious consideration involved.

c. The representative of the Willys-Overland Company and the Ford Motor Company were called in and encouraged to make major expenditures for engineering development work, after telephone consultation and verbal approval of Colonel Aurand to the Commanding Officer of the Holabird Quartermaster Depot.

d. The probable requirement of this vehicle are not less than 11,800 for procurement before June 30, 1941, in the event that the service test proves these vehicles satisfactory. It is extremely desirable that adequate and competitive sources of production be developed for this vehicle. It is the considered opinion of the Quartermaster General's office that the American Bantam Car Company cannot furnish these requirements and insure a continuing service organization. Note that the American Bantam Car Company wanted an advance payment of approximately thirty percent or $52,000 on the original contract for seventy-two cars. Note also the following extract from paragraph 1.c of the communication of the Infantry representative of October 21, 1940: "it is understood that failure on the part of the government to support the manufacturer who has developed this vehicle with adequate contracts may result in the elimination of that source entirely."

e. The American Bantam Car Company has been fully paid for development work to date. The original award for 70 trucks was $171,185.75.

f. The division of this quantity of 1500 between two or three manufacturers will not delay production. The communication of the Quartermaster General dated October 22nd, paragraph 3.a (2) stated specifically, "Negotiations should not be allowed to delay production of the 1500 vehicles." On the contrary this proposed program was specifically designed to expedite the procurement of the eventual requirements. It is expected that either Ford or Willys will eventually themselves go into production of axles and transfer cases so as to break the present Spicer bottle-neck. The Willys pilot model is expected to arrive at Holabird Quartermaster Depot November 1, 1940, and the Ford pilot model not later than November 15, 1940. It is essential that the Quartermaster General have final authorization to negotiate an award of 500 trucks to The Ford Motor Co. and also to the Willys-Overland Motors, Inc. upon completion of satisfactory tests of the pilot models submitted by these companies. It is not sufficient, in view of the action of Mr. Payne referred to in paragraph a above, to assume that when the pilot model has been approved authority to make the award will be forthcoming.

g. Any objection to approving the original recommendation to divide this award that is based on the fact that The Ford Motor Co. and the Willys-Overland Motors, Inc. have not yet submitted pilot models is not justified because communication of the Quartermaster General of October 22, 1940, stated in paragraph 3.a (1) "Negotiations recommended in sub-paragraph 2 in Recommendations in basic report should be based upon the prior approval and acceptance of the pilot model submitted for test." Consideration should also be given to the fact that the proposed award to American Bantam Co. is not based upon the submission of a satisfactory pilot model, but upon the completion of tests of a preliminary engineering model, most of the parts of which were made in the tool room and which represents an assembled vehicle designed primarily by the engineers of the Holabird Quartermaster Depot, the unit manufacturers and the engineer of the Bantam Company; for example, the present body design was based entirely on drawing furnished by Holabird, and the axles and transfer case were designed by Spicer Mfg. Corporation.

h. To consider the American Bantam Car Company as the only source of quarter-ton trucks for substitution for motorcycles with sidecars is contrary to the spirit and letter of the general principles governing defense contracts, particularly with respect to the effect of the Army program upon the peace-time economy. This is evidenced by the following paragraph from the letter of the American Bantam Company to the Secretary of War dated October 14, 1940:

"We have practically stopped all commercial business in order to devote all our time to National Defense and to give the Army exactly what they want in the shortest time and at the lowest possible price. This, however, is not true of the others, such as Ford, Overland, etc., who, besides being engaged in their commercial business, are also developing aircraft motors, accessories, and other products. Our plant is open exclusively for the development and output of this one mighty item in National Defense."

j. The unusual amount of publicity released by American Bantam Company considered in conjunction with present financial situation of the company give cause for suspicion that the possibility of army contracts is being used as a basis for stock promotion.

2. Based on the above, reconsideration of the action directed in paragraph 3 of 1st Indorsement is urgently requested and it is recommended that:

a. Procurement of 1500 vehicles of this type in addition to the 70 now ordered be authorized for extended service test. Funds for the procurement of these vehicles be taken from those previously set aside for procurement of motorcycles with sidecars during the fiscal 1941.

b. The Quartermaster General be directed to procure these 1500 additional vehicles as expeditiously as possible bearing in mind the development of adequate sources for possible future development.

3. The action directed, in paragraph 5, which comprises the elements of delay in this procurement, has been initiated and will be carried out as expeditiously as possible.[414]

In summary Gregory stated:

- his thinly veiled disdain for Payne,

- the "considered opinion of the Quartermaster General's Office" that Bantam could not meet the production needed,

- the Butler manufacturer's lack of funds,

- the downplaying of the Pennsylvania car maker's role in developing the specifications for the July 11, 1940, request for bids, and

- accused Bantam officials of "stock promotion"

The memo also reveals that the decision to include Willys and Ford originated at the QMC. They had "a carefully considered plan initiated by the office of the Quartermaster General so as to ensure the proper engineering development, and, in addition, the development of adequate productive facilities to produce this type of car in the quantities that may be needed". Moreover, the Quartermaster Corps' foresight to include the two larger companies led to: "the representative of the Willys-Overland Company and the Ford Motor Company were called in and encouraged to make major expenditures for engineering development work, after telephone consultation and verbal approval of Colonel Aurand to the Commanding Officer of the Holabird Quartermaster Depot."[415]

Figure 77: Major General Richard C. Moore, deputy to Chief of Staff General Marshall.

Gregory also penned a three-page scathing memo to Major General R. C. Moore, Chief of Staff Marshall's deputy, on November

5, 1940, going around the AG altogether and making his case to the Army's highest levels. In his document the QMG formally made known his belief that the awarding of 1,500 units only to Bantam constituted a major error, stating, "I wish to go on record now with you that I do not consider the above procedure in the best interest of the government", and that the Bantam Company, "is a small company with no productive facilities of any importance and their financial status is entirely inadequate for any substantial production program," and that the decision rendered came about based upon, "misinformation furnished by the representative of the Bantam Company."[416]

He compared Bantam's sorry state to Willys and Ford asserting, "This office definitely recommended that an amount of 500 vehicles be made to the Ford Company and Willys-Overland Company. Both of these companies have adequate production facilities and their financial standing is such that there is no question of their ability to produce cars in volume if the War Department so desires."[417] Further criticizing Bantam's fitness for the task at hand Gregory opined, "I doubt the ability of the Bantam Company to turn out 50 cars a day, even if axles are provide[d], without additional financing to expand their present facilities." However, he again praised Willys and Ford stating, "There is no question of the ability of the Ford and Willys companies to produce cars as fast as axles can be provide[d]."[418]

The QMG reiterated that Fenn and company should only receive an order for 500 vehicles; that Ford and Willys should receive an order for 500 upon acceptance of their pilot models; he deeply regretted that the War Department embarked on a procurement from a company with no national organization and is not prepared to render any service on the vehicles purchased; and undermined Bantam once again by asserting the Pennsylvania firm, "was paid very liberally for the development of a pilot model," while Willys and Ford developed their pilots at their own expense (conveniently leaving out Willys' unsuccessful bid in July 1940 and Ford's refusal to bid then); and lastly, again, as with the AG, asserting Holabird's engineers did the majority of the vehicle's design and the BRC had been primarily built with purchased parts.[419]

These two documents represent a major turning point for both near and far-term events in the development of the Jeep. Bantam had obviously lost any goodwill with the QMG and Quartermaster Corp. staff, if any ever existed. More far-reaching, if Fenn's firm ever had a chance to receive volume production, the Quartermaster General himself had now gone on record to both the AG and the Deputy Chief of Staff stating his belief that the Butler firm could not manufacture to the Army's needs. Gregory's statements concerning Payne, and stock manipulation show further contempt for the Butler car maker. After making these assertions could the QMG ever support awarding another large contract to Bantam? While the Butler manufacturer may have won the battle to solely receive a fifteen hundred unit order they had lost the war of ever receiving another order after the 1,500.

These documents from the QMG clearly shows QM bias for the larger firms and lends credence to Rice's testimony that the Army's procurement arm suggested Willys build a pilot model at their own expense. The AG's response to the QMG's November 1, 1941, appeal, labeled "Immediate Action," came on November 5, 1940, and included:

- o Rejection of QM's "urgent request" to overturn the decision to award only 1,500 to Bantam,

- o not to delay the order to Bantam, and,

- o not to order any large quantities from a manufacturer until a pilot model was delivered and tested.[420]

The Adjutant General did leave the door open for Willys and Ford as the purchasing of 1,500 cars from Bantam did not prevent developing other sources and, "upon satisfactory completion of tests of Ford and Willys pilot models, recommendations for purchase of vehicles for extended service test for those companies will be entertained."[421] However, the AG made sure Gregory knew this was the final say, and pulled rank, as the memo closed with, "in view of the foregoing, the directive contained in 1st Indorsement is reaffirmed and **will** (emphasis added) be executed. By order of the Secretary of War:"[422]

Kenny Rogers famously stated, "know when to hold 'em, know when to fold 'em" and the Quartermaster General knew when to follow a direct order. That same day a directive, also labeled "immediate action," went out from QM Headquarters Washington to Holabird to immediately secure pricing from Bantam for 1,500 BRC's and to submit to headquarters for approval. The memo indicated that Spicer had already been notified of a 1,500 axle order coming, which assuredly was warmly received by that organization.[423] November 6, 1940, Ingram requested the quote from Fenn who responded the same day in a letter which included pricing ($995.59 per unit) and a delivery schedule.[424] Ingram notified QM headquarters that same day the procuring of the quote. When the time comes, no matter one's differences, when the top says "immediate action", it gets done![425]

November 6, 1940, began the final victory lap for the Butler car maker as the AG notified Deputy Chief of Staff Moore of the 1,500 procurement from Bantam and noted, "this office will now see to obtaining from the Bantam Company their definite proposal as to price and time of delivery of 1,500 cars which we have been directed to procure. Of course, you understand that this proposal must be approved by the National Defense Advisory Commission before an award can be made."[426] Gregory notified Knudsen on November 7, 1940, noting that the Assistant Secretary of War had approved the contract that date.[427] Informal approval was sent to Bantam by wire on November 16, 1940, with the official notification completed on November 25, 1940.[428]

Willys and Ford, like the QMG, also sprang into action after the AG's October 29th decision. Rice sent a telegram, on November 7, 1940, directly to Chief of Staff Marshall stating "it is contemplated giving Bantam Motor Car Company entire educational order 1500 quarter ton 4x4's [...] because they had convinced someone high up in Army authority that they had done all the pioneer work on this model... we were low on first bid [...] convinced our ability to manufacture and Army's needs being large, spent fifteen thousand dollars of our own money building two test trucks that are ready to go to Holabird Quartermaster Depot for trial now [...] believe we are entitled to full consideration on [a] competitive price basis and would appreciate such consideration."[429]

Willys sales manager testified he found out about this situation from, "one of the Bantam boys," that he communicated the information to Toledo, sent the telegram and he did so because he "wanted it (the order) for myself." He stated that the Chief of Staff wired back that if a satisfactory pilot model was produced then an order might be given.[430] Ford sent a letter directly to Gregory on November 9, 1940, that presented a quote of $975.00, a delivery schedule, and that the Dearborn firm understood the desirability to diversify the sources of axles.[431]

Figure 78: John D. Biggers

On November 14, 1940, a decision came down that altered the direction of Jeep history as the Advisory Commission to the Council of National Defense intervened in the ¼-ton, 4x4 Command Reconnaissance truck procurement. John D. Biggers, Director of the Production Division, Office of Production Management for said organization, penned a letter to Gregory stating approval of Bantam's 1,500 contract, but "we" (meaning Knudsen and himself) agreed with the multi-vendor approach, and that this viewpoint explained to Moore in a meeting at his office that very morning.[432] General Moore considered the facts and decided to "promptly" authorize the QMG to negotiate contracts for 1,500 vehicles from Ford and Willys subject to approval of their pilot models! This would satisfy their "contention for multiple sources of supply" consistent with the procurement of other trucks.[433]

How much Rice's telegram to Marshall or Gregory's missives to the AGO and Deputy Chief of Staff impacted events cannot be calculated; however, Ingram testified that "my recollection for the reason of that was the Army contemplated buying 1,500 vehicles, altogether, and there was enough pressure brought to bear by the various companies interested that a decision was made to give 1,500 to each of the companies."[434] Regardless of how it came about, this decision placed Willys and Ford back onto equal footing with Bantam, (ending any advantage the Butler manufacturer had) and with the negotiations and approval of the contracts for 1,500 from these firms it would then come down to how well the larger firm's pilot models performed under Holabird's grueling tests.

With the top individuals in the food chain (Knudsen and Moore and by extension Marshall) authorizing 1,500 each from Willys and Ford the denouement on this phase for the Dearborn manufacturer proved anticlimactic. Ford revised their November 9 quote on November 18, approval given verbally by Moore on November 18 with the condition of testing and acceptance of Ford's pilot model, approval obtained from the Assistant Secretary of War November 19, approval sought from Knudsen also November 19, and the Advisory Commission to the Council of National Defense approved the deal shortly thereafter.[435]

Ford now was officially back in the game! Testing on their pilot model was completed and reported to Ingram on January 6, 1941. The vehicle's acceptance triggered approval for the Dearborn firm to begin preparations for building 1,500 more.[436] Table 12 (page 212) contains the complete evaluation of Ford's initial vehicle.

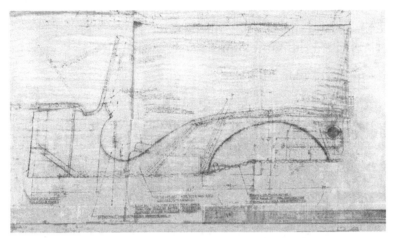

Figure 79: Quartermaster Drawing QM08501-Z, October 26, 1940.
Source: United States National Archives, College Park, Maryland.

Willys' contract would take slightly longer beginning with Rice writing Ingram on November 21 detailing conversations with Roos over chassis and body issues that might impact the quote. The issues arose from a new body drawing, QM08501-Z, issued by the QM on October 26, 1940.[437] Roos and Rice worked out the kinks and on November 27 Rice quoted Ingram a unit price of $959.00 with the stipulation that Willys was taking a gamble on this bid as their actual costs without profit or overhead came in at $989.00.[438] Verbal approval from Lt. Colonel Aurand of G-4 (Moore's staff) was given to Lt. Colonel Dow of the QMC on December 3rd with the condition, similar to Ford, of test and acceptance of their pilot model.[439]

The Chief of Staff's office approval did contain possible trouble ahead for the Toledo manufacturer. "Lt. Col Aurand mentioned that the pilot model now on hand would not be acceptable to the users but he was in favor of a contract similar to the Ford contract to be handled just as that one was handled."[440] Request and approval from the Assistant Secretary of War would come on that same day in early December. Not wasting any time, Ingram immediately notified Willys that they had a contract for 1,500 vehicles, even though final approval by Knudsen came shortly thereafter.[441] In one final twist of fate, the QMG would have to defend Willys' higher price to the Assistant Secretary of War and successfully did so.[442] With grit and determination, and some deft political maneuvering, Willys survived their second near-death experience in the truck ¼-ton 4x4 light procurement.

November 1940–February 1941—Camp Holabird, Maryland, Toledo, Ohio and Washington, D.C.

Willys' pilot model began testing in November 1940. Hausmann, the general foreman who helped drive the vehicle to Maryland, remained at Holabird, to act as their first Jeep mechanic, observing the tests and making any necessary repairs.[443] Most likely both the Ford and Willys pilot models received the same punishment as the BRC.

Kenower described one particular trial.

> The next part of the test was what they called cross-country. This was run in a field, at the camp, which they had fixed up to simulate extremely rough country, ditches, hills, etc. Our job had light springs and rode fairly well. The result was that they drove it about twice as fast as they did other similar vehicles, as the speed was regulated by how fast it was possible to go and still stay *in the job*!

> During the cross country test that field became a mud lake due to continuous hard rains. At that time we found the oil bath air cleaner was not properly mounted, and permitted dirt to get into the engine through the air inlet. Before this was discovered, the engine had been damaged, and in order to continue the test and avoid delay an engine was taken out of a Willys passenger car and installed in the pilot model, and it was again running on the course in a few hours.[444]

Whatever other manner of testing they performed, the Quartermaster Corps came to the stunning conclusion, detailed in a January 8, 1941, report, that the Toledo firm's pilot model had failed! Just weeks after surviving the 1,500 contract showdown, Willys now faced its gravest threat to date in the ¼-ton, truck 4x4 light race. Table 13 (page 214) contains the complete evaluation of the Toledo manufacturer's initial vehicle.

The AG apparently became aware of the Willys pilot model test situation before the official memo came out. On January 7, 1941, the AG ordered that before any further truck procurement from Willys proceeded, the Quartermaster Technical Committee's recommendation and report, must "be forwarded to the Adjutant General for approval."[445] This memo also included a handwritten note dated January 8, 1941, to Biggers informing him, "this was phoned to Holabird," and that the AG's request significantly impacted the Toledo manufacturer.

> It has the effect of holding up any action on the Willys pending approval by the Staff of acceptability to the Tech Committee. When Holabird is ready to report on the Willys, we will have to call Tech Comm to review the report &

probably go to Holabird again to look it over. I think someone objects to Oseth acting alone on this.[446]

Obviously, someone at the AGO felt it necessary to informally keep the Advisory Commission to the Council of National Defense in the loop on Willys' latest crisis.

The QMC Technical Committee, Sub-Committee on Motor Transport met on January 14, 1941, to discuss the Toledo firm's pilot model's fate. The report contained a litany of issues including:

- engine failure,
- transmission failure,
- unusual number of spring failures,
- windshield failure and,
- starting pin failure.[447]

Harking back to the very beginnings of the truck 4x4 light procurement the overriding concern centered squarely on the vehicle's weight and Willys' fateful decision to build their pilot model with the Go-Devil engine.

> The major objection in deviation from specification requirements in the case of the Willys-Overland ¼-Ton 4x4 Truck is the excessive weight. In this connection, it was pointed out that the Bantam Company originally offered a vehicle of 2,030 pounds, but now has added 130 pounds to make the required 2,160 pounds. Ford has guaranteed to meet the weight limitation of 2,175 pounds. Willys-Overland have stated in writing that they will guarantee a weight of 2,300 pounds, and will build down as near to 2,200 pounds as possible. **It is believed that in order for Willys-Overland to meet the weight limitation of 2,175 lbs., it will be necessary to use a smaller size engine** (emphasis added). It was the consensus opinion of the members of the Sub-Committee present that the maximum weight should not exceed 2,160 pounds without the machine gun base, and with 5.50-16 inch tires, or 2,175 pounds with the machine gun base, and the 5.50-16 inch tires.[448]

However, the committee did throw Willys a lifeline.

> Further discussion was to the effect that, following the usual procedure, when we complete a pilot model test we indicate to the manufacturer the changes necessary to meet specification requirements for a satisfactory vehicle. **Generally speaking, the Willys-Overland ¼-Ton, 4x4, Truck is considered as possible for correction to a satisfactory vehicle, provided the weight can be reduced to not to exceed 2,160 pounds without machine gun base plate and with 5.50-16 inch tires. The smaller engine offers the only method of reducing**

the weight (emphasis added). However, the Willys-Overland Company so far has not met specification requirements, and apparently is not immediately prepared to do so. **It is doubtful they will be able to meet specified weight requirements as long as they insist on using the heavy motor** (emphasis added). Therefore, it appears that the Willys-Overland Company will have to submit an entirely new pilot model.[449]

Given the facts as they stood the group recommended the following:

That no satisfactory pilot model has been submitted by the Willys-Overland Company to date, and that therefore the present requirements and authorization be used for the purchase of the total 4,500 vehicles from the two concerns which have submitted satisfactory pilot models, these being the Ford Motor Company and the American Bantam Company, and that the contract of the Willys-Overland Company become operative upon acceptance by the Quartermaster Technical Committee of the pilot model from this company, which must be within the weight restriction of 2,160 pounds without machine gun base and with 5.50-16 inch tires.[450]

The Sub-Committee duly forwarded the report to the Adjutant General, per the January 7, 1941, directive, on January 21, 1941.[451] The full QM Technical Committed approved the Sub-Committee's findings on January 22, 1941.[452] Willys would not receive a 1,500 unit contract and the Toledo manufacturer had to develop another pilot model with no idea how long that would take, and if they succeeded, no guarantee that it would pass testing. In late January 1941 another round of high-stakes negotiations took place at the highest levels to once again determine Willys-Overland Motors, Inc. fate in the competition.

On January 21, 1941, Eugene Rice sent a telegram to Chief of Staff Marshall stating (not exactly accurately) that, "our pilot model passed satisfactory test." The Willys Fleet and Government sales representative continued by asserting that, "ordered tendered for 1500 units on which all items satisfactory except we are now told weight over 2175 pounds not acceptable. This is lightest weight one of three manufacturers have been able to figure he can attain and develop after original impossible weight specification of 1,300 pounds and consistent advice of responsible officers in charge that we build our weight down to as near 2000 pounds as possible. **We can guarantee maximum weight of 2270 pounds as our heavier and more powerful engine entails basic additional weight and we believe certain desirable advantages** (emphasis added)."[453]

The Chief of Staff ordered an investigation into Rice's allegations. In a memorandum for Marshall dated January 24, 1941, one Colonel Meyer stated he reviewed the QM's Technical Committee's Subcommittee's January 14, 1941, report and highlighted the engine and weight issues described above.[454] The Acting Assistant Chief of Staff included the recommendation to split the 4,500 order between Bantam and Ford and delay Willys' contract until a satisfactory pilot model had been submitted and accepted.[455]

Colonel Meyer disputed Rice's test claim stating, "Contrary to statements contained in Mr. Rice's telegram, subject vehicle has not passed satisfactory tests, as is evidenced by the foregoing views of the Quartermaster Technical Subcommittee. The order for 1,500 units was tendered prior to the test and was subject to acceptance of the pilot."[456] In a devastating blow to Willys, "G-4 concur in the foregoing findings and recommendation of the subcommittee of the Quartermaster Technical Committee, except for the purchase of additional vehicles from Ford and Bantam."[457] The memorandum then states that the Secretary of War directed the drafting of a letter to Rice which would contain language used in Meyer's memo and detailed below in the AG's response.

The Toledo firm had made their play and would once again live or die on their Go-Devil engine. However, this gambit, unlike the one two months prior, proved unsuccessful as Major General E.S. Adams, the Adjutant General—not a subordinate, replied to Rice on January 28, 1941, using the language directed by the January 24, 1941, Chief of Staff's investigation memo. The letter stated a thorough investigation had been undertaken. Moreover, taking a swipe at Rice's test assertion (as directed) Adams stated, "As you know, the order for 1,500 units was tendered prior to completion of the test and was contingent upon acceptance of a pilot model. The pilot model can be said to have passed satisfactory tests only after representatives of the using arms have found it acceptable."[458]

Adams further asserted that the QM Technical Committee had found that their pilot model was unsatisfactory due to excessive weight and it was unlikely that Willys could meet the specified requirement, **"as long as it continued to insist on using the heavy motor** (emphasis added)."[459] Then striking at the heart of Roos' design (again as directed by the Secretary of War) he continued, "Weight is critical in this vehicle. The War Department believes that the Willys-Overland pilot provides power with a sacrifice of reduced weight. It is considered that **more engine power is provided than is necessary** (emphasis added) and the resultant weight increase undesirable." Then the Major General put the arrow through Willys' heart by concluding that the action of the subcommittee appeared "reasonable and proper," and the contract for 1,500 would only become operative upon acceptance of a pilot model that met the 2,160 lbs. limit.[460]

With their all or nothing gambit to the top in shambles, the Toledo manufacturer appeared doomed. Then, on January 31, 1941, QMC General Barzynski, most likely with Gregory's approval, wrote the Adjutant General and Deputy Chief of Staff Moore pleading Willys' case, thus disregarding the recommendations of his own committee!

The QMC had gone to great lengths, and at the highest levels, in November 1940, to justify the QM's multi-vendor approach. At that same time, Gregory threw more than a pinch of doubt and dispersion on Bantam. He clearly communicated his lack of faith in Bantam as a viable supplier. Therefore, one could reasonably conclude that the QM General would not let his organization's carefully crafted plan to have multiple vendors compete for this vehicle, let alone allow the disparaged and despised Bantam company have an order for even more vehicles. He would not go down without a fight, even if that meant overriding his own subordinates!

In astonishing detail Barzynski disputes the arguments of his own Technical Committee, even, like Rice, at best fudging how Willys' pilot model had tested, and even sings the praises of that vehicle!

> The record shows that the pilot model, ¼-ton, 4x4 trucks, submitted by Willys-Overland Company under their current contract has completed test at the Holabird Quartermaster Depot, Baltimore, Md., satisfactorily with the exception of a failure to meet weight limitation of 2,160 lbs. without machine gun base and with 5.50-16 inch tires and that the performance of that vehicle in spite of the added weight has been in all respects equal to that of the pilot models submitted by the other two manufacturers holding contracts for this type of truck. **It is believed that the importance of maximum weight is not as critical in actuality as has been stressed by certain using services and that the product offered by Willys-Overland Company being in all other respects equally satisfactory as the other two competing makes will serve the purpose for which intended in an excellent manner** (emphasis added)."[461]

These assertions by Barzynski elicit astonishment as the weight requirement drove the entire ¼-ton truck 4x4 light procurement from the very beginning. Suddenly now that requirement "is not as critical in actuality as has been stressed by certain using arms." Despite the Toledo firm's pilot model failures—described in detail in the January 8, 1941, test evaluation, as well as in the January 14, 1941, QM Technical Committee Sub-Committee report—Barzynski claims the "product offered by Willys-Overland Company, being in all other aspects equally satisfactory as the other two competing makes will serve the purpose for which intended in an excellent manner." All of it comes across as disingenuous at best, and downright false at worst. The arguments indicate his intention to prop up Willys in favor of other agendas, the aforementioned multi-vendor approach, and blatant QM animus for Bantam.[462]

The QM Brigadier General recommended the acceptance of the Willys pilot model based on "satisfactory performance despite a weight slightly higher than the specified limitation" and the contract for 1,500 triggered.[463] The Willys pilot weighed hundreds of pounds over the revised weight limit. He was brushing that off as just "slightly higher" in a vehicle where that very requirement took center stage from day 1? In another amazing downplay of the weight issue, he argued that these vehicles, "may not prove even more desirable at the higher weights involved, than vehicles built to a definite weight limit at the sacrifice of ruggedness and performance.[464] The Quartermaster Corp. at its highest levels had once again done everything in its power to save Willys.

It remained up to Moore and the Adjutant General to decide Willys' fate. In rather brief fashion for such a momentous decision in Jeep history, the first reply came from the AG on February 8, 1941. With no supporting rationale he wrote: "the recommendation of the Quartermaster General for clearance of the Willys-Overland pilot model ¼-ton, 4x4 truck as acceptable and suitable on the basis of satisfactory performance are approved. The vehicle will be released for production with the changes as indicated by the pilot model test report. This release applies only to the current contract of 1,500 units for the Willys-Overland Company."[465]

Moore overrode his own subordinates too as a memo described as "for record only" states, "following submission of study from G-4, G-429265-64, dated February 5, 1941, to Deputy Chief of Staff Moore, in which G-4 recommended against release of Willys-Overland contract for 1,500 units until such time as the pilot model was accepted by the using arms as satisfactory, verbal instructions were received from Gen. Moore to approve the recommendations of TQMG as contained in the 1st Ind. hereon. Action above complies with that directive.[466]

Moore followed-up his "verbal instructions" on February 8, 1941, with a memorandum to the QMG explaining his actions supporting Gregory's recommendation to award Willys a 1,500 contract stating that, "I did this primarily because I felt that an equity had been established in favor of the contractors, due to various conversations during the course of negotiations between the contracting officer and the contractor, and that this equity would be sustained in case of an appeal to the Comptroller General."[467] The Deputy Chief of Staff did chastise Gregory and his office for the controversy surrounding weight.

> However, Army Regulations provide that military characteristics of all equipment, or changes in military characteristics, must be approved by the Chief of Staff. In this case it would appear that, in effect, the contracting officer had usurped the functions of the Technical Committee and the Chief of Staff in assuming military characteristics that have not been previously approved.[468]

> When it became apparent that it would be impracticable to obtain a satisfactory military vehicle with a minimum weight of 1300 or 1400 pounds, some other minimum weight should have been sought through proper channels as a change in military characteristics.[469]

After the dust settled Gregory wrote Moore on March 5, 1941, with a copy to Biggers at Knudsen's office, explaining that the Biggers November 1940 memo had established an equity in favor of Willys-Overland (i.e. a higher authority than the Chief of Staff) and that Aurand of G-4 had given verbal authorization on December 3, 1940, to approve Willys' contract.[470] He addressed the military characteristics with a history lesson harking back all the way to June 19, 1940, that the weight issue finally resolved by the QM Technical Committee on February 14, 1941, authorizing an increase in weight, after all pilot model tests were completed.[471]

The QMG finished by asserting that, "there was and is no intention on the part of the

Quartermaster General to usurp the functions of the Technical Committee or the Chief of Staff" because the present procurement (1,500) was an extension of the original seventy awarded and that all the events of the fall 1940 and winter 1940–1941 were a "means for working out further revisions of military characteristics," presumably completed on February 14, 1941. With this first step now completed, further changes would occur, as directed by the Adjutant General on July 5, 1940, from the service tests then underway.[472]

Regardless of hard feelings, unprecedented actions, twists and turns, 11th-hour reprieves, and everything in between, the decision to award Willy's a 1,500 vehicle contract, despite the failure of their pilot model, significantly impacted the course of Jeep history. The official notification of their salvation came on February 11, 1941, when Ingram wrote Willys that, "your pilot model is accepted as suitable for military usage and therefore released for production with the other changes as indicated by the pilot model inspection report dated January 8, 1941."[473]

Ingram's final directive meant that Willys had to produce a vehicle which not only met the weight requirement, but also fixed all the issues detailed in the test report. For Roos, and the rest of the Toledo firm's team, this meant a significant redesign of the truck, which placed them significantly behind Bantam and Ford, with no idea, in February 1941, how long it would take to catch up.

February 1941–June 1941—Toledo, OH

Although Roos and company had put in a tremendous effort to design and build a suitable pilot model their first attempt failed. In February 1941 Willys stood at a crossroad with their truck ¼-ton 4x4 light design and the decisions on how to make it acceptable to the Army would fall to the Vice President of Engineering and his subordinates.

Figure 80: "The engineers tore it down and then rebuilt." Source: United States National Archives, College Park, Maryland.

After the pilot model returned to Toledo on January 10, 1941, the engineers tore it down for "careful inspection of all parts and then rebuilt."[474] However, the initial monumental decision needed before beginning the work on a new pilot model would come from the top. It revolved around what to do with the engine, which the Army had made a defining issue, and had recommended replacing the Go-Devil.

In an incredible show of faith in their product and decision making, and in complete defiance of the Army's recommendation, Willys would not bow to the military's demands. Frazer recalled the momentous decision.

> Mr. Roos and I had a very serious discussion as to whether or not we would abandon our engine, buy a Continental engine and reduce the weight, we said no, that we felt this was the proper vehicle for the armed forces, and we would rise or fall on showing the superiority of this vehicle, we wouldn't back down.[475]

Triumph Over Adversity—The Willys MA is Born

The die was cast and now Roos and his engineering team went to work. Though it would take to May 1941 to produce a new pilot model and June 7, 1941, to go into production, the result would prove worthy of their efforts. Roos would outline the significant changes made to build a new vehicle.

> Our pilot model went through its test, and before the conclusion of the test we were advised that some more orders were going to be given. I don't know exactly when we got the information, but a number of meetings were held in December and technical discussions were had between the engineers at Holabird, and Mr. Rice kept in touch with me, and the principal thing centered around the fact that we were going to have an order of 1500 vehicles and that we would have to meet a specified weight of 2175 pounds. The orders for those vehicles were held up for some time. In the meantime, we were getting reports back on the test of our vehicle and were making use of that fact to plan whatever changes we were going to make if we had an opportunity to build the 1500 additional vehicles, which we were told would be considered.
>
> Then you went to work on this order for 1500?
>
> **That's right. That entailed much more difficulty and a harder task then the first design** (emphasis added).
>
> Why was that?
>
> Because we had to make our basic pilot model design and, without sacrificing any of the fundamental items in it, we had to get the weight down to 2175 pounds from 2450 pounds […] we were informed if it did exceed that weight, we wouldn't get any more orders, so it was up to us to get the weight down.
>
> Will you outline, Mr. Roos, the salient changes which were made when you redesigned the vehicle to fill the order for 1500?

The whole front, as you see from the photograph was changed. That was in the interest of saving weight. The frame was completely redesigned. We changed the frame and used light gauge steel with reinforced upper and lower flanges following accepted bridge construction in order to dispose the material where it was most effective […] with the weight that we had.

The gasoline tank was taken out from the back of the rear seat and put under the driver's seat. The gauge of the body was lightened in certain spots. In the frame two cross tubes were taken out and we substituted channel sections for them. We changed the so-called single bow top, which the Army had originally specified, to a double body top. That was at our own suggestion because the single body top was unsatisfactory. We had to follow some further specifications of the Army as regards to instruments we used, so there was some change in the dash instruments. We put an effective propeller shaft brake on the back of the transfer case. **Most of our work, outside of that, was in the way of weight reduction, and I would have to submit a tabulation which we have made showing the weight taken out of each part of the original pilot model in order to make this model** (emphasis added).

The engine remained the same, but there was some changes in accessories. The carburetor was changed because the Government put in a specification that the engine would have to operate satisfactorily on a 60-percent grade both facing up and facing down, one on a twenty-percent grade both right and left hand, and some difficulty had been encountered with the pilot model in meeting that specification. That was corrected in the specification and manifolding [sic] of the 1500.[476]

McCaslin would add additional insight into this process.

Well, the frame, we reduced the frame weight by reducing the gauge of the metal, and using a higher tensile strength steel, and then by adding strips of metal on the top and bottom sides to give us the best section modulus we could get out of a given section. We also reduced the wall thickness of the manifold on the engine. We reduced the wall thickness of the water outlet elbow. We reduced the weight of our radiator by using gauges of metal that was…gave us all the strength required, and at the same time getting a radiator that was suitable for the job, we did likewise, or had Spicer do likewise in their wall thickness of their transfer cases and their axles.

We reduced the metal gauge thickness of the wheels. We reduced the gauge of the muffler, and also we reduced the gauges of the metal in the bodies. And in so doing we were able to get down to, I believe, the final weight was 2,155 pounds. And there is others, we took off a little weight here and there all over the job. I can't just enumerate them all.[477] Table 14 (page 216) presents a complete structural analysis of the new vehicle.

Through painstaking detail, part by part, and the other modifications, Roos and his team reduced the weight from 2450 pounds to 2154 pounds an amazing achievement given they refused to take the easy route and replace the engine. Willys, by June of 1941, had a truck that not only made weight, but did so with a more powerful engine than Bantam and Ford. This provided an advantage in performance as Roos had argued from the very beginning and made Willys' redesigned vehicle a formidable competitor! They would christen their vehicle the MA, M for military and A for the first model and thus an icon was born, the Willys M series of Jeeps!

Figure 81: 1941 Willys-Overland MA.

By June of 1941 over a year had gone by in the tale of the ¼-ton truck 4x4 light reconnaissance car. A small peace-time Army in the spring of 1940, only beginning to understand the magnitude of the coming conflict, embarked on a procurement to solve the problem of a light car to replace the mule to carry troops and light payloads. No one at the beginning could have imagined the epic proportions the seemingly insignificant procurement for seventy BRC vehicles from Bantam would morph into and the story remained unfinished even as Willys delivered the MA.

A synopsis of events that occurred during the spring, summer and fall of 1941, detailed in the epilogue to follow, will provide a brief history of "the rest of the story."

PAUL R. BRUNO

Epilogue

The Jeep Name

One of the enduring legacies of the Jeep story remains how these vehicles morphed from the "Bantam Reconnaissance Car", the "Willys Quad" and the "Pygmy" into all bearing the name "Jeep". If an opportunity ever existed to solve the mystery, the Federal Trade Commission case, adjudicated just a few years after the events of 1940, presented the best opportunity to discover the answer. However, even this meticulous look into the early Jeep saga could not draw any definitive conclusions.

Application of the Word "Jeep" To the ¼-Ton 4x4 Truck

There is a conflict in the testimony as to what and when a vehicle of this ¼-ton 4x4 type was first called a "jeep." The factory superintendent and driver of the American Bantam Car Company, who delivered its pilot model to Camp Holabird, Maryland, on September 23, 1940, and who, at the time of testifying, were no longer employees of, or in anywise connected with, that company, stated that the enlisted men at Camp Holabird called the vehicle a "jeep" several days after its arrival, among them three sergeants and the captain in charge of the tests (TR. 2848-2850, 2906-7). They also testified that it was referred to as blitz-buggy, puddle-jumper and various other names, but most commonly as "jeep." One of these sergeants, (at the time of testifying, a lieutenant) called by respondents in rebuttal, testified that he never heard the name "jeep" applied to the Bantam-built pilot by others and had never applied the name to it himself (TR. 3417-18). One of the other men referred to, the captain, was reportedly killed in action in Italy, and the other two were not called as witnesses.

The driver and repairman of Willys-Overland Motors who delivered its pilot model to Camp Holabird, Maryland, on November 13, 1940, testified for respondents that it was first called a Bantam but thereafter referred to by enlisted personnel on the post as a "jeep" (Tr. 1387-89, 1409-12).

Two retired master sergeants, stationed at Fort Oglethorpe, Georgia, testified for the Commission that eight or ten Bantam-built vehicles (part of the 69 remaining on the first contract) were received at Fort Oglethorpe just before Christmas 1940 for tests and that upon their arrival and thereafter while they remained at that post, they were referred to generally as "jeeps" (Tr. 2737-47).

Both stated that the Dodge ½-ton truck had previously been called a "jeep" but that after the arrival of the Bantam-built vehicles, the latter acquired that name. One of these witnesses testified that the commanding officer of that post also referred to the Bantam-built vehicle as a "jeep," but in a letter from that officer received in evidence without cross-examination, the officer stated that the Bantam-built vehicles were not called "jeeps" until several months after their arrival and that March of 1941 was the best of his recollection as to this date (RX 221). There is no dispute in the record that a Bantam-built "jeep" at Fort Knox was referred to as a "jeep" at that post in November 1940 (Tr. 2913-16); and was so-called at Fort Meade, Maryland, in January of 1941 (Tr. 2920) and at Fort Benning, Georgia, in February of 1941 (Tr. 2118, 3342).[478]

The summary above would suggest that the application of the name "Jeep" to the ¼-ton 4x4 trucks began sometime in the fall of 1940, after the delivery of the Bantam pilot model, first by whom and why not known. Without the unlikely surfacing of new information on this subject the commission's conclusion remains one of the best answers to the mystery.

As a postscript addition to the above, in previous years to 1940, the Quartermaster mechanics and test-drivers generally applied the generic term to a new machine under review as "jeep". As a matter of fact, the term reportedly had been floating around U.S. Army motor pools as far back as 1914. First World War-era doughboys were known to refer to **any army utility truck or car** (emphasis added) by the slang term "jeep."[479]

Figure 82: The Willys-Overland 1942 MB. 360,000 units were manufactured for the War.
Source: jeep.com

The "Rest of the Story"

The arrival of the Willys MA in mid-1941 represented a major milestone in early Jeep history. The events that occurred in the ¼-ton tale during the year that ended with the bombing of Pearl Harbor could fill an entire book; however, for purposes of this tome a brief summary suffices to complete the narrative.

Ford and Bantam built their 1,500 units during the first half of 1941 and some of these entered service in Army units around the country for field testing while others went overseas as part of Lend-Lease.[480] Willys began volume production on the MA in June 1941 and these began life as part of the assessment by the military.[481]

In July 1941 the Army decided not to wait for the completion of the analysis of the three vehicles and requested bids for 16,000 units, winner take all for standardization; therefore, whoever received this order would most likely end up building the "jeep" thereafter.[482] In August 1941, the award went to Willys, who then had to make significant changes requested by the Army to the truck. The newly minted car, due to the many changes, became the Willys MB, the legend of World War II![483]

In October 1941, with war imminent, the Army decided they needed a second source of supply and asked Willys to allow Ford to build their vehicle under license, thus the Ford Jeep for the Second World War.[484] In the end Willys built 360,000 Jeeps, and Ford 277,000.[485] Bantam produced only 2,675.[486]

American Bantam survived the war by building trailers some of which most likely pulled by the vehicle they had a significant hand in creating.[487] They never built cars again after 1940 and eventually went bankrupt in 1956.[488]

Willys would build cars, trucks and Jeeps after the war with varying degrees of success.[489] In 1953 Kaiser Motors Corporation purchased the firm's operating assets and renamed the company Willys Motors.[490] The rest of the 1950s saw the Toledo firm's passenger car business dry up although they still had success selling trucks and Jeeps.[491] However, by the early 1960s sales figures showed that the former automotive giant now existed as a marginal player in the market.[492] While some improvement came during the Kennedy Administration, the end of the Willys name in the automotive world came swiftly in 1963 when the Kaiser Industries' board of directors changed Willys Motors to Kaiser Jeep Corporation.[493]

Kaiser carried the Jeep legacy until 1970, when they sold the legend to American Motors Corporation (AMC), who eventually sold out to Renault in 1979.[494] In 1987 Chrysler Corporation acquired AMC (and the Jeep brand) from the French automaker. Then in 1998 Daimler-Benz acquired Chrysler. Bankruptcy in 2007 led to acquisition of Chrysler by Cerberus Capital Management. Eventually the Jeep product became a division of Fiat Chrysler Automobiles (FCA) and recently transferred to the new firm created by the merger of FCA and Peugeot, where it remains as of this writing.[495]

Ford ceased production of Jeeps in June 1945.[496] However, they built one more series of Jeeps, the M151, beginning in the 1950s and kept it in service through the 1990s.[497] The Dearborn manufacturer remains an international giant in the automotive industry as of the second decade of the 21st century.

Conclusion

20th century mechanized warfare had made animal transportation too slow, cumbersome and vulnerable. The need to replace that outdated mode of transportation provided the genesis (chapter 3) that led to the development of the truck ¼-ton 4x4 light. The testimony to the success of that endeavor, and the Jeep's transformational greatness, came from a German soldier who fought the Allies at Normandy on June 6, 1944, four years to the day from the date of Infantry's memo which launched the endeavor.

> One thing in particular struck many of us as amazing: all along the beach, there were no horses!

> This was a surprise for you?

> Yes, we found it astounding. This huge army had brought with it not one single horse or pack-mule! All their transport was mechanized. It may sound bizarre today, but this impressed us greatly, showing that the Allies had no need of horses anymore, as they had such huge oil resources and production capacity. Because, of course, the German armies used horses for transport on quite a large scale right up until the end of the war, due to limited fuel and constraints on mechanized vehicle production. Every German unit had its stables and veterinarian officer, and here were these English without that need at all. For us, this symbolized the Allied capabilities.[498]

The procurement that resulted in the creation of the first Jeeps demonstrates that when a dire need intersects with unusual circumstances (the beginning of World War II) the extraordinary can occur. These endeavors represent the right people, in the right place, at the right time overcoming every obstacle to create a vehicle so outstanding that the Army credited it as one of the primary reasons the Allies won World War II. That legacy, in and of itself would, for most products, rank as more than enough. The fact is, however, that descendants of Bantam's, Willys' and Ford's work still roam the highways and byways of the world many decades later. It provides further testament to the once-in-a-lifetime achievement these individuals and companies brought to life.

Time Line

1918–January 1940:	Project Genesis, research into a light vehicle
February–Mid-May 1940:	Discussions on light vehicle general characteristics
Mid-May–June 6, 1940:	Coalescing and documentation of vehicle general characteristics
June 6–June 20, 1940:	Initial work to develop a detailed vehicle specification
June 21–July 2, 1940:	Development and documentation of detailed vehicle drawing and specification
July 3–July 11, 1940:	Preparation and finalization of invitation for bids
July 12- July 21, 1940:	Bid preparation by manufacturers
July 22, 1940:	Bid opening and award to Bantam
July 22–July 24, 1940:	Willys given permission by QMC to build a pilot model at their own expense
July 23-August 5, 1940:	Finalization of bid award and contract award for Bantam
August 5-Sept. 21, 1940:	Bantam pilot model built and christened "Bantam Reconnaissance Car" (BRC)
August 15–November 4, 1940:	Willys pilot model built and named the Quad
September 23, 1940:	BRC delivered to Camp Holabird
Sept. 24-Oct. 23, 1940:	BRC tested at Camp Holabird
October 4, 1940:	Ford representatives, on invitation from the QMC, meet with QMC representatives who request they build and submit a pilot model

October 4–November 21, 1940:	Ford pilot model built and dubbed the Pygmy
October 4–December 3, 1940:	Order for 500 from each manufacturer becomes 1,500 from each contender
Oct. 23-29, 1940:	Inspection, test and final reports on Bantam pilot model completed
October 30, 1940:	BRC officially accepted and order for next sixty-nine placed
November 13, 1940	Willys Quad delivered to Camp Holabird
November 23, 1940	Ford Pygmy delivered to Camp Holabird
November 1940–January 1941:	Bantam builds the other 69 from original contract; Willys Quad and Ford Pygmy tested at Camp Holabird
January 6, 1941	Ford pilot model accepted and order for 1,500 vehicles commences
January 8–28, 1941:	Willys pilot model rejected and order for 1,500 cancelled
January 31–February 11, 1941:	Willys 1,500 unit order restored
February–June 1941:	Bantam and Ford build their 1,500
February 1941–May 1941:	Creation of the Willys MA
June 1941:	Willys MA goes into volume production
July 1941:	RFP for 16,000 vehicles
August 1941:	Award for 16,000 trucks to Willys-Overland Motors
August–October 1941:	Creation of the Willys MB
October–November 1941:	Formalization of agreement between, Willys, Ford and the QMC for Ford to build the MB under license

Tables

From Chapter 5, page 79

Table 1: ¼-Ton Truck 4x4 Light – Specification ES–No. 475

Army Requirement
A. Applicable Specifications
A-1. The following current specifications and drawings in effect on date of Invitation to Bids, shall form a part of this specification.
A-2. Responsibility for obtaining copies of the latest revisions of Specifications and Drawings listed under A-1 rests with prospective bidders.
B. General
B-1. Quartermaster Corps Specifications ES – No. 459 applies.
C. Service Requirements
C-1. General – see above
C-2. Abilities. The truck, fully equipped and loaded, shall demonstrate the following speeds:
C-2a. A level road maximum speed of not less than fifty(50) miles per hour, at a corresponding engine speed that shall not exceed the peak horsepower speed.
C-2b. A level road minimum speed of not more than three (3) miles per hour, at engine maximum torque speed.
C-3. Cruising range – The truck, fully equipped and loaded, shall be capable of making an average day's run of one hundred fifty (150) miles, at an average speed of thirty-five (35) miles per hour, on good roads over average rolling terrain, on one initial filling of the gasoline tank and without requiring the addition of oil.
C-4. Traction devices – Tire chains will be required for use on the driving wheel tires, and the truck construction shall permit the satisfactory installation and use of the tire chains.
D. Specifications
D-1. Chassis. The chassis shall be of sturdy construction capable of withstanding the strains of the service.
D-1a. Weights and loads – The weight of the truck, fully equipped and serviced (less only the payload), shall not exceed 1275 pounds (amended to 1300 pounds) and every effort, consistent with the best recognized engineering practices, shall be made to minimize weight. The truck shall have a nineteen hundred (1900) pound gross weight allowance to provide at least a six hundred twenty-five (625) pound payload carrying capacity.
D-1b. Dimensions – The wheelbase shall be the minimum practicable, not more than eighty (80) inches. Ground clearance under the axles eight and one-half (8 ½) inches, clearance under transmission, transfer case skid shoe, gas tank, battery and propeller shaft brake clearances shall be sufficient to permit operations over unimproved roads and cross country terrain the clearance under the lowest unit to be at least nine and one-half (9 ½) inches. Angle of approach not less than forty-five degrees, angle of departure not less than 40 degrees. Overall height not to exceed 40 inches. Radiator shell, engine hood, cowl and front fenders and headlight

mounting permit a driver of average height, 68 inches, to properly see road at a distance of not more than ten feet.
D-2. Frame—The chassis frame shall support the maximum gross loads imposed under the most severe operating conditions.
D-3. Power unit—The power unit shall consist of an engine, clutch and transmission embodied in a unit power plant.
D-4. Engine—shall be internal combustion, four-stroke cycle type, no less than 4 cylinders, piston displacement not less than 85 cubic inches, fuel knock rating not more than 68 octane number, cylinder heads not made of aluminum, crankshaft counter balanced, supported by at least 3 main bearings.
D-4a. Governor – if install, set to manufacturer limit, but not hinder engine operation at speeds of 55 miles per hour
D-5. Cooling system – shall be of the type using a circulating pump.
D-6. Lubricating system – Manufacturer's standard – oil filter detailed requirements, chassis lubricating system high pressure type.
D-7. Ignition system – Complete battery and generator ignition system, 6 volt potential.
D-8. Fuel System – 1 gasoline tank, 10 gallon capacity, flexible fuel line.
D-9. Exhaust system – substantial leak-proof, amply proportioned, securely mounted.
D-10. Clutch – torque capacity at least equal to maximum engine torque.
D-11. Transmission – no less than 3 forward, 1 reverse speeds, can provide 4 speeds.
D-12. Transfer case – 2 speed type having a high range ratio of 1.0 and low range reduction of approximately 2.0 to 1.0 if 3 speed, gear ratio 1.0 – 1.0 for 4 speed.
D-13. Propeller shaft – rugged construction and positively lubricated, universal joints latest design, length to manufacturer specifications.
D-14. Axles – single reduction type, identical tread front and rear, front axle full floating type.
D-15. Springs – strength adequate to sustain the gross speed loads, without evidence of overload or permanent set.
D-16. Shock absorbers – Hydraulic, double acting, of adequate capacity on both axles, side frame mounting, brackets not to protrude below axle housing.
D-17. Bogie – does not apply.
D-18. Wheels and tires
D-18a. Wheels – pressed steel ventilated disc or steel spoke type interchangeable on axle hubs.
D-18b. Tires – balloon type, size 5.50-16 4 ply with mud and snow tread design.
D-18c. Inner tubes – heavy duty type, bullet sealing type.
D-18d. All wheels, tires and tubes same size.
D-19. Brakes – safely control fully equipped and loaded truck under all operating conditions.
D-19a. Service brakes – hydraulic application type, brakes and drums on all wheels, sufficiently control and hold fully equipped vehicle on 50 percent grade, complete stop at deceleration equivalent to a stop within 30 feet from speed of 20 miles per hour on dry, hard, approximately level road, free from loose material. No evidence of excessive fading.
D-19b. Parking brake – hand lever operated mounted at rear end of transfer case main (top) shaft.
D-20. Electrical equipment – chassis equipped with complete electrical starting and lighting system, 6 volt

potential.
D-21. Chassis equipment – complete including enumerated articles
D-21a. Engine hood – water proof, readily removable, easy access.
D-21b. Instrument panel – speedometer, recording odometer, fuel gauge, ammeter, engine heat indicator, direct reading oil pressure gauge. Carburetor choke control, ignition lock, hand throttle control, spark control (when provided) located convenient reach of operator.
D-21c. Tool equipment – Type I, Q.M. Specification ES – No 422, 4 chains required.
D-21d. Accessory equipment – at least rear view mirror, windshield wiper, locks, electric horn
D-21e. Lighting equipment – best commercial grade, 2 head lamps, 1 combination service tail and service stop, license plate, "black-out" tail lamp, sketch of all lamp mountings, all lamps moisture, dust and rust proof, standard and "black-out" switch best commercial grade, I.C.C. regulation reflectors.
D-22. Controlling mechanism – steering mechanism withstand strains of cross country operation.
D-23. Operating mechanism – all controls within convenient operator reach, clutch, brake and accelerator pedals spaced so operated properly without interference, accelerator pedal located to the right of brake pedal.
D-24. Name, caution and shifting plates – name plate with specified information, caution plate with maximum road speeds, shifting plate with specified information, plates etched with black background.
D-25. Body – conform to specification Q.M. 08370-Z.
D-26. Special operating equipment – rear pintle, brush guard, towing hooks.
D-27. Painting – key components clean and dry before primer, polished finish conform to requirements specified, surface primed, surface coated and finish painted, at least 2 coats of synthetic enamel meeting Quartermaster specifications.
D-28. Marking – War Department Registration Numbers stenciled in block letters and figures 4 inches in height in white synthetic enamel, on each side of the engine hood.
E. Test Requirements – preliminary tests at manufacturer's plant under government supervision.
F. Questionnaire – A summary of Bantam's questionnaire presented in chapter 7.

From Chapter 6, page 90

Table 2: Bantam Main Bid and Two Alternative Bids

Item No.	Articles or Services	Quantity	Unit	Unit Price	Amount Dollars	Amount Cents
1.	Trucks, Motor, Gasoline, Light Reconnaissance and Command Car (Four Wheels—Four Wheel Drive), in accordance with Quartermaster Corps. Tentative Specification ES-No. 475, dated July 2, 1940, attached	62	each	2260.50	140,151	00
		70	each	2260.50	158,235	00
a.	Alternative bid is requested for	62	each	2415.50	149,761	00

	Trucks under Item No. 1 equipped with Full-Floating Type Rear Axle (Par. D-14.a.)					
	Alternative bid is requested for furnishing eight (8) Trucks under Item No. 1. Or 1.a., equipped with Four-wheel steering mechanism (pars. D-14.b. and D-22.a.).					
		70	each	2415.50	169,085	00
b.	Item #1	8	each	2673.00	21,343	00
	Item NO. 1.a	8	each	2823.00	22,584	00

From Chapter 6, page 91

Table 3: Bantam's Response to Army Requirements

F-1. Truck. Make Bantam, model 40, overall length 126 inches, overall width 54 inches overall height 71.5 inches shipping weight 1,273 pounds (exactly as Probst remembered!), 4 wheel steer shipping weight 1,323 pounds, dunnage in shipping weight 85 pounds.
F-1a. Trucks loaded on freight car, item 1, 8, 50' Auto Box Car, item 2, 8 50' Auto Box Car, item 3, 6 – 9, per truck by our own transport trucks
F-1b. Weight of truck fully equipped, 1,300 pounds, 4-wheel steer 1,350 pounds, gross weight allowances specified.
F-1c. Wheelbase 79 inches, with truck fully equipped and loaded: ground clearance under following units, front axle 8.5 inches, rear axle 8.5 inches, transmission 11.25, transfer case skid shoe 9.5 inches, gas tank 21 inches, battery 21 inches, propeller shaft brake 9.5 inches, angle of approach 45 degrees, departure 36 degrees, truck will comply with overall height specification, driver vision requirement will be met.
F-2. Frame will support maximum gross loads and be suitably braced.
F-3. Power unit – Will the engine, clutch and transmission be embodied in a unit power plant, yes; will the engine be so mounted that it will not be damaged form distortion, yes; will the transfer case be mounted as a unit with the transmission, yes; will it be so mounted that it will not be damaged by frame distortion, yes.
F-4. Engine make Bantam 40; model 40; number of cylinders 4; displacement 113.1 cubic inches; maximum peak horsepower 40H.P.at 5500 r.p.m.; maximum operating speed guaranteed by the engine manufacturer 3300 r.p.m.; maximum torque, less only fan and generator operating 79 lbs./ft.; will this torque be developed while using fuel having a knock rating of not more than 68 octane, yes; will engine operating be satisfactory using fuel of this octane number, yes; the torque quoted above was developed employing what compression ratio, 5.4 plns to 1.0; is this the compression ratio that will be furnished, yes; cylinder head material, cast iron; will the crankshaft be counterbalanced, yes; number of main bearings, three.
F-4a. Will a governor be provided on the engine, no.
F-5. Cooling system – will the requirements of paragraph D-5 herein regarding cooling, be fully complied with, yes; will a thermostat be provided, yes.
F-6. Lubricating system – Method of lubricating: crankshaft main bearings, pressure; connecting rod lower

bearings, pressure; camshaft bearings, pressure; piston pin bearings, splash; cylinder walls, splash, timing gears or chain, spray; capacity of engine oil reservoir, 5 quarts; is this capacity sufficient to meet the cruising range requirements of paragraph C-3 herein, yes; lubrication system will function satisfactorily on side slopes up to, 22%; and on longitudinal slope to, 59%.

F-6a. Oil filter – Make, as specified; model, as specified; type, as specified; will the filter comply with the requirements of paragraph D-6 herein, yes; will the requirements concerning oil lines be fully complied with, yes.

F-6b. Type of chassis lubricating system, alemite; type of fittings alemite h.p.; will the system be of a design that will permit the ready attachment of the grease gun, yes.

F-7.   Ignition system – Make, auto-lite; potential 6 volts. Is automatic or hand control for spark advance provided, automatic.

F-8.   Fuel system – fuel tank, capacity ten gallons; will this capacity be sufficient to meet the cruising range requirements of paragraph C-3 herein, yes; will the tank be so mounted that it will not be damaged by frame distortion, yes; tank mounting location, rear of body; fuel pump make, A.C.; model, 1523306; type A.F, will it include sediment bowl or chamber, yes; strainer, yes; hand primer, yes; will the pump be so located that its operation will not be objectionably affected by exhaust heat, yes;

F-8.   Fuel system – auxiliary filter, make Zenith; model M22X-2-B2; recommended mounting location, at tank; air cleaner, make, A.C.; model, as specified; is it oil bath type, yes; oil capacity, as specified; will it meet the efficiency requirements of paragraph D-8 herein, yes; will fuel line requirements be fully complied with, yes; will the lines be arranged to prevent vapor-lock, yes; the fuel system will function satisfactorily on slide slopes up to, 20%; longitudinal slope to, 50%.

F-9.   Muffler – will the requirements of paragraph D-9 herein be fully complied with, yes.

F-10. Clutch – Make, long; model, 8½ CB-C; type, single plate; guaranteed to transmit torque of 90 lbs./ft.; will automatic means be provided for lubricating the throwout bearing mechanism, no; if not, will a lubricating fitting be provided at a readily accessible location which does not require the removal of toe or floor board, yes.

F-11. Transmission – Make, Warner Gear; model, T 84 E; guaranteed to transmit a torque of 80 bls./ft.; reductions, 1st 2.93 to 1.000; 2nd, 1.70 to 1.000; 3rd 1.000 to 1.000; reverse, 3.90 to 1.000 to 1.0.

F-12. Transfer case – Make, Spicer; model, 40; reductions, high range 1. To 1.; low range 2. To 1.0; guaranteed to transmit a torque of 325 IN lbs./ft.; will the transfer case include front axle drive declutching mechanism, yes; will the declutching mechanism be properly lubricated from the transfer main case, yes; will controls be readily operatable from the driver's seat, yes; will the controls detract from driving comfort; no; will transfer case noise be effectively minimized, yes.

F-13. Propeller shaft – Make, Spicer; model, 40; front Spicer 23 ¾ inch; rear, Spicer 23 ¾ inch; between transmission and transfer case, none; guaranteed to transmit a torque of, front, 325; rear 325; transmission-transfer case, none lbs./ft.; maximum angle at which universal joints are guaranteed to continue operation, 20 degrees; maximum angle that will exist in universal joints with truck in the fully equipped, loaded and level position (for momentary operation, 10 degrees; are the joints all of the same make and type, yes; are they of metal construction; yes; will the propeller shaft lengths conform to the manufacturer's recommendation, yes.

F-14. Axles – type, hypoid reduction; gear ratio, 5.25 to 1.0; Ratio of impact resistance between horizontal and vertical planes of axles housing, 1. To 1. To 1.0; will axle bowl covers be so constructed that they will not be damaged in cross country operations, yes; will they be bolted to the axle housings, yes; will differential assemblies be interchangeable between front and rear axles, yes; will housing breathers be provided, no; will gear lubricant be confined to the differential bowls, yes; will high pressure lubrication fittings be provided in the hubs, yes; will high pressure lubrication fittings be provided in the hubs, yes; if so, will the hubs include the

required relief fittings, yes.
F-14. Front axle – Make, Spicer; model, 40; input torque capacity 325 lbs./ft.; will it be of the full floating type which a wheel will not be released if an axle shaft fails, optional; axle shaft diameter over the splines, 1.125 inches; number of splines, 10; steering drive ends, joint make, Bendix-Weiss; type C.V.; size, 3 ¼ inch; outside spherical diameter, 6 inches; will steering pivots be equipped with roller bearings, yes; offset between king-pin center and tire center, at ground 1 ¾ inches; front wheel maximum cramping angle, at the wheel on the inside of the turning circle, 30 degrees; will axle stops be of the required design and welded, yes; steering tie rod, outside diameter, 1 1/8 inches; wall thickness 3/16 inch; will the ends be threaded as required …; tread 47 ½ inches.
F-14. Rear axle – 2 wheel steer trucks – make, Spicer; model 40; type, optional i.e. full floating or semi-floating; if a semi floating rear axle is offered at the bid price, has the increased cost (per truck) been quoted in the bid, for the provision of a full floating axle of a type with which the wheel will not be released if an axle shaft fails, yes; input torque capacity, 325 lbs./ft. axles shaft diameter over the splines, 1.125 inches; number of splines, 10; tread, 47 ½ inches.
F-14. Rear axle – 4 wheel steer trucks – make, Spicer; model 41; will the steering drive ends be identical to those provided on the front axle, yes; input torque capacity 325 lbs./ft.; tread, 47 ½ inches.
F-15. Springs – will the requirement concerning spring to spring stop clearances be fully complied with, yes; will the required spring leaf clips be provided, yes; is it guaranteed that the spring suspension will be suitable for the required service conditions, yes.
F-16. Shock absorbers – Make, Gabriel; model, 40; total number provided, 4.
F-17. Does not apply.
F-18. Wheels, tires and tubes – wheels, make, motor wheel; type, steel ventilated; will they be so constructed that they will not be damaged in cross country operations, yes; will they be interchangeable on all axle hubs, yes.
F-18. Rims – Make, Motor Wheel; size 16 – 5.50; type, Dr. Center; will they permit proper mounting of tires containing bullet seal tubes, yes.
F-18. Tires – Make offered for selection, Firestone; type, Ground gripper; size 16 X 5.50; number of plies, 4; type of tread design, ground gripper; loaded radius, 12 ¾ inches.
F-18. Inner tubes – Make, Firestone; type, regular.
F18. Tire, tube, flap wheel assemblies will be balanced to within 35 inch-ounces. Will the tires be balanced dotted, yes.
F-19. Brakes – Service brakes – application type, hydraulic; brakes and drums provided on 4 wheels; hydraulic line maximum pressure 1000 lbs. per square inch; brake size, front 9 X 1-1/2; rear 9 X 1-1/2
F-19. Parking brake – make, Spicer; type, external band; actual location, rear of transfer case; will the parking brake be operatable at all times on the rear wheels, yes.
F-20. Electrical equipment – potential, 6 volts; battery – capacity 80 ampere hours at a 20-hour rate; make U.S.L; model, AB-13; generator, make, Auto-Lite; type, voltage controlled; guaranteed maximum output capacity (when hot), 25 amperes; generator regulation apparatus box, make Auto-Lite; model, as specified; type, as specified; will the requirements concerning wiring be fully complied with, yes.
F- 21. Chassis equipment – will the requirement concerning engine hood, bumpers, instrument panel, tool, tire chain and accessory equipment be fully complied with, yes; are the requirements concerning lighting equipment thoroughly understood, yes; will they be fully complied with, yes; will reflectors be furnished as required, yes.
F-22. Controlling mechanism – Steering gear – make, Ross; model T 12; rated for easy steering in connection

with a driving front axle and a load of, 724 lbs on the front tires at the ground; is the control mechanism guaranteed to be of a capacity adequate for the intended service, yes; steering wheel diameter, 17 inches.

F-22. Controlling mechanism – 4 wheel steer trucks – will the steering mechanism provide delayed steering on the rear wheels, yes; maximum cramping angle on front wheels, 30 degrees; on rear wheels, 23 degrees; will the design of the steering mechanism preclude weaving of the rear end of the truck and any tendency to over-steer, yes; will the mechanism be substantially constructed and so installed that it will not be damaged in cross country operations, yes.

F-23. Operating mechanism – will the requirements of paragraph D-23 herein, be fully complied with, yes.

F-24. Name, caution and shifting plates – will the plates be provided, inscribed as required, yes; will drawings of the plates be submitted for approval, yes; will they be mounted at approved locations, yes.

F-25. Body – will the body conform to the requirements of drawing 08370-Z, yes; is a body drawing being furnished for approval, yes.

F-26. Special operating equipment, rear pintle, make, as recommended; will it be installed as required, yes; will towing hooks be furnished, no; if not will the front bumper be so designed and mounted that it can be used for towing purposes, yes; will the truck construction permit the satisfactory installation and use of tire chains, yes.

F-27. Painting – will the painting requirements be fully complied with, yes.

F-28. Markings – will the trucks be marked as required, yes.

F-29. Maximum road speed, truck fully equipped and loaded, 50 m.p.h.

F-30. What grade abilities will be demonstrated with the truck fully equipped and loaded – with transmission in direct gear and transfer case in high range – 2 wheel steer truck 15%; 4 wheel steer truck, 14%; with transmission in low gear and with 2 speed transfer case in low range, 2-wheel steer truck, 75%; 4-wheel steer truck, 70%

F-31. Will a pilot model truck or trucks, be produced for inspection and tests at the Holabird Quartermaster Depot, yes; describe the type of trucks that will be produced for pilot model tests, light reconnaissance and command car 4x4

F-32. Has the service facility list been included with the bid, no; if not has it been filed with the Purchasing and Contracting Officer, will be.

F-33. Have drawings been included with the bid, chassis assembly, yes; frame, yes; body, yes; have engine certified power curves been included with the bid, yes; do the curve sheets indicate what compression ratio and octane numbered fuel were employed, yes.

F-34. Bidders shall signify compliance with the requirements of this specification by supplying herewith the following data required as proof of the fact that compliance is intended:

F-34a. As required by paragraph E-2. Specification ES- No. 459, has the manufacturer of the trucks offered under this bid been continuously engaged in the production of motor truck chassis for a period of 2 years immediately prior to the opening date of this Invitation to Bid, yes; and does he possess the facilities necessary to produce trucks meeting the requirements of this specification, yes.

F-34b. Have the guarantees as required by paragraph E-3 specification ES-No. 459, been carefully considered and are they fully agreed upon, yes.

F-34c. If any exceptions are contemplated in the specifications requirements, have they been completely listed below, as required under paragraph E-3 specification ES-No. 459, yes; is it clearly understood that in the event exceptions are not listed below, the right is reserved to demand a full and complete compliance with the specification requirements, yes.

F-34d. Exceptions to specification requirements are listed below:
Tie rod will be placed in front of the front axle and above the center line. It is impossible to place the tie rod in the rear of the axle and secure the minimum ground clearance as specified.
We can supply spare tire mounting and bumperettes as specified. We would prefer, however, to extend the side rails of the frame to the rear and to mount a rear bumper duplicating the front. We would then propose to mount the tire between the rear bumper and the body. This change will raise the tire 1 ¼ inches, but will have the advantage of better rear protection and also the ability to mount the pintle hook so as to be accessible without the removal of the bumper or the spare tire.
We can provide the instrument panel with two glove compartments as specified, but it is our opinion that it would be better to use the instrument panel we are now using in Bantam cars, as we feel this would make it possible for the men in the two bucket seats to enter and leave the car much more easily.
In all preliminary conversations upon which the 4-wheel drive equipment were based, there was no mention made of the parking brake on the rear of the transfer case; in as much as parking brakes are already included on the 4-wheel hydraulic brakes and we naturally assumed the parking brake properly shielded against brush, etc. would be entirely satisfactory. We believe this specification should be changed as the specified parking brake will, in our opinion, not be effective or meet your requirements.

From Chapter 7, page 95

Table 4: Technical Analysis of Bids Submitted
In Response To
Invitation for Bids No. 398-41-9
Bidder No. 2 – American Bantam Car Company, Butler, Penna

Findings / Exceptions / Deviations	Recommendation
Shipping weights	The shipping weights quoted appear reasonably correct.
Exception: Tie rod will be placed in front of the front axle and above the centerline. It is impossible to place the tie rod in the rear of the axle and secure the minimum ground clearance specified.	The tie rod location offered is contrary to the specification requirements but is the most desirable place available. Mounting behind the axles housing will result in less than the minimum ground clearance, which is believed will be more hazardous than the mounting offered. It is recommended that the specification requirement be waived and the construction offered considered acceptable.
Exception – We would prefer to extend the side rails of the frame to the rear and mount a rear bumper duplicating the front, this in lieu of furnishing spare tire mounting and bumperettes as specified.	Demand compliance with specification requirements.
We can supply the instrument panel with two glove compartments as specified, but it is our opinion that it would be better to use the instrument panel we are now using on Bantam cars.	Require two glove compartments be supplied as called for in the Invitation for Bids.

Exception – A cut-in type parking brake is offered in lieu of the transmission brake specified.	It is recommended that the specification requirement be waived and the parking brake offered be accepted provided it meets the performance requirements of paragraph D-19. b.
Deviation – The chassis drawings which accompanied the bid discloses a number of features which do not conform to the requirements of drawing 08370-ZA (is this the drawing we have?) Thermo-syphon type engine cooling system instead of pump circulated system. Same volume radiator core apparently will be used with the larger engine that is used with the engine of less than one-half the size of the one offered.	Hand written notes acknowledging deviations
The cooling fan diameter is shown to be greater than the height of the radiator. The blades extend below the core.	
The head lights are not placed in a protected or desired location.	
The engine hood does not slope as required to give road vision. However, this is probably due to the use of the larger engine.	

General Recommendations
The product described in the bid submitted by the American Bantam Car Company most nearly meets the specification requirements, is lowest in price and since this is an experimental development, award is recommended to be made to this firm.
There are a number of controversial questions which can and will be adjusted at the time of award.
It is suggested that the personnel of the interested using arm be consulted regarding the importance of the Exceptions and Deviations and their reactions thereto incorporated in the directive award.
This office recommends acceptance of the alternate bid which includes full floating axles.
If the alternate bid which covers four wheel steering is acceptable, it is recommended that the delivery time be extended the amount requested by the bidder.
The bid submitted by Willys-Overland, Inc. while basically low, actually is higher, due to the addition of liquidated damages because of excessive delivery time over the limit of seventy-five (75) days.
Suggested changes in specification – this specification should be reviewed as soon as the results of field tests are available.

From Chapter 7, page 97

Table 5: Contract—Additional Requirements

1. You took exception to mounting the tie rod behind the front axle. You will be permitted to mount the tie rod ahead of the front axle housing, provided that it is adequately protected from damage.

2. You will be permitted to extend the frame side rails to the rear to support a full width rear bumper, provided that the front and rear bumpers will properly overlap. If necessary, bumper guards may be used to provide compliance with overlap requirements.

3. The two (2) glove compartments are desired and it is requested that you make an effort to supply compartments that will not interfere with entrance and egress from the vehicle, Additional data are desired covering the compartments.

4. Regarding the parking brake it is desired that you submit for approval a layout portraying clearly the type of cut-in brake you would provide, bearing in mind that the control mechanism must be effectively protected from damage.

5. You have quoted an engine compression ratio of 5.4 plus. It is desired that you quote the actual compression ratio figure you intend to employ.

6. In your bid questionnaire you state that the cooling system requirements of paragraph D-5. will be complied with. However, your chassis print R-100001 indicates that the thermo-syphon system of circulating the cooling medium will be employed. This is contrary to the specification requirements. A circulating type pump must be furnished on the vehicles.

7. The chassis print shows the cooling fan extending above the radiator core necessitating a housing in the radiator upper tank. Also, the fan blades extend below the radiator lower tank which indicates that the installation is one in which a large engine and fan assembly are utilized with a radiator core designed for a smaller engine. While the design as illustrated, is acceptable, you are cautioned that the cooling medium temperature differential requirement at the top of the radiator must be complied with.

8. You have not named the brand of oil filter you intend to furnish. In this connection it is suggested that you investigate the metal edge type filter now under development by the Zenith Carburetor Corporation. It is understood that a filter of light weight might be obtained suitable for use on this light weight vehicle. Comment and data are desired.

9. The specification drawing requires a gasoline tank having a capacity of at least ten (10) usable gallons. Your chassis print shows a tank of ten (10) gallons capacity but it may be possible that all ten (10) gallons are not usable. You are cautioned that the usable gallonage must be at least that required.

10. You have quoted the transfer case torque capacity as 325 inch-pounds. It is assumed that this is an error. It is desired that adequacy of this unit be substantiated.

11. It is requested that data covering the propeller shaft universal joints be furnished together with the shaft angles that will actually exist with the vehicle in the level and loaded position.

12. You have quoted the steering drive and universal joints as of 3-¼" size, and outside spherical diameter of 6". Obviously steering drive universal joints of the spherical diameter stated could not possibly be assembled in the axles offered in the vehicle. It is requested that the correct size joint together with a print of same be furnished this office.

13. The steering tie rod must be threaded to permit a fine toe-in adjustment, i.e. fine and coarse threads at the right and left hand ends of the rod respectively. You have failed to answer this question but it is assumed that you contemplate such a construction.

14. You offer Firestone "Ground Gripper" tires. The specification stipulates that the tread design must not require directional operation. Will the tire you contemplate using be one that does not require directional operation to insure satisfactory life? It is desired that data covering the tread design be furnished this office for approval.

15. The chassis assembly print shows only one auxiliary shift handle. Since the two speed transfer case requires separate shift handles for range gear and declutching mechanism two shift handles must be furnished and provided with simple means to prevent low range gearing being utilized when the front axle drive is

disengaged. This can be in the form of a lip extension placed on the range gear shift handle so that the transfer case cannot be shifted into low range unless the front axle drive is engaged.

16. It is desired that a more suitable location be selected for the mounting of the auxiliary gasoline filter. The filter must be accessible for servicing.

17. With the 3300 r.p.m. engine maximum operating speed, tires having a 12-3/4" loaded radius, and 5.25 axle ratio, the vehicle road speed will be less than 50 m.p.h. It is desired that the road speed at the 3300 r.p.m. engine speed shall definitely exceed 50 m.p.h. Accordingly, it is requested that you advise whether an axle ratio of approximately 4.7 to 1.0 can be furnished in lieu of the 5.25 ratio.

18. The construction and arrangement of the tool boxes are not in accordance with bid drawing #08370-ZS. You are advised that the construction must be that shown on the above mentioned drawing.

19. It is desired that the body be made slightly wider to more properly cover the rear tire equipment. This as you have increased the axle tread beyond that contemplated. It is further desired that the wheel housing side panels be moved closer to the tires resulting in a wider cargo space between the wheel housings and wider rear seat.

20. In the case of the four wheel steer vehicles it will be necessary, of course, to provide proper clearance for tire chains when the rear wheels are cramped either to right or left.

21. It is noted from your layout that when the front wheels are cramped there does not appear to be sufficient tire chain clearance with respect to the frame. You are cautioned that sufficient clearance must be provided.

22. You are requested to furnish as promptly as practicable detailed prints of the engine, transmission and transfer case, front and rear axles, and a print clearly showing the four wheel steer layout actually installed in your chassis.

23. A sample of the dull and lusterless paint you propose to employ together with the name and address of the manufacturer, must be furnished this office.

24. The headlight mounting location you selected is not considered the most appropriate one, It is requested that you submit sketches showing any optional mountings you could provide. The tail lights must be mounted flush in the body rear panel.

From Chapter 7, page 110

Table 6: Parts: ¼-Ton, 4x4 Truck ("Jeep")
American Bantam Car Company Butler, Pennsylvania
Contract W-398-QM-8269

Part No.	Part Name	Vendor	P.O. No.	P.O. Date	First Date	Receipts Quantity
R-10259	Fuel Pump	A.C. Spark Plug Divn.	13617			
10044	Clutch Throwout Bearing	Aetna Ball Br. Mfg. Co.	13516	8/23/40	9-9-40	70
10290	Rear View Mirror	American Automatic Device Co.	13528	8-27-40	8-23-40	1

10027	Accelerator Pedal	American Automatic Device Co.	13528	8-27-40	8-23-40	1
	Wiring	American Wire Division, Electric Auto-Lite Co.				Wiring for Pilot model made at Bantam and fitted on car by representative of American Wire Division, Electric Auto-Lite Co.
10048	Gas Tank	O.L. Anderson Co.	13521	8-23-40	9-4-40	2
	Wheel & Rim Assemblies	Budd Wheel Company	13521	8-23-40	9-19-40	2 sets
	Hand Brake Assembly	Butler County Motor Co.	13535	8-28-40	8-28-40	1
	Tail Lamps-Service, Stop & Blackout	Corcoran-Brown Lamp Divn.	13583	9-19-40	9-17-40	1 Pr.
	Head Lamps	R.E. Dietz Co.	13555	9-5-40	9-1-40	1 Pr.
	Ignition Lock	H.A. Douglas Mfg. Co.	13548	9-3-40	9-15-40	2
	Side Rails	Dreyer Metal Products Co.	13510	8-23-40	8-29-40	4
	Tires & Tubes	Firestone Tire & Rubber Co.	13532	8-28-40	9-10-40	1 Set
10015	Brake & Clutch Pedals	Fort Pitt Steel Casting Co.	13534	8-28-40	9-5-40	4
	Front Axle	Spicer Manufacturing Company	13509	8-22-40	9-18-40	1
	Speedometer	Stewart-Warner Corporation	13541	8-23-40	9-16-40	2
	Fuel Filter	Zenith Carburetor Divn.	13525	8-26-40	8-30-40	2
10107	Pedal Shaft Bushings	Cleveland Graphite Bronze Co.	13578	9-18-40	9-23-40	13
	Hood & Fenders	Cutler Metal Products	13580	9-19-40		Sheet Metal Parts for Pilot model made at Bantam

						and fitted on car by their representative.

Note: In addition to this list of components, many small items were picked up at local automobile supply houses, numerous small parts were fabricated in our plant and some standard Bantam parts were used. Some sample parts were also\` used and standard nuts, bolts, washes, etc. were obtained from our inventor, or purchased locally.

The detailed list of components clearly indicated that Bantam followed the guidelines as specified in the Invitation to Bids to use only American made parts. Therefore, the pilot model, in many respects, was "America's Car."

From Chapter 8, page 116 (1 of 3)

Table 7: Inspection Report on Pilot model ¼-Ton, 4x4 (Bantam) Chassis
Light Reconnaissance and Command Car
October 23, 1940
Comments Broken Down By Paragraph Section Specification ES-475

Par. B-1. The truck as received had one-sixteenth (1/16) inch toe out on the front tires, loaded. Care must be taken to see that wheel alignment is correct on the production trucks.

Par. D-1 Weights – Vehicle – front – 975 lbs, rear 1,055 lbs., total 2,030 lbs. Gross – front 1,060 lbs., rear 1,570 lbs. total 2,630 lbs. Note – The specification limited the vehicle weight to thirteen hundred (1,300) pounds, based on the provision of an engine developing approximately sixty-five (65) lbs./ft. torque. Every effort was made to minimize weight, but in the hand built sample vehicle a two thousand thirty (2,030) pound weight resulted when material was used of a size adequate for cross-country service. To offset this, eighty-three (83) lbs./ft. engine torque was provided. The weight that will result in production is not yet known, but efforts will be made to keep the weight under two thousand (2,000) lbs.

Par. D-2. Both side members in the frame failed at the point of support of the rear of the engine, transmission and transfer case. The strength of the side member at this point is not adequate for the load imposed. The design of the side member must be suitably altered and adequacy guaranteed.

The right side member was damaged by the right front spring striking the engine front support bolt. This interference must be eliminated. The frame lower flanges were damaged by severe bottoming of the rear spring bumper blocks. Alterations to be made in spring and bumper block designs must prevent the frame members being damage.

The engine rear mountings, transmission and transfer case support member failed at the points of attachment to the frame side member. The member design must be altered and so reinforced as to adequately support the load imposed. As this member also serves as a skid-shoe under the transfer case, its lower edges should be generously rounded to permit the member skidding more readily over obstructions in the terrain.

The left front spring bracket failed. The bracket design is not considered satisfactory. The manufacturer must suitably alter spring bracket designs.

The engine right front support bracket failed twice during the tests. A suitable type bracket must be furnished on the production vehicles.

Par. D-4. The intake manifold carburetor attaching flange cracked and had to be repaired. It is understood this was caused by the mounting of the air filter, which was not equipped with the brace, and is to be included in production. The thickness of the flange stock shall be increased and the brace provided in the production trucks.

To prevent damage to the engine oil pan, a skid plate, of the general type of the one added during the tests, must be furnished on the production vehicles.

The crankcase oil filler pipe opening must be accessibly located.

Par. D-5. Truck cooling system originally furnished did not meet the specification cooling requirements. Several cooling tests were run using various combinations of pulleys, fans and radiator cores. It was finally decided that the most satisfactory combination of meeting the requirements was a six (6) blade fan, assembly and high efficiency core. The production trucks must include the six (6) blade fan and the improved radiator core. To increase the cooling efficiency, louvers more provided in the right hood side and in the fender skirt. An adequate number of louvers must be included in the production trucks.

The radiator upper unit was fractured and had to be repaired. It is believed that the fracture was caused by the location of the radiator tie rod bracket. A suitable tie rod bracket of improved design must be provided.

Par. D-7. The ignition system is not effectively weather sealed. On several occasions the system failed because of water accumulating on the spark plugs and coil. Means to effectively weather seal these units must be provided.

Par. D-8. The auxiliary fuel filter must be installed in the fuel line between the fuel tank and the fuel pump.

The carburetor throughout the test became inoperative due to the entrance of water and dirt. This was due to an unnecessarily large hole where the accelerator plunger link enters the carburetor body. This difficulty had not been satisfactorily remedied at the time of the completion of test.

Flexible fuel line from the fuel filter to the carburetor was damaged due to connecting adjacent units. It was necessary to replace the line. On the production trucks, fuel lines shall be placed in a protected position.

Par. D-9. The exhaust muffler originally furnished with the truck was damaged beyond repair. A muffler of smaller diameter which provided more ground clearance was installed, and was found satisfactory.

Par. D-13. The front propeller shaft front universal joint cross failed during the tests. The broken cross must be inspected by the joint manufacturer, the cause of failure determined and remedied.

The front propeller shaft tube strikes the engine bell housing. This interference must be properly corrected.

Par. D-14. Axles: Caskets must be supplied under axle drive shaft flanges.

The front axle steering drive universal joints were removed at the completion of the tests and found to bind unduly when cramped. The axle manufacturer must see that the joints operate satisfactorily when installed in the front axles.

In the production vehicles the front axle stops must be set to limit the cramping angle (at the wheel on the inside of the turning circle) to 26 degrees, plus 1 degree, minus 0 degrees, and the stop screws and check nuts must then be so welded that the setting cannot be readily altered.

The horizontal rib on the right hand side of the front differential housing, struck and damaged the fan drive pulley. The shape of the ribs was altered to eliminate the interference. The interference must be properly eliminated.

Par. D-15. Spring eye bolts and nuts should include cotter pins. Double nuts must be provided on front and rear U bolts.

Springs of the type furnished as original equipment were not satisfactory for cross-country operation. Several springs were broken and, due to front spring weakness, fan blade tips, fan shroud and fan drive pulley, were damaged by contacting the axle housing, and spring bumper blocks failed due to continual bottoming. The manufacturer must provide springs that will eliminate objectionable bottoming, install bumper blocks that will prevent interferences that cause damage, and guarantee the adequacy of the spring suspension and bumpers furnished in the production vehicles.

Par. D-16. The manufacturer must see that the shock absorbers are properly installed and adjusted.

Par. D-18. Wheel mounting studs must include serrated shoulders, to prevent the studs turning in the brake drums and hub flanges.

Tire wear on the pilot model vehicle was considered excessive. In view of this it is recommended that the manufacturer consider furnishing approximately fifty (50) percent of the vehicles with the Firestone mud and snow tread as furnished on the pilot model, the remainder to be supplied with Goodyear All-Service mud and snow tread, without delay in delivery and additional cost to the Government.

Par. D-19. The emergency brake handle lever pall will not release properly. The contractor must properly improve this construction. Emergency brake system as furnished on pilot model was not satisfactory in operation. A proper emergency brake must be provided.

Par. D-20. Trouble was experienced with the lighting cable harness assembly. To expedite the test certain of the electrical units were rewired. It is understood that harness is not the one that will be used on the production vehicles. A suitable wiring harness must be provided.

The ammeter is not registering properly. It shows "discharge" when a test ammeter indicates a "charge." Indicating instruments must operate accurately.

The generator pulley exploded during operations. This was apparently due to a bad pulley as the second one installed went through the remainder of the test without failure. Suitable generator pulleys must be furnished on production vehicles.

The voltage regulator should be properly grounded directly to the generator, providing a separate wire for this purpose.

Par. D-21.a. The front bumper length does not comply with Q.M. Drawing 08370-Z. The bumper shall be suitably altered.

Hood side panels must be reinforced by the addition of a transverse tie-rod.

b. The speedometer cable must be properly installed and clipped. The cable as installed is too sharply bent where it connects to the transmission. This condition has damaged the cable case.

c. A front and rear axle wheel bearing nut wrench was not included with the tool equipment. This item must be provided in production tool sets. Inspectors will be instructed to check the wrench for suitability. The pliers and adjustable auto type wrench were not branded with an identification number. The marking must be applied. This requirement also applies to the above wheel bearing nut wrench.

d. The horn should be mounted in a more suitable protected position.

e. The entire black-out wiring system is not working properly. This is probably caused by failure of certain wiring in the harness. The dimmer switch must be so positioned that the proximity of the emergency brake lever will not prevent its being readily operated. Loom should be provided on tail light wires. Tail lamp plugs must include the required metal parts.

Par. D-24. Name, caution and shifting plates were not installed on the pilot model truck. The plates must be mounted at the appropriate locations where they will be readily seen by the operator.

Par. D-25. The body, cowl, windshield, hood, front fenders, headlights, gas tank and brush guard, will be commented on in a supplemental report, which will be forwarded from this office on October 23, 1940.

Par. D-28. The vehicle marking shall be applied using blue drab color paint complying with specification ES-No. 510. A sample color chip was furnished Mr. Frank Fenn.

Production of the chassis only is authorized subject to proper correction being made of defects enumerated herein.

Table 8: Test Report on Bantam, ¼-Ton, 4x4, Pilot Model
Contract No. W-398-QM-8269 (Invitation for Bids 398-41-9) American Bantam Car Company (October 23, 1940)

1. The operations test on the Bantam Pilot model was commenced on September 27, 1940 and terminated on October 16, 1940. The types of operations were as follows:

   Highway operation: 247 miles

   Test truck operation: 1,894 miles

   Cross country operation: 901 miles

   Bad road operation: 244 miles

   Miscellaneous tests: 124 miles

   Total: 3,410 miles

2. The following difficulties were developed during the operation test.

a. Tire wear was very excessive. This could have been due to operation on the test track which is very severe on tires but is believed that the wear as demonstrated was excessive.

b. Interference of the crank shaft fan pulley with a reinforcing web of the front axle caused breakage of the pulley. This was corrected by the manufacturer's representative by grinding away a portion of the web and installing stiffer springs. The corrective action was sufficient as no more difficulty was experienced.

c. The generator pulley exploded during operations. This was apparently due to a bad generator pulley as the second one installed went through the remainder of the test without failure.

d. The windshield was inadequately braced and failed early in the test. The windshield wiper needs stops to prevent its being pulled off the windshield during operation.

e. The carburetor throughout the test became inoperative due to the entrance of water and dirt. This was due to an unnecessarily large hole where the accelerator plunger link enters the carburetor body. This difficulty had not been satisfactorily remedied at the time of completion of test.

f. Considerable difficulty was experienced in grounding out the ignition system at any time the vehicle entered water above a foot and a half in depth. This is due to the fan turning the water and splashing it about the spark plugs and distributor coil. Proper shielding of the ignition system with rubber shields should correct this difficulty. This had not been corrected at the completion of the test.

g. The emergency brake as furnished on the pilot model was not satisfactorily in operation and it is understood that a new type of emergency brake will be furnished on production vehicles.

h. The headlight bracket tore loose from the fender during the test. This must be braced more adequately.

i. The crank case was fractured on two occasions by rocks and other obstructions on the course. A skid plate was brazed to the crank case and no more difficulty encountered. A proper skid plate protecting the crank case is a necessity on this vehicle.

j. Chain clearance on the rear wheels is inadequate. Space between the rear wheels and body must be increased.

k. No satisfactory springs were submitted for test. The last springs furnished were the best but require more strength. The mortality on rubber bumper blocks was very high. The weak springs used may have contributed to this bumper block failure.

l. The exhaust muffler was torn off during the test.

m. The fenders and grills loosened during the test.

n. Difficulty was experienced keeping the headlight lens in its frame due to loosening of the clamping screw.

o. There was interference between the front drive shaft and the clutch bell housing. This interference was not serious but should be corrected.

p. The rear motor support cracked twice. This needs to be strengthened.

q. One shock absorber had to be replaced at the end of the 3,394 miles of operation.

r. Several shorts developed in the electrical system. This may have been due to the fact that this was a hand built vehicle but care should be exercised in production vehicles to prevent chaffing of the electrical system.

s. The rear spring hanger of the left front spring failed during the test. This unit should be strengthened.

t. The test was terminated due to the failure of both frame side members at the rear motor support. This was undoubtedly due to the combined weight of the operating personnel, the transfer case and the weight of the rear end of the motor, all of which are supported at this point. The frame must be reinforced to prevent this type of failure.

3. Remarks

a. Some type of handle at the rear and side of the body to assist in lifting the vehicle when it becomes mired in mud or extreme terrain conditions will materially assist in removing the vehicle when it becomes bogged down.

b. The vehicle demonstrated ample power and all requirements of the Service.

From Chapter 8, page 117 (3 of 3)

Table 9: Final Inspection Report on Pilot model ¼-Ton, 4x4 (Bantam) Chassis Light Reconnaissance and Command Car
October 28, 1940

The following comments covering body, cowl, windshield, hood, front fenders, headlights, gas tank and brush guard are furnished in addition to the Inspection Report on Pilot model

¼ –Ton, 4x4 (Bantam) Chassis, Light Reconnaissance and Command Car, submitted under date of October 23, 1940:

Par. D-25. a. The brush guard must be of stronger construction and shall include the headlight guards required by Drawing 08570-Z.

The original front fender equipment was not suitable and will be replaced by fenders of a designed stipulated below.

The hood catch would not remain latched when the car was resting on uneven terrain. A suitable catch shall be provided at the front and safety catches must be mounted on each side of the hood.

Louvres must be inserted in the hood sides on production trucks.

The design of the windshield is not satisfactory. The manufacturer shall furnish a windshield assembly of adequate strength and suitable design on the production trucks.

The windshield wiper was placed too near to the left side of the windshield. Stops must be provided to prevent the blade being rotated off the windshield.

The headlight brackets cracked the fender skirt to which they were attached and the headlight lens clamp screws loosened from vibration, permitting the lens to become loose. The left front headlight interfered with opening and closing of the hood. Headlights properly placed and brackets of a suitable design must be provided.

Running boards required by Q.M. Drawing 08370-Z., extending from the front fenders to the side panels with their outer edges extending in a straight line with the outer edges of the fenders and extending rearward for a distance of at least fifteen (15) inches shall be provided.

The body was not mounted squarely on the chassis. Bodies must be properly mounted.

Sufficient body clearance must be provided at the tires for the use of tire chains. It is suggested that at least one and one half (1-1/2) inch additional clearance be provided between the tire and sides of the wheelhousings. The body as provided did not have sufficient tire clearance when operating without tire chains.

The bucket seats were not sufficiently rugged and must be of stronger construction. Both original seats supplied were in bad condition at the end of the test.

The seat cushions have a semi-circular front, the forward portion of which is useless. It is requested that the front of the seat cushion be cut back approximately two (2) inches.

The forward edge of the wheelhousing must be well rounded or shaped to prevent tearing of clothing or hurting occupants when entering truck.

The body rear corner braces prevented the proper lowering of the lazy back as required. The lazy back must lower as shown in Q.M. Drawing 08370-Z.

The bucket seat backs are three (3) inches higher than shown in Q.M. Drawing 08370-Z. It is desired the seat backs extend eighteen (18) inches above the seat cushions.

The canvass cover and fasteners did not fit properly. The cover was poorly sewed with edges not properly hemmed. A serviceable cover must be provided. It is desirable to have two (2) straps over the right wheelhousing, arranged to hold the cover when not in use.

The tool box drawer under the driver's seat should be increased in size to accommodate the hand tools (excepting the jack, wheel wrench and crank), including the hammer and monkey-wrench.

The stud threads on the tire carrier and nuts were not protected from rust and the threads of one stud were stripped.

The gasoline tank filler spout is inaccessible. The spout must be accessibly placed on production vehicles.

New springs must be of a design that will not raise any portion of the truck beyond the specified limits.

The body floor shall be reinforced adequately for the mounting of a machine gun midway between the rear panel and cowl, approximately on the chassis longitudinal centerline.

The pintle hook was mounted incorrectly. The rearmost portion of the pintle must be one-half (1/2) inch forward of the rear surface of the rear bumper and be accessible for testing.

Channel section at rear of body to which tire carrier bracket is attached shall be twelve (12) gauge instead of twenty-two (22) gauge.

r. In addition to the corrections listed above, you are authorized to proceed with the following design changes. The cost of these was quoted in our letter of October 17, 1940 and agreed upon in conference with your Mr. K. K. Probst, Mr. C. M. Payne and personnel of this office. A formal Change Order will be forwarded to you at the earliest practicable date and will cover a total of sixty-eight (68) trucks, complete with bodies, the remaining two (2) chassis to be shipped to the body manufacturer, as outlined in our letter of October 26, 1940.

Two braces extending from the dash to the instrument panel shall be provided.

The glove box in the instrument panel shall have the bottom cut back two (2) inches to provide more leg room.

Larger pedestal on driver's seat shall have a two (2) inch side drawer beneath.

A two (2) inch Latex pad on each front seat and a one (1) inch Latex pad on the adjustable back rest over the rear seat to be properly applied and covered with O.D. Duck

Clips shall be provided for retaining the wheel nut wrench and crank.

Two (2) handles shall be provided on each side of body. The handles shall be applied so that they will enable lifting of the rear of truck by crew.

The rail forming the top bow shall be 1-1/16 inch O.D. pipe instead of ¾ inch O.D. pipe and its brackets changed accordingly.

Provide a 1-inch Latex covered pad at each side of each bucket seat back; also an 18 X 18 inch (approximate) pad at each side of body interior directly adjacent to each front seat. Panel pads shall have a plywood backing and O.D. Duck covering corresponding to that used on the seats.

Driver's seat to be stationary.

Assistant driver's seat must have a stationary back. The seat must be hinged to fold forward.

Fenders, hood and brush guard as shown in Cutler Metal Products Company Drawing E-5.

From Chapter 9, page 131

Table 10: Willys' Response to ES-475 Requirements

Willys' Response to Army Requirements
Section F of Bid – Questionnaire
F-1 Truck. Make Willys; model, overall length 127 inches, overall width 56 inches overall height 71 inches shipping weight 1,750 pounds, dunnage in shipping weight 100 pounds.
77F-1a Trucks loaded on freight car, Item No. Quantity 0

F-1b – weight of truck fully equipped, 1,700 pounds,

F-1c – wheelbase 80 inches, with truck fully equipped and loaded: ground clearance under following units, front axle 8.5 inches, rear axle 8.5 inches, transmission 10 inches; transfer case skid shoe 9.5 inches, gas tank over 18 inches, battery over 12 inches, propeller shaft brake X inches, angle of approach 45 degrees, departure X degrees, Will the overall height of the truck comply with the requirements of Q.M. Drawing 08370-Z, Yes. Will the requirements of paragraph D-1. B. herein, concerning driver vision ahead of the front of the truck, be fully complied with? Yes.

F-2 – Will the frame be of such a design and construction that it will support adequately the maximum gross loads imposed under the most severe operating conditions, Yes. Will the frame rear end be suitably braced for pintle mounting, Yes.

F-3 – Power unit – Will the engine, clutch and transmission be embodied in a unit power plant yes; will the engine be so mounted that it will not be damaged form distortion, yes; will the transfer case be mounted as a unit with the transmission, yes; will it be so mounted that it will not be damaged by frame distortion, yes.

F-4. Engine make N-C, model 44; number of cylinders 4; displacement 137 cubic inches; maximum peak horsepower 2600 r.p.m.; maximum operating speed guaranteed by the engine manufacturer 4000 r.p.m.; maximum torque, less only fan and generator operating 100 lbs./ft.; will this torque be developed while using fuel having a knock rating of not more than 68 octane, yes; will engine operating be satisfactory using fuel of this octane number, yes; the torque quoted above was developed employing what compression ratio, 6.1 to 1.0; is this the compression ratio that will be furnished, yes; cylinder head material, C.1; will the crankshaft be counterbalanced, yes; number of main bearings, 8.

F-4a – Will a governor be provided on the engine, yes. Make Haunty; type WG. Set to limit the speed to 3600 r.p.m. Will this governor setting permit a 55 m.p.h truck road speed without causing erratic engine operation, yes.

F-5. Cooling system – will the requirements of paragraph D-5 herein regarding cooling, be fully complied with, yes; will a thermostat be provided, yes.

F-6. Lubricating system. – Method of lubricating: crankshaft main bearings, pressure; connecting rod lower bearings, pressure; camshaft bearings, pressure; piston pin bearings, splash; cylinder walls, splash; timing gears or chain, pressure; capacity of engine oil reservoir, 5 quarts; is this capacity sufficient to meet the cruising range requirements of paragraph C-3 herein, yes; lubrication system will function satisfactorily on side slopes up to, 25%; and on longitudinal slope to, 50%.

F-6a. Oil filter – Make, DeLay Products Corp.; model, DeLux, type, X will the filter comply with the requirements of paragraph D-6 herein, yes; will the requirements concerning oil lines be fully complied with, yes.

F-6b. – Type of chassis lubricating system, Zink; type of fittings X; will the system be of a design that will permit the ready attachment of the grease gun, yes.

F-7. Ignition system – Make, autolite; potential 6 volts. Is automatic or hand control for spark advance provided, automatic.

F-8. Fuel system – fuel tank, capacity 12 gallons; will this capacity be sufficient to meet the cruising range requirements of paragraph C-3 herein, yes; will the tank be so mounted that it will not be damaged by frame distortion, yes; tank mounting location, rear of unit; fuel pump make, A.C.; model, will it include sediment bowl or chamber, yes; strainer, yes; hand primer, yes; will the pump be so located that its operation will not be objectionably affected by exhaust heat, yes;

F-8. Fuel system – auxiliary filter, make A.C. model 1529769; recommended mounting location, at tank; air cleaner, make, A.C.; model, as specified; is it oil bath type, yes; oil capacity, as specified; will it meet the efficiency requirements of paragraph D-8 herein, yes; will fuel line requirements be fully complied with, yes; will the lines be arranged to prevent vapor-lock, yes; the fuel system will function satisfactorily on slide slopes

up to, 10%; longitudinal slope to, 50%.
F-9 – Muffler – will the requirements of paragraph D-9 herein be fully complied with, yes.
F-10 – Clutch – Make Abbott: model Singlelife; type 1, single plate; guaranteed to transmit torque of 100 lbs./ft.; will automatic means be provided for lubricating the throwout bearing mechanism, yes; if not, will a lubricating fitting be provided at a readily accessible location which does not require the removal of toe or floor board X.
F-11 – Transmission – Make, Warner Gear; model, T 84 G; guaranteed to transmit a torque of 100 bls./ft.; reductions, 1st 2.665 to 1.000; 2nd, 1.564 to 1.000; 3rd 1;1; reverse, 3.554 to 1.0.
F-12 – Transfer case – Make, Spicer; model, special; reductions, high range 1. To 1; low range 2. To 1.0; guaranteed to transmit a torque of 354 lbs./ft.; will the transfer case include front axle drive declutching mechanism, yes; will the declutching mechanism be properly lubricated from the transfer main case, yes; will controls be readily operatable from the driver's seat, yes; will the controls detract from driving comfort; no; will transfer case noise be effectively minimized, yes.
F-13 – Propeller shaft – Make, Spicer; model, special; front Spicer yes; rear, yes; between transmission and transfer case, none; guaranteed to transmit a torque of, front, 390; rear 390; transmission-transfer case 390 lbs/ft.; maximum angle at which universal joints are guaranteed to continue operation, 10 degrees; maximum angle that will exist in universal joints with truck in the fully equipped, loaded and level position (for momentary operation, X degrees; are the joints all of the same make and type, yes; are they of metal construction; yes; will the propeller shaft lengths conform to the manufacturer's recommendation, yes.
F-14 – Axles – type, hypoid reduction; gear ratio, 4.0 to 1.0; Ratio of impact resistance between horizontal and vertical planes of axles housing, not required To 1. To 1.0; will axle bowl covers be so constructed that they will not be damaged in cross country operations, yes; will they be bolted to the axle housings, yes; will differential assemblies be interchangeable between front and rear axles, yes; will housing breathers be provided, vent; will gear lubricant be confined to the differential bowls, no; will high pressure lubrication fittings be provided in the hubs, no; if so, will the hubs include the required relief fittings, X.
F-14 – Front axle – Make, Spicer; model, special; input torque capacity 390 lbs./ft.; will it be of the full floating type which a wheel will not be released if an axle shaft fails, sans flat; axle shaft diameter over the splines, 1 1/8 inches; number of splines, 10; steering drive ends, joint make, Bendix-Weiss; type Ball.; size, 3 1/2 inch; outside spherical diameter, 6 1/2 inches; will steering pivots be equipped with roller bearings, yes; offset between king-pin center and tire center, at ground 2 39/64 inches; front wheel maximum cramping angle, at the wheel on the inside of the turning circle, 28 degrees; will axle stops be of the required design and welded, yes; steering tie rod, outside diameter, 7/5 inches; wall thickness 1/8 inch; will the ends be threaded as required, yes; tread 11/16 – 18th inches.
F-14 – Rear axle – 2 wheel steer trucks – make, Spicer; Special; type, Hybro Sun i.e. full floating or semi-floating; if a semi floating rear axle is offered at the bid price, has the increased cost (per truck) been quoted in the bid, for the provision of a full floating axles of a type with which the wheel will not be released if an axle shaft fails, no; input torque capacity, 390 lbs./ft. axles shaft diameter over the splines, 1 1/8 inches; number of splines, 10; tread, 43 inches.
F-14 – Rear axle – 4 wheel steer trucks – make, will the steering drive ends be identical to those provided on the front axle, X input torque capacity X; tread, X inches.
F-15 – Springs – will the requirement concerning spring to spring stop clearances be fully complied with, yes; will the required spring leaf clips be provided, yes; is it guaranteed that the spring suspension will be suitable for the required service conditions, no.
F-16 – Shock absorbers – make, Monroe; model, Hydraulic, total number provided, 4.
F-17 – does not apply.

F-18 – Wheels, tires and tubes – wheels, make Relsayor Build; type, Slulluc; will they be so constructed that they will not be damaged in cross country operations, yes; will they be interchangeable on all axle hubs, yes.
F-18 – Rims – Make, Firestone; size 3.5 X 16; type, X; will they permit proper mounting of tires containing bullet seal tubes, yes.
F-18 – Tires – Make offered for selection, Kelly Springfield or equivalent; type X; size 5. 50 X 16; number of plines, 4; type of tread design, X; loaded radius, X.
F-18 – inner tubes – Make, Kelly Springfield; type, Std.
F18 – Tire, tube, flap wheel assemblies will be balanced to within X inch-ounces. Will the tires be balanced dotted, yes.
F-19 – brakes – Service brakes – application type, hydraulic; brakes and drums provided on 4 wheels; hydraulic line maximum pressure 1000 lbs. per square inch; brake size, front 9 X 1-3/4; rear 9 X 1-3/4
F-19 – parking brake – make, Bendix; type, two shoe; actual location, rear whell; will the parking brake be operable at all times on the rear wheels, yes.
F-20 – electrical equipment – potential, 6 volts; battery – capacity 80 ampere hours at a 20-hour rate; make U.S.L; model, Std.; generator, make, Auto-Lite; type G.O.J.; guaranteed maximum output capacity (when hot), 18 amperes; generator regulation apparatus box, make Auto-Lite; model, VRR; type X; will the requirements concerning wiring be fully complied with, yes.
F- 21 – chassis equipment – will the requirement concerning engine hood, bumpers, instrument panel, tool, tire chain and accessory equipment be fully complied with, yes; are the requirements concerning lighting equipment thoroughly understood, yes; will they be fully complied with, yes; will reflectors be furnished as required, yes.
F-22 – Controlling mechanism – Steering gear – make, Ross; model T 12; rated for easy steering in connection with a driving front axle and a load of, 1110 lbs on the front tires at the ground; is the control mechanism guaranteed to be of a capacity adequate for the intended service, yes; steering wheel diameter, 17 inches.
F-22 – Controlling mechanism – 4 wheel steer trucks – will the steering mechanism provide delayed steering on the rear wheels, X; maximum cramping angle on front wheels, X degrees; on rear wheels, X degrees; will the design of the steering mechanism preclude weaving of the rear end of the truck and any tendency to over-steer, X; will the mechanism be substantially constructed and so installed that it will not be damaged in cross country operations, X.
F-23 – Operating mechanism – will the requirements of paragraph D-23 herein, be fully complied with, yes.
F-24 – Name, caution and shifting plates – will the plates be provided, inscribed as required, yes; will drawings of the plates be submitted for approval, yes; will they be mounted at approved locations, yes.
F-25 – Body – will the body conform to the requirements of drawing 08370-Z, yes; is a body drawing being furnished for approval, not with bid.
F-26 – Special operating equipment, rear pintle, make, X; Will the brush guard be substantially constructed, yes; will it be installed as required, yes; will towing hooks be furnished, yes; if not will the front bumper be so designed and mounted that it can be used for towing purposes, yes; will the truck construction permit the satisfactory installation and use of tire chains, yes.
F-37 – Painting – will the painting requirements be fully complied with, yes.
F-28 – Markings – will the trucks be marked as required, yes.

F-29 – Maximum road speed, truck fully equipped and loaded, 550 m.p.h.	
F-30 – What grade abilities will be demonstrated with the truck fully equipped and loaded – with transmission in direct gear and transfer case in high range – 2 wheel steer truck X; 4 wheel steer truck, X with transmission in low gear and with 2 speed transfer case in low range, 2-wheel steer truck, X 4-wheel steer truck, X.	
F-31- Will a pilot model truck or trucks, be produced for inspection and tests at the Holabird Quartermaster Depot, X; describe the type of trucks that will be produced for pilot model tests, X	
F-32 – Has the service facility list been included with the bid, no; if not has it been filed with the Purchasing and Contracting Officer, no.	
F-33 – Have drawings been included with the bid, chassis assembly, X; frame, X; body, X; have engine certified power curves been included with the bid, X; do the curve sheets indicate what compression ratio and octane numbered fuel were employed, X.	
F-34 – Bidders shall signify compliance with the requirements of this specification by supplying herewith the following data required as proof of the fact that compliance is intended:	
F-34a – As required by paragraph E-2. Specification ES- No. 459, has the manufacturer of the trucks offered under this bid been continuously engaged in the production of motor truck chassis for a period of 2 years immediately prior to the opening date of this Invitation to Bid, X; and does he possess the facilities necessary to produce trucks meeting the requirements of this specification, X.	
F-34b – Have the guarantees as required by paragraph E-3 specification ES-No. 459, been carefully considered and are they fully agreed upon, X.	
F-34c – if any exceptions are contemplated in the specifications requirements, have they been completely listed below, as required under paragraph E-3 specification ES-No. 459, X; is it clearly understood that in the event exceptions are not listed below, the right is reserved to demand a full and complete compliance with the specification requirements, X.	
F-34d – Exceptions to specification requirements are listed below:	
D-1-A - Weight 1300 lbs. – too low.	
D-4 – Engine – specified larger engine.	
D-11 – Gear Box	
D-14 - Axle	

From Chapter 10, page 140

Table 11: Willys-Overland Motors, Inc. Key Pilot Model Parts ¼-Ton, 4x4 Truck ("Jeep")

Name of Part Part No.	Purchase Order No.	Date Issued	Date Received
2 FRONT AXLES complete with Hubs, double anchor Bendix 9 X 1-3/4" Brakes, 16" Budd Spicer Mfg. Co. Toledo, Ohio	37409	8/21/40	10/19/40 1st 10/26/40 2nd

2 REAR AXLES complete with Hubs, double anchor Bendix 9 X 1-3/4" Brakes, 16" Budd Wheels and Rims Spicer Mfg. Co. Toledo, Ohio	37409	8/21/40	10/19/40 1st 10/26/40 2nd
2 TRANSFER CASE complete with PROPELLER SHAFT, Brake and Drum (for mounting on 2 Warner Gear Company Transmission T-84 for overdrive) Spicer Mfg. Co. Toledo, Ohio	37409	8/21/40	10/19/40 1st 10/26/40 2nd
2 Pair – COMBINATION SEAL BEAM HEA LAMPS with BLACKOUT PARKING LAMPS PART No. E-37756 Corcoran Brown Lamp Company Cincinnati, Ohio	37941	8/21/40	10/4/40
2 Pair - COMBINATION SERVICE, TAIL, STOP, LICENSE PLATE and BLACKOUT LAMPS PART No. E-37757 Corcoran Brown Lamp Company Cincinnati, Ohio	37941	8/21/40	10/4/40
2 Pair - COMBINATION BLACKOUT TAIL AND BLACKOUT STOP LAMPS PART No. E-37758 Corcoran Brown Lamp Company Cincinnati, Ohio	37941	8/21/40	10/4/40
8 Pair – Red Reflectors PART No. E-37759 Corcoran Brown Lamp Company Cincinnati, Ohio	37941	8/21/40	10/4/40
1 STARTER MOTOR Part No. E-37761 Auto Lite #E-06152 Electric Auto-Lite Co. Toledo, Ohio	37947	8/26/40	9/1/9/40
1 GNERATOR WITH 3 ½ inch Pulley Part No. E-37762	37947	8/26/40	9/1/9/40

Auto Lite #E-04479 Electric Auto-Lite Co. Toledo, Ohio			
1 VOLTAGE REGULATOR Pat No. E-37763 Auto Lite #VRP-06 Electric Auto-Lite Co. Toledo, Ohio	37947	8/26/40	9/1/9/40
2 GASOLINE STRAINERS Part No. AE-107 Zenith Carburetor Company Detroit, Michigan	37948	8/29/40	9/16/40
2 STEERING WHEEL Part AE-106 Sheller Manufacturing Company Portland, Indiana	37950	8/29/40	9/16/40
2 CLUTCH PRESSURE PLATE ASSEM. Part No. 638992 Incorporate into this Pressure Plate, Clutch Pressure Spring #638993. Blue Prints Attached Auburn, Mfg. Co. Auburn, Indiana	37954	9/6/40	9/12/40
2 BLACKOUT SWITCH Part No. AE-110 Delco-Remy Part #1994509 Delco-Remy Anderson, Indiana	37955	9/6/40	10/2/40
2 BLACKOUT KNOB Part No. AE-111 Delco-Remy Part #1994504 Delco-Remy Anderson, Indiana	37955	9/6/40	10/2/40
2 CONTROL BUSHING ASSEM. Part No. AE-112 Delco-Remy Part #1990545 Delco-Remy Anderson, Indiana	37955	9/6/40	10/2/40
2 TRANSMISSION ASSEMBLY to have special main shaft and washer.	37961	9/9/40	9/18/40

Part No. AE-115 Total cost not to exceed $100 Warner Gear Corporation Muncie, Indiana			
10 TIRES 5:50 X 16 4-Ply Part No. AE-135 and valve caps Firestone Tire & Rubber Co. Akron, Ohio	37974	9/17/40	9/17/40
2 FRAME ASSEMBLIES Part No. AE-116 Total cost of two frames and hand tools not to exceed $920 Truscon Steel Company Cleveland, Ohio	37969	9/17/40	10/18/40
2 INTAKE MANIFOLD CASTINGS Part No. AE-124 Wilson Foundry & Machine Co. Pontiac, Michigan	37933	9/19/40	6/30/40
2 CYLINDER HEAD WATER OUTLET ELBOW Part No. AE-125 Wilson Foundry & Machine Co. Pontiac, Michigan (Pattern to be the property of Willys Overland Motors, Inc.)	37984	9/23//40	10/5/40
2 SAMPLE WINDSHIELD ASSEMBLIES, including MOUNTING BRACKETS. Must be in Willys-Overland Motors, Inc., Oct. 4, 1940 Motor Products Detroit, Michigan	37990	9/25/40	10/25/40 1st 10/30/40 2nd
2 OVAL MUFFLERS 4" x 9" x 15" 1-5/8" Exhaust Pipe Opening Part No. A-6118 Maremont Muffler Company Chicago, Illinois	37922	9/26/40	10/7/40
1 STEERING GEAR ASSEM. Complete for two wheel steer. This steering gear to be furnished complete	37993	9/27/40	10/8/40

with steering wheel, jacket tube, horn button and Pitman arm. Part No. AE-137 Ross Gear & Tool Co. Lafayette, Indiana			
1 STEERING GEAR ASSEM. Complete for four wheel steer. This steering gear to be furnished complete with 17" Steering wheel, jacket tube, Horn button and Pitman Arm. Part No. AE-138	37993	9/27/40	10/22/40
4 FRONT SPRINGS Part No. AE-131 Mather Spring Company Toledo, Ohio	37998	10/1/40	10/18/40
4 REAR SPRINGS Part No. AE-132 Mather Spring Company Toledo, Ohio	37998	10/1/40	10/18/40
2 RADIATOR ASSEMBLIES with shrouds, to be equipped with Hot Climate Core Part No. AE-186 Jamestown Metal Equipment, Inc. Jamestown, N.Y.	37997	10/1/40	10/2/40
2 AUTO-LITE BATTERIES with moulded manifold Part No. 638763 U.S.L. Battery Company Niagara Falls, N.Y.	38886	10/3/40	10/15/40
2 OIL FILTERS with 1/8" Pipe Taps Part No. AE-202 Zenith Carburetor Company Detroit, Michigan	38895	10/4/40	10/14/40
2 AIR CLEANER ASSEMBLY Oil type, with will include ring – and air cleaner gasket Part No. AE-272 United Specialties Co. Chicago, Illinois	38925	10/16/40	10/18/40

From Chapter 11, page 167

Table 12: Ford Pilot Model Test Report
Preliminary Report of Pilot Model ¼-Ton, 4x4 Ford Truck
Contract Number W-398-QM8887 January 6, 1941 Comments Broken Down by
Paragraph Section Specification ES475

C-4. Tire chains were not submitted with the Pilot Model Vehicle, therefore not possible to check them. It is recommended that a set of chains be forwarded to this depot at the earliest opportunity for proper inspection and for installation on the Pilot Model vehicle.

D-1. Weights –

Front – 1185

Rear – 1215

Total – 2400

Gross Weight

Front – 1210

Rear – 1790

Total – 3000

Gross weight was taken with a payload of 600 pounds.

D-1b Ground clearance of rear axle was 7 1/2 inches. Specification requirement is 91/2 inches. It is believed that this requirement can be waived in as much as no difficulties were experienced in all types of operations.

D-2. No difficulty was experienced with the frame. The frame was reinforced after 4,895 miles of operation and it is understood that in production, frames would be constructed of high tensile steel. The final fame design is considered satisfactory.

D-5. Copies of the test determining the cooling differential of this vehicle are attached in Exhibit A. Cooling test was passed successfully.

D-6. Oil filter was not marked at outlet and inlet. An oil filter properly marked will be required.

D-7. The distributor position as originally furnished is not satisfactory. Recurrent failures occurred due to water shorting out the distributor. Numerous efforts were made to correct this condition but were unsuccessful. A redesigned distributor was installed after 5,619 miles of operations and intake has proved satisfactory. It is understood that the distributor will be raised an additional 4 inches. This should further improve this performance as it is believed that the difficulty of previous experiences was chiefly due to low position of distributor.

D-8. The fuel tank filler cap was chained to the body. This cap must be chained to the gas tank.

D-11. The studs mounting; the transmission to the clutch bell housing; loosened during operations. The heads of these studs are only acceptable from within the clutch bell housing. It is understood that these studs are secured by lock washers. A more positive means of locking must be provided. There is some question as to the adequacy as to size of these studs. The manufacturer should be cautioned to provide studs of ample size securely locked in place by wiring or equally effective means.

D-12. The declutch lever was broken during operation. A sufficiently rugged lever must be provide.

D-14. The steering drive end universal joints have failed to date. This vehicle had 6.00 tires installed previous to breakage of these steering drive ends. The manufacturer must assure himself that the steering drive end joints furnished are of adequate capacity for intended service.

The axle stops on the Pilot Model Vehicle were not welded. After the axle stops have been set in accordance with the specification, lock nuts muse be welded.

D15. The springs as originally furnished were inadequate. Redesigned springs have just recently been installed (after 5,169 miles of operation). The springs have not been operated sufficiently to date to form any conclusion as to their adequacy. Considerable trouble was experienced with spring hangers loosening from the frames. Adequate springs must be furnished and the spring hangers must be more securely attached to the frame.

D21b. The instrument panel on Pilot Model vehicle is inaccessible from the rear. Consideration should be given to improving accessibility of the instrument panel.

D21c. No tool equipment was furnished with the Pilot Model vehicle. Steps should be immediately be taken to have complete set of tool equipment forwarded to this depot for inspection.

D24. Name, caution and shifting plates were not furnished with Pilot Model Vehicle. These plates should be submitted for approval at an early date.

D25. Due to changes in body drawings the body as submitted was not in accordance with latest specifications. AS soon as a body built according to requirements of QM Drawing 08501 Z revised January 6, 1941 is completed this office should be notified, in order that inspection may be accomplished.

D26. Towing hooks were not furnished on Pilot Model vehicle, nor was the frame properly gusseted for towing. Proper towing hooks must be supplied and the frame properly reinforced for towing.

D27. Pilot Model body was apparently not properly primed as paint is chipped off on various parts of the body. In provision of Par. D-27 relative to painting, must be strictly complied with.

C-4. Manufacturer must assure himself that there is ample tire chain clearance with wheels in maximum cramped position both right and left. Although tire chains for this vehicle were not available there is some question as to adequate chain clearance under all conditions. Adequate chain clearance under all conditions must be provide.

D20. The battery ground cable was broken during operation. This was due to cable being too short. A cable of proper length will be furnished.

Electric Wiring cable passes directly under the battery box subjecting the cable to corrosion by battery acids. Consideration should be given to the improvement of the location of this cable.

2. The vehicle has been operated to date a total of 5,743 miles.

From Chapter 11, page 168

**Table 13: Willys Pilot Model Test Report
Report of Pilot Model Vehicle
¼-Ton, 4x4 Command Reconnaissance Truck
Contract Number W-398-qm-8888 (Willys Overland)
January 8, 1941
Comments Broken Down By Paragraph Section Specification ES475**

D-1a. Weights –

Front – 1230

Rear – 1290

Total – 2520

Gross Weight:

Front – 1285

Rear – 1835

Total – 3120

Gross weight was taken with a payload of 600 pounds including driver.

D-1b Ground clearance of rear axle is only 8-¼". Results of operating tests show that this clearance is adequate.

D-2. After 5184 miles of operations, the right side rail of the frame was fractured. This was reinforced and operations resumed. After 776 more miles of operation, the left side rail was fractured and the right side rail fractured at both ends of reinforcement previously installed. Frame was reinforced and operation continued. Vehicle was operated an additional 880 miles and no further frame failures resulted.

The frame as originally submitted is not sufficiently rugged for service intended. A frame of sufficient strength must be provided.

D-4. After 5011 miles of operations the engine cylinders were badly worn. It was not possible to determine the exact cause, but improper functioning of the air cleaner was suspected. The worn engine was replaced by an engine which had been driven for 3731 miles in an Americar. This engine operated for 1316 miles when the same failure occurred and cylinders badly worn. It was observed at this time that there was considerable mud in the oil pan. It was also noted that the end of the oil filler pipe is located directly in front of the vacuum spark control mechanism, and that mud was caked around the top of the oil filler pipe and wedged between oil filler pipe and automatic spark control mechanism. It is possible that when the oil filler pipe cap was removed during operation, that mud was allowed to fall on the filler pipe. A new motor was installed, and special care was exerted during the remainder of the operation to prevent possible entrance of mud into the filler pipe. Vehicle was operated an additional 513 miles and no engine failures occurred. While it is the opinion of this office that these failures were due to entry of mud through the crankcase filler pipe, there is not sufficient evidence to be absolutely certain. The manufacturer should carefully check his air cleaner system and further investigate these failures. A longer filler pipe which will make more difficult entry of foreign substance must be provide.

D-5. The cooling system as originally furnished was not satisfactory, the temperature rise being excessive. After installation of larger core and proper shrouding the cooling system satisfactorily passed the test. (See Exhibit "A")

D-6. The oil filler pipe must be lengthened.

D-7. The ignition system can be made more efficient against "drowning out" by the installation of rubber protectors over spark plugs and distributor, (similar to the type used to protect motorcycle engines against water). It is recommended that these protectors be installed.

D-10. The clutch driven plate in the first replacement motor failed. It is understood that this was an experimental plate which was inadvertently installed. No difficulty was experienced with clutch plates in the original or second replacement engine.

D-11. After 5354 miles of operation the transmission was seriously damaged due to error on the part of one of the operators. Apparently an effort was made to shift gears without disengaging the clutch. A new transmission was installed and after 2335 miles of operation this transmission failed while being operated on sand grades. Inspection disclosed that teeth were broken on sliding cluster gear, pilot shaft gear and that cluster gear was frozen to its shaft. Failure was apparently caused by a lack of lubrication of the cluster gear bushing. This failure should be further investigated by the manufacturer.

The gear shift lever as originally furnished had the bias spring so located that it was necessary to exert downward pressure on the lever in order to shift into second and third gears. This resulted in constant shifting into reverse and low gears when it was intended to shift into second and high gears. The bias spring as later installed, which requires upward pressure to shift into low and reverse was satisfactory, and this bias spring loading must be furnished on production vehicles.

D-12. After 6109 miles of operation, the transfer main shaft bearings failed, and main shaft was galled. This was probably caused by mud and sand entering bearings. Damaged parts were replaced, and no further difficulties encountered. No gears were replaced. More effective means to protect the transfer case bearings must be employed.

D-15. Spring failure was encountered throughout the test. The last set of springs installed, were operated for 865 miles without failure. It is not felt that this is sufficient operation to base a conclusion on the strength of these springs. However, as the last set of springs developed are the result of 6000 miles of test operation and the experience of several failures, it is possible they will be adequate.

Springs of sufficient strength for the intended service will be furnished.

D21c. D-21C. Tool equipment was satisfactory except the following items which were not inspected:

a. Grease gun

b. Wheel nut wrench

c. Spark plug wrench and handle.

The above tools should be forwarded to this depot for inspection.

D22. After 1814 miles of operation, the steering pin mounted on the front axle failed. This pin was mounted in a bushing. An improved pin assembly was installed employing roller bearings. This pin was loose at the completion of test. Study should be made with a view to improving the construction of this pin assembly, or providing a ready means to take up wear.

D25. The windshield stanchions failed after 1640 miles of operation. These were bronze castings, so no conclusion can be drawn of the strength of the production stanchions. Rugged stanchions must be furnished.

Due to recent changes in the body drawing the pilot model vehicle did not conform as to body.

At such time as a body is completed in accordance with Q.M. Drawing 08501Z, Revised January 6, 1941 this office should be advised, in order that inspection may be made.

From Chapter 11, page 176

Table 14: Willys MA General Specifications

GENERAL SPECIFICATIONS	
Willys Model MA ¼-4x4 Truck	
Wheelbase	80"

Track	48¼"
Overall Length	132¼"
Overall Width	62"
Silhouette Cowl	40"
Road Clearance	81/2"
Angle of Approach	32.5 degrees
Angle of Departure	35 degrees (at bumper)
Frame	
Willys MA ¼—4x4 — Specifications	
Side Members - open channel sections	
Length — side members	122-38"
Depth — side members	4"
Width — main side members	1¾"
Thickness — main side member stock	.093 to .083
Cross Members — Front Tubular Section	
All other channels and rear "K" is attached to top of rear channel with center of supporting pintle hook.	
Frame outside diameter(Without side Brackets or bumpers)	29-"
Frame material side members made of NAX-high tensile steel with reinforcing strip of SAE-1025 Steel spot-welded to lower flange to increase strength with minimum added weight – all other parts 20 to 25 carbon steel.	
Springs	
Willys MA 1/4—4x4 — Specifications	8
Front Springs	13/4"
No. of leaves	.206
Width	
Thickness	.194 thick
Parabolic section steel except bottom leaf flat	
Second leaf has Military wrapping at both ends	
Center to center lengths	36¼"
Willys MA ¼—4x4 — Specifications	
Rear Springs	
No. of leaves	
Width	9
Thickness – main leaf	1-4/4"
Thickness – 2, 3, 4, leaves	.251"
Thickness – 5, 6, 7, 8 leaves	.228"
Parabolic section steel except No. 9 – bottom leaf flat	.206"

Spring shackles same as on Willys Pilot Model	.214" thick

[To convert 2 columns to 1: select both columns in the row. Right click, right select merge cells. Type as needed. Height of column will expand to accommodate any height you need.]

Front Axle

Willys MA ¼—4x4 — Specifications

Modified Spicer diameter hypoid gear This is the same axle as for the Willys Pilot model. The differential housing is on the right side of the axle and the right front spring inner-clip rests on the differential housing.

The steering arm and tie rods are arranged the same as on the Willys Pilot Model, the drag link being above the axle tube and the tie rods connecting to the axle steering arm from the bell crank mounted near the center of the axle and above the tube.

Rear Axle

Willys MA ¼—4x4 — Specifications

Spicer Design with 7-3/4" diameter hypoid gear. This axle is the same as for the Willys Pilot Model with the differential housing at the right of the center of the axle because the design of the vehicle.

Clutch

Willys MA ¼—4x4 — Specifications

Same as for the Willys Pilot Model

Transmission

Willys MA ¼—4x4 — Specifications

Warner Gear Company Model T-84-J. This was the same as specified for Willys Pilot Model. Shift is by remote control on steering column operating through 2 shift levers on side of gear box.

Transfer Case

Willys MA ¼—4x4 — Specifications

Made by Spicer Manufacturing Company and identical with design used in Willys Pilot Model.

Engine

Willys MA ¼—4x4 — Specifications

Willys Model MA (modified 442 production engine). The specifications and accessories for this engine are the same as listed for the Willys Pilot Model.

Muffler

Willys MA ¼—4x4 — Specifications

Cylindrical Type 3-14" in diameter by 22-3/4" long. Attached to body outside of side rail on left side and connected with exhaust pipe through flexible tubing to permit engine movement without shaking muffler in a similar manner as on the Willys Pilot Model.

Radiator

Willys MA ¼—4x4 — Specifications

Jamestown cellular type. Core 2¼" thick, 20-1/2" wide X 13¼" high.

Radiator cap conventional type without pressure valve. Fan Shroud ring 16-1/2" in diameter.

Sheet metal and felt baffles at top and sides to prevent re-circulation of under hood air.

Fan-Hayes Industries 4 blades riveted to a spider, 15" outside diameter.

Steering Gear

Willys MA ¼—4x4 — Specifications	
Ross Model T-12 Cam and Lever-Twin pin lever.	
Variable ratio 14-12 – 14 to 1.	
Wheel has 3 spokes and is 17¼" in diameter.	
Mounted on inside of left side rail with straight tie rod to bell crank pivoting on pin located on upper side of front axle tube.	

Electrical

Willys MA ¼—4x4 — Specifications	
Starter Auto-Lie MZ-4108 with 10 tooth Bendix Pinion Gear operated by Solenoid mounted starting motor.	
Generator Auto-Lite GDA-4810-A.	
Voltage Regulator – Auto-Lite Model VRP-4009-D – mounted on inside of right fender.	
Ignition Coil – Auto-Lite Model IG-4090-A – mounted on right side wall of engine.	
Battery - Auto-Lite Type AD-1-12-R – Capacity 80 ampere hours- mounted on right side rail under hood, just back of radiator.	
Horn – Sparks-Withington Model B-9288 – mounted on front of dash at left under hood.	
Headlight sealed beam – 5-1/2" in diameter.	
Distributor - Auto-Lite Model GW-4129 with vacuum and automatic spark advance.	
Spark Plugs – 14 Millimeter.	

Instruments

Willys MA ¼—4x4 — Specifications	
The instruments are arranged in 3 groups and are the same as used on the Willys Pilot Model	

Body Dimensions

Willys MA ¼—4x4 — Specifications	
Inside of Body	57 inches wide
Between wheelhouse panels	31-1/8 inches
Body length – dash to rear panel	79 inches
Body width – overall	62 inches

Driver's Seat

Willys MA ¼—4x4 — Specifications	
Cushion Top	9-1/2 inches from floor
Cushion Top	10 inches from steering wheel
Front of seat back	41 inches to dash
Front of seat back	32¼ inches to pedals
Front of seta back	12 inches from steering wheel
Seat is tubular frame and metal panel construction and is mounted solid to the floor. A 10 gallon gas tank is located under the seat.	

Front Passenger Seat

Willys MA ¼—4x4 — Specifications

Tubular frame and panel construction. The entire seat pivots forward at the floor.

Rear Seat Cushion and Back

Willys MA ¼—4x4 — Specifications

Cushion is 30-5/8" wide and 15" deep, tubular frame and panel construction. The back is 24¼" above the floor, steel frame and panel construction. The cushion frame is hinged at the back so that the cushion assembly can be folded up and back. The steel back frame can be released by thumb screws and the back dropped down so that top of back is flush with rear body panel.

Rear Floor Design

Willys MA ¼—4x4 — Specifications

Rear floor is 3-1/2" above front floor with base for machine gun provided but otherwise similar to the Willys Pilot Model.

Front Floor Design

Willys MA ¼—4x4 — Specifications

The floor is a drawn panel with transmission and transfer case clearance drawn in panel and floor reinforced with channel sections.

Tool Compartment

Willys MA ¼—4x4 — Specifications

Two large compartments, one in each wheelhouse back of rear wheel with compartment lids in top of wheelhouse.

Windshield

Willys MA ¼—4x4 — Specifications

This is similar to and can be described the same as for the original Ford Windshield except for slight modifications made to fit the Willys MA ¼-4x4 Truck.

Top Bows and Tops

Willys MA ¼—4x4 — Specifications

Two bow tops, the forward or number one bow pivots on the front side of the rear bow. The bows when folded and in down position for a double body rail with one bow on top of the other. The bows are held in down position by thumb screws through sides of sockets, and are set in rear sockets to form a support for the top. The bows are tubular.

Hood

Willys MA ¼—4x4 — Specifications

The hood is of two piece construction consisting of one formed top piece and one front panel spot welded to the top piece, and it is hinged on one piano type hinge at the rear of the hood, and is held down by 2 spring loaded hooks engaging through holes in the front wheel.

Grille and Headlamp Guards

Willys MA ¼—4x4 — Specifications

Band Iron construction mounted on top of frame side rails and attached to front fenders and to small grilles on top of fenders that protect headlamps.

Front Fender

Willys MA ¼—4x4 — Specifications

The fender is of two pieces; that is, fender top panel, and fender rear panel, with a rolled edge along the outside edge of the top and rear. The top is flat and the rear panel is also flat and angles down to the rear at approximately 60 degrees. There is no fender skirt.

From the Author for further reference

Table 15: Comparison Chart—General Specifications of Original Jeeps

	Original Bantam	Original Ford	Willys Pilot Model
Wheelbase	78-1/2	80	80
Track	48-1/2	48	48¼
Overall Length	129"	129	132¼
Overall Width	62-1/2	62"	62"
Silhouette Cowl Windshield	42¼ 62-3/4	38-3/4	42¼
Road Clearance	8"	8"	8-1/2
Angel of Approach	40 degrees	40 degrees	32.5 degrees
Angle of Departure	30 degrees (at pintle hook)	34 degrees (at bumper)	28 degrees (at pintle hook)

Bibliography

Books

Eckhertz, Holger. *D Day Through German Eyes: Eyewitness Accounts by German Soldiers of June 6th 1944.* DTZ History Publications, 2016.

Foster, Patrick and Bill Tilden. *Willys: The Complete Illustrated History 1903 – 1963.* Enthusiast Books, 2016.

Overy, R. J. *The Origins of the Second World War, Second Edition.* London and New York: Addison Wesley Longman Limited, 2013.

Rifkind, Herbert R. *Jeep – Its Development and Procurement Under the Quartermaster Corps, 1940 – 1942.* Tallahassee, Florida: Robert V. Nortman, 2011.

Risch, Erna. *United States Army in World War II – The Technical Services – The Quartermaster Corps: Organization, Supply and Services – Volume 1.* Washington, D.C.: Center of Military History – United States Army, 1995.

Taylor, Blaine. *Volkswagen Military Vehicles of the Third Reich.* Cambridge Center, Massachusetts: Da Capo Press, 2004.

Thomson, Harry C. and Linda Mayo. *United States Army in World War II – The Technical Services – The Ordnance Department: Procurement and Supply.* Washington, D.C.: Office of the Chief of Military History – Department of the Army, 1960.

Underwood, John W. *Whatever Became of the Baby Austin.* Sun Valley, California: Heritage Press, 1965.

Watson, Mark Skinner. *Chief of Staff: Prewar Plans and Preparation.* Washington, D.C.: Historical Division United States Army, 1950.

Wells, Albert Wade. *Hail to the Jeep.* New York, New York: Harper and Brothers, 1946.

Articles

Bennett, Ralph Kinney. "The Elegant Jeep." *American Magazine,* 9 April 2010.

Chester Hempfling as told to Bob Lindsey. "A Personal Interview of Chet Hempfling." 27 July 1988.

Domer, George Edward. "Good Things Did Come in Small Packages – The History of the American Austin and Bantam." *Automotive Quarterly,* XIV, no. 4 (Fourth Quarter, 1976), 404 – 429.

Domer, George Edward. "Harold Crist – The Man and His Machines."— http://www.willys-overland.com/documents/198203-04%20-%20Looking%20Back%20-%20Harold%20Crist%20-%20The%20Man%20and%20His%20Machines%20-

%20George%20Domer.htm

Johnson, Wendell G. "The Howie Machine-Gun Carrier." *Infantry Journal,* (November – December 1937).

Probst, Karl K. with Charles O. Probst. "One Summer in Butler – Bantam Builds the Jeep." *Automotive Quarterly,* XIV, no. 4 (Fourth Quarter, 1976), 430– 439.

Ralph Turner as told to Bob Lindsey. "We Were Beaten by the Roosevelt's." December 1982.

Public Documents

Bantam Jeep Festival, www.bantamjeepfestival.com/about/history

Federal Trade Commission, In the Matter of Willys-Overland Motors, Inc., Toledo, Ohio, *United States National Archives, College Park, Maryland.*

https:www.allpar.com/corporate/bios/willys.html

https://www.britannica.com

https://encyclopedia.densho.org

http://en.wikipedia.org

United States National Archives, College Park, Maryland.

militaryhistorynow.com

Endnotes

Chapter 1

1 http://en.wikipedia.org/wiki/Causes_of_World_War_I#Over_by_Christmas; http://en.wikipedia.org/wiki/World_War_I.

2 http://en.wikipedia.org/wiki/George_Washington%27s_Farewell_Address; http://en.wikipedia.org/wiki/The_war_to_end_all_wars.

3 http://en.wikipedia.org/wiki/Treaty_of_versailles; http://en.wikipedia.org/wiki/Fourteen_points; http://en.wikipedia.org/wiki/Ferdinand_Foch.

4 http://en.wikipedia.org/wiki/Fourteen_points.

5 http://en.wikipedia.org/wiki/Woodrow_Wilson.

6 R. J. Overy, The Origins of the Second World War, Second Edition, (London and New York: Addison Wesley Longman Limited, 2013), 8 – 9; http://en.wikipedia.org/wiki/Warren_Harding.

7 Ibid., http://en.wikipedia.org/wiki/Calvin_Coolidge; McElvaine, 23.

8 Overy, 11; E. H. Carr, International Relations Between The Two World Wars (1919 – 1939), (New York: Saint Martin's Press, 1961), 93 – 98, 117.

9 McElvaine, 89 – 90, 163 – 164, Mitchell, 10 – 16, Overy, 8.

10 Overy, 8.

11 Overy, 12, 36 – 42.

12 Overy, 12 – 18, 25 – 32.

13 Overy, 16 – 22.

14 Overy, 39 – 42.

15 Overy, 25 – 32.

16 Overy, 25 – 32, 63 – 84.

17 Overy, 63 – 84.

18 Overy, 84 – 87.

19 Mark Skinner Watson, Chief of Staff: Prewar Plans and Preparation, (Washington, D.C.: Historical Division United States Army, 1950), 15-56.

20 Ibid., 23.

21 Ibid., 24.

22 Ibid., 23 – 31.

23 Ibid., 23 – 36.

24 Ibid., 24, 31 – 33; http://www.history.army.mil/books/AMH-V2/AMH%20V2/chapter2.htm, 59.

25 Ibid., 34.

26 Ibid., 43.

27 Ibid., 37-38.

28 Ibid., 30.

29 http://en.wikipedia.org/wiki/Neutrality_Acts_of_1930s

30 Watson, 209.

31 Ibid.

32 Ibid., 209-210.

33 Ibid., 52.

Chapter 2

[34] George Edward Domer, "Good Things Did Come in Small Packages – The History of the American Austin and Bantam," *Automotive Quarterly*, Vol. XIV, no. 4, (Fourth Quarter 1976), 405.

35 Ibid.

36 Ibid.

37 Ibid.

38 Ibid.

39 Ibid.

40 Ibid.

41 Ibid.

42 Ibid.

43 John W. Underwood, Whatever Became of the Baby Austin?, (Sun Valley, California: Heritage Press, 1965), 8.

44 Domer, 405.

45 Underwood, 8.

46 Ibid., 8 – 9.

47 Domer, 407.

48 Underwood, 9.

49 Domer, 408 – 409.

50 Ibid.

51 Ibid., 411 – 413.

52 Ibid., 413.

53 Ibid.

54 Underwood, 12.

55 Ibid., 16.

56 Domer, 417.

57 Ibid., 417 – 418.

58 Underwood, 16, 20.

59 Domer, 418.

60 Ibid.

61 Ibid.

62 Ibid.

63 Ibid.

64 Ibid.

65 Ibid., 422-423.

66 Ibid., 423.

67 Underwood, 21.

68 Ibid.

69 Domer, 423.

70 Ibid.

71 Ibid., 425.

72 Ibid.

73 Ibid.

74 Ibid.

75 Ibid.

76 Ibid.

77 Ibid., 425 – 426.

78 Ibid., 426.

79 Ibid.

80 Ibid., 426 – 428.

81 Underwood, 28.

Chapter 3

82 Herbert R. Rifkind, Jeep–Its Development and Procurement Under the Quartermaster Corps, 1940-1942, (Tallahassee, Florida: Robert V. Notman, 2011), 6.

83 Ibid.

84 Chief of Infantry to Adjutant General, 26 July 1938, United States National Archives, College Park, Maryland.

85 Rifkind, 6–7.

86 Ibid., 7, 11.

87 Ibid., 8.

88 Federal Trade Commission, In the Matter of Willys-Overland Motors, Inc., Toledo, Ohio, United States National Archives, College Park, Maryland, 2410–2411.

89 Ibid., 2412.

90 Ibid., 2418.

91 Ibid., 2420-2421, 2432-2437.

92 Ibid., 2437-2438.

93 Ibid., 2439-2441.

94 Ibid., 2451-2454.

95 Federal Trade Commission, In the Matter of Willys-Overland Motors, Inc., Toledo, Ohio, Respondents Exhibit 203–Report 850 Dated 3-26-36, United States National Archives, College Park, Maryland.

96 Ibid.

97 Rifkind, 10.

98 Captain Wendell G. Johnson, Infantry, "The Howie Machine-Gun Carrier," Infantry Journal, (November–December 1937).

99 Ibid.

100 Ibid.

101 Ibid.

102 Chief of Infantry to Adjutant General, 26 July 1938, United States National Archives, College Park, Maryland.

103 The Infantry Board to Chief of Infantry, 12 February 1938, United States National Archives, College Park, Maryland.

104 Ibid.

105 The Infantry Board to Chief of Infantry, 1 March 1938, United States National Archives, College Park, Maryland.

106 Ibid.

107 Chief of Infantry to Adjutant General, 26 July 1938, United States National Archives, College Park, Maryland.

108 Blaine Taylor, Volkswagen Military Vehicles of the Third Reich, (Cambridge Center, Massachusetts: Da Capo Press, 2004), 15.

109 Ibid.

110 Ibid., 53–59.

111 Quartermaster General to Commanding Officer Holabird Quartermaster Depot, 2 June 1938, United States National Archives, College Park, Maryland.

112 Ibid.

113 Quartermaster General to Commanding Officer Holabird Quartermaster Depot, 10 August 1938, United States National Archives, College Park, Maryland.

114 The Cavalry Board to Chief of Cavalry, 8 November 1938, United States National Archives, College Park, Maryland.

115 Ibid.

116 Adjutant General to Chief of Infantry, 13 October 1938, United States National Archives, College Park, Maryland.

117 This same report detailed the problem as discussed in the Introduction to this chapter and the report's conclusion that the Marmon-Herrington ½ ton 4x4 truck met Infantry needs was presented in the "1938: Vehicle Testing" section of this chapter.

118 Ibid.

119 Ibid.

120 Frank H. Fenn to Col. H. C. Lawes, 25 September 1939, United States National Archives, College Park, Maryland.

121 Ibid.

122 Ibid.

123 Ibid.

124 H. J. Lawes to Quartermaster General, 12 December 1939, United States National Archives, College Park, Maryland.

125 Erna Risch, United States Army in World War II–The Technical Services–The Quartermaster Corps: Organization, Supply and Services–Volume 1, (Washington, D.C.: Center of Military History–United States Army, 1995), 246, 253.

126 Harry C. Thomson and Lida Mayo, United States Army in World War II–The Technical Services–The Ordnance Department: Procurement and Supply, (Washington, D.C.: Office of the Chief of Military History– Department of the Army, 1960), 268.

127 Ibid., 267.

128 Ibid., 268-269.

129 Ibid., 270.

130 Ibid., 267.

131 Rifkind, 16.

132 Thomson and Mayo, 271–272.

133 Risch, 51–52.

134 Rifkind, 13.

135 Ibid., 13–14.

136 Ibid., 15–17.

137 Ibid.

Chapter 4

138 Federal Trade Commission, In the Matter of Willys-Overland Motors, Inc., Toledo, Ohio, United States National Archives, College Park, Maryland, 2924.

139 Ibid.

140 Ibid., 2928.

141 Ibid., 2931–2936.

142 Ibid., 453.

143 Ibid., 460–463.

144 Ibid., 383.

145 Ibid., 454.

146 Ibid., 363–365.

147 Ibid., 457, 463–464.

148 Ibid., 369–370.

149 Ibid., 467.

150 Ibid., 365–366.

151 Ibid., 465–466.

152 Ibid., 366–367.

153 Ibid., 1650.

154 Ibid., 1632–1634.

155 Ibid., 1636–1637.

156 Ibid., 1641.

157 Ibid.

158 Ibid., 1645.

159 Ibid., 1645–1646.

160 Ibid., 1648.

161 Ibid., 1648–1649.

162 Ibid., 1650–1652.

163 Ibid., 1652.

164 Ibid., 1654–1656.

165 Ibid., 1656–1659.

166 Ibid., 1660.

167 Ibid., 1661–1662.

168 Ibid., 1737.

169 Ibid., 1740.

170 Ibid., 1743.

171 Ibid., 1663.

172 Chief of Infantry to Adjutant General (THROUGH The Chief of Cavalry), 6 June 1940, United States National Archives, College Park, Maryland.

173 Ibid.

174 Ibid.

175 Ibid., 1665–1666.

176 Ibid.

177 Federal Trade Commission, 1652–1653.

178 Ibid., 1664.

Chapter 5

179 Chief of Cavalry to Adjutant General, 8 June 1940, United States National Archives, College Park, Maryland.

180 Adjutant General to The Quartermaster General AND the Chief of Ordnance, 14 June 1940, United States National Archives, College Park, Maryland.

181 Federal Trade Commission, In the Matter of Willys-Overland Motors, Inc., Toledo, Ohio, United States National Archives, College Park, Maryland, 2935-2936.

182 Quartermaster General to Commanding Officer, Holabird Quartermaster Depot, Baltimore, Md., 14 June 1940, United States National Archives, College Park, Maryland.

183 H. J. Lawes to Quartermaster General, 12 December 1939, United States National Archives, College Park, Maryland.

184 War Department General Staff to Adjutant General, Quartermaster General, Chief of Cavalry, Chief of Infantry and Chief of Ordnance, 15 June 1940, United States National Archives, College Park, Maryland.

185 Adjutant General to Chief of Ordnance and The Quartermaster General, 15 June 1940, United States National Archives, College Park, Maryland.

186 Ordnance Sub-Committee on Ordnance to The Ordnance Committee, Technical Staff, 17 June 1940, United States National Archives, College Park, Maryland.

187 Adjutant General to Chief of Ordnance, 18 June 1940, United States National Archives, College Park, Maryland.

188 Federal Trade Commission, 2752-2753.

189 Ibid., 481-482.

190 Ibid., 2936-2942.

191 Ibid., 2943-2947.

192 Ibid., 2943, 2947-2949.

193 Sub-Committee on Automotive Equipment to The Ordnance Committee, Technical Staff, 22 June 1940, United States National Archives, College Park, Maryland.

194 Ibid.

195 Ibid.

196 Federal Trade Commission, 1442, 1438.

197 Ibid., 1438-1439.

198 Ibid., 1442-1449.

199 Ibid., 1455.

200 Ibid., 1456-1457.

201 Ibid., 1460-1463.

202 Ibid., 1465-1466.

203 Ibid., 1669-1672.

204 Ibid., 1672-1674.

205 Ibid., 2961-2964.

206 Ibid., 2776-2768.

207 Federal Trade Commission, 1675.

Chapter 6

208 War Department General Staff to Adjutant General, Quartermaster General, Chief of Cavalry, Chief of Infantry and Chief of Ordnance, 27 June 1940, United States National Archives, College Park, Maryland.

209 Federal Trade Commission, In the Matter of Willys-Overland Motors, Inc., Toledo, Ohio, United States National Archives, College Park, Maryland, 1724.

210 Ibid., 2949.

211 Ibid., 1561.

212 Ibid., 1573.

213 Holabird Quartermaster Depot to Quartermaster General, 3 July 1940, United States National Archives, College Park, Maryland.

214 Quartermaster General to Chief Motor Transport, 5 July 1940, United States National Archives, College Park, Maryland.

215 Adjutant General to Chief of Ordnance and The Quartermaster General, IN TURN, 5 July 1940, United States National Archives, College Park, Maryland.

216 Charles H. Payne to Colonel J. H. Johnson, 9 July 1940, United States National Archives, College Park, Maryland.

217 Chief of Infantry to The Quartermaster General, 9 July 1940, United States National Archives, College Park, Maryland.

218 Quartermaster General to The Assistant Secretary of War, 10 July 1940, United States National Archives, College Park, Maryland.

219 Quartermaster General to Commanding Officer, Holabird Quartermaster Depot, 11 July 1940, United States National Archives, College Park, Maryland.

220 Federal Trade Commission, 1534.

221 Ibid., 676, 689.

222 Karl K. Probst with Charles O. Probst, "One Summer in Butler-Bantam Builds the Jeep" Automotive Quarterly, Vol. XIV, no. 4, (Fourth Quarter 1976), 432.

223 Ibid.

224 Ibid.

225 Federal Trade Commission, 213, 255.

226 Ibid., 689, 696.

227 Probst, 432.

228 Ibid., 433.

229 Federal Trade Commission, 695.

230 John W. Underwood, Whatever Became of the Baby Austin?, (Sun Valley, California: Heritage Press, 1965), 30.

231 Federal Trade Commission, 708-709.

232 Probst, 433.

233 Ibid.

234 American Bantam Car Company reply to Invitation to Bids No. 398-41-9, 22 July 1940, United States National Archives, College Park, Maryland.

235 Ibid.

236 Ibid.

237 Ibid.

238 Ibid.

239 Quartermaster General, Specification ES–No. 475, 2 July 1940, United States National Archives, College Park, Maryland.

240 American Bantam Car Company reply to Invitation to Bids No. 398-41-9, 22 July 1940, United States National Archives, College Park, Maryland.

241 Probst, 433.

242 D. G. Roos to J. Van Ness Ingram, Q.M.C, 20 July 1940, United States National Archives, College Park, Maryland.

243 Ibid., 433.

244 Ibid.

245 Underwood, 31.

246 Federal Trade Commission, 1720–1721.

Chapter 7

247 Quartermaster General to Commanding Officer, Holabird Quartermaster Depot, 25 July 1940, United States National Archives, College Park, Maryland.

248 Contact No. W-398-qm-8269 (O.I. #137) Invitation to Bids No. 398-41-9, 1 August 1940, United States National Archives, College Park, Maryland.

249 Ibid.

250 Ibid.

251 Federal Trade Commission, In the Matter of Willys-Overland Motors, Inc., Toledo, Ohio, United States National Archives, College Park, Maryland, 2952-2960.

252 Ibid., 2961.

253 George Domer, "Looking Back: Harold Crist–The Man and His Machines," http://www.willys-overland.com/documents/198203-04%20-%20Looking%20Back%20-%20Harold%20Crist%20-%20The%20Man%20and%20His%20Machines%20-%20George%20Domer.htm

254 Federal Trade Commission, 680.

255 George Edward Domer, "Good Things Did Come in Small Packages–The History of the American Austin and Bantam," Automotive Quarterly, Vol. XIV, no. 4, (Fourth Quarter 1976), 418, 422.

256 Ralph Turner as told to Bob Lindsey, "We Were Beaten by the Roosevelt's", December 1982, http://www.willys-overland.com/documents/198212%20-%20We%20Were%20Beaten%20by%20the%20Roosevelts%20-%20%20as%20told%20by%20Ralph%20Turner%20-%20by%20%20Bob%20Lindsey.htm

257 Karl K. Probst with Charles O. Probst, "One Summer in Butler-Bantam Builds the Jeep" Automotive Quarterly, Vol. XIV, no. 4, (Fourth Quarter 1976), 435.

258 Probst, 433.

259 Ibid., 432.

260 John W. Underwood, Whatever Became of the Baby Austin?, (Sun Valley, California: Heritage Press, 1965), 31.

261 Chet Hempfling as told to Bob Lindsey, "A Personal Interview of Chet Hempfling," 27 July 1988, http://www.willys-overland.com/documents/19880726%20-%20A%20Personal%20Interview%20of%20Chet%20Hempling%20as%20told%20to%20Bob%20Lindsey.htm

262 Ralph Kinney Bennett, "The Elegant Jeep," American Magazine, 9 April 2010.

263 Turner to Lindsey.

264 Domer, "Looking Back: Harold Crist–The Man and His Machines."

265 Turner to Lindsey.

266 Hempfling to Lindsey.

267 Probst, 435.

268 Underwood, 431.

269 Bennett, "The Elegant Jeep."

270 Probst, 432.

271 Ibid.

272 Federal Trade Commission, 235.

273 Probst, 432.

274 Federal Trade Commission, 221- 222.

275 Ibid., 214, 255.

276 Ibid., 255 – 260.

277 Probst, 435.

278 http://www.bantamjeepfestival.com/about/history/

279 Probst, 435.

280 Underwood, 32.

281 Domer, "Looking Back: Harold Crist–The Man and His Machines."

282 Federal Trade Commission, 682, 2846, 2967.

283 Probst, 435.

284 Underwood, 32.

285 Federal Trade Commission, 682.

286 American Bantam Car Company reply to Invitation to Bids No. 398-41-9, 22 July 1940, United States National Archives, College Park, Maryland.

Chapter 8

[287] Federal Trade Commission, In the Matter of Willys-Overland Motors, Inc., Toledo, Ohio, United States National Archives, College Park, Maryland, 2906, 2908, 2912.

[288] Ibid., 3415, 3432, 3443.

[289] Ibid., 3415-3416.

[290] Ibid., 3417.

[291] John W. Underwood, Whatever Became of the Baby Austin?, (Sun Valley, California: Heritage Press, 1965), 32- 33.

[292] Probst, 437.

[293] Memorandum For the Chief of Staff: Subject: Demonstration of Light Weapons Carrier, 26 September 1940, United States National Archives, College Park, Maryland.

[294] Underwood, 33-34.

[295] Federal Trade Commission, 2847.

[296] Ibid., 2882- 2883.

[297] Ibid., 2910, 3424- 3425, 3435.

[298] Quartermaster General to The Adjutant General: Procurement of Fifteen Hundred (1500) Trucks, ¼-ton (4x4) Light Command-Reconnaissance Truck, 22 October 1940, United States National Archives, College Park, Maryland.

Chapter 9

[299] https:www.allpar.com/corporate/bios/willys.html, 1-3.

[300] Ibid.

[301] Ibid.

[302] Ibid.

[303] Allpar.com, 3-4; Patrick Foster and Bill Tilden, Willys: The Complete Illustrated History-1903-1963, (www.enthusiastbooks.com), 8.

[304] Allpar.com, 8; Foster, 10-12.

[305] Allpar.com, 8; Foster 12-22.

[306] Allpar.com, 8-9; Foster, 22-40.

[307] Allpar.com, 12, Foster, 40-50.

[308] Allpar.com, 12, Foster, 49-61.

[309] Ibid.

[310] Federal Trade Commission, Exhibit 91B-91C.

[311] Ibid., 78-80, 107.

[312] Ibid., 129.

[313] Ibid., 1209-1212.

[314] Ibid., 1212-1213.

[315] Ibid., Exhibit 91C-91D.

[316] https://encyclopedia.densho.org/Walter_Short/

[317] Federal Trade Commission, 191.

[318] Ibid., 192-193.

[319] Ibid., 193-194.

[320] Ibid., 129-130.

[321] Ibid., 131-132.

[322] Ibid., Exhibit 91-D.

[323] Ibid., 132-133.

[324] Ibid., 182-183.

[325] Ibid., 133-134.

[326] Ibid., Exhibit 92-M.

[327] Ibid., Exhibit 92-W, 56-57.

[328] Ibid., 1220-1221.

[329] Ibid., 1285-1286.

[330] Ibid., 195.

[331] Ibid., 82.

[332] Ibid.

[333] Ibid., Exhibit 91-E.

[334] Ibid., 82.

[335] Ibid., 195.

[336] Ibid., 83.

[337] Ibid., 330.

[338] Ibid., 333.

[339] Ibid., 134.

[340] Ibid., 134-135.

[341] Ibid., 197.

[342] Ibid., 1683.

Chapter 10

[343] Federal Trade Commission, 244 – 266.

[344] Ibid., 1001 – 1003.

[345] Ibid., 1002.

[346] Federal Trade Commission, 1002;
https://en.wikipedia.org/wiki/American_Expeditionary_Force,_Siberia

[347] Federal Trade Commission, 1002 – 1004.

[348] Ibid., 1061 – 1062.

[349] Ibid., 1078 – 1079.

[350] Ibid., 136.

[351] Ibid., 145 – 146.

[352] Ibid., 171 – 172.

[353] Ibid., 1029 – 1031.

[354] Ibid., 1080.

[355] Ibid., 1080, 1082, 1089.

[356] Ibid., 1083.

[357] Ibid., 137 – 138.

[358] Ibid., Exhibit 91-E.

[359] Ibid., 1221 – 1222.

[360] Ibid., 1222 – 1223.

[361] Ibid., 219 – 220.

[362] Ibid., 261 – 262.

[363] Ibid., 173.

[364] Ibid., 169.

[365] Ibid., 221.

[366] Ibid., 265 – 266.

[367] Ibid., 1214.

[368] Ibid., 1214 – 1215.

[369] Ibid., 1215.

[370] Ibid., 1216 – 1217.

[371] Ibid., 1041, 1135 – 1147.

[372] Ibid., 1249 – 1258.

[373] Ibid., Exhibit 91-G.

[374] D. D. Stone to Milton Boesel, 12 March 1945, United States National Archives, College Park, Maryland.

[375] https://www.britannica.com/topic/Ford-Motor-Company

[376] Ibid.

[377] Federal Trade Commission, 597.

[378] Ibid., 644 – 645.

[379] Ibid., 646 – 647.

[380] Ibid., 595.

[381] Ibid.

[382] Ibid., 597.

[383] Ibid., 598 – 599.

[384] Ibid., 615.

[385] Ibid., 616 – 617.

[386] Ibid., 617.

[387] Ibid., 599.

Chapter 11

[388] Frank Fenn to J. Van Ness Ingram, 4 October 1940, United States National Archives, College Park Maryland.

[389] Ibid.

[390] Federal Trade Commission, 332 – 333.

[391] Ibid., Exhibit 112-D.

[392] Ibid., 335, - 338.

[393] Ibid., 336.

[394] Ibid., Exhibit 126-A.

[395] Ibid. Exhibit 121-A.

[396] Ibid.

[397] Ibid., 340.

[398] Ibid., 424 – 425.

[399] Ibid., Exhibit 126-A.

[400] Ibid.

[401] Ibid.

[402] Ibid., 413 – 414.

[403] Ibid., 419.

[404] Ibid., 420, 422.

[405] Ibid., Exhibit 117-D.

[406] Ibid., Exhibit 117-E.

[407] Ibid., 1493.

[408] Ibid., Exhibit 117-F.

[409] Ibid., Exhibit, 117-G.

[410] Ibid., Exhibit 117– H – J.

[411] Ibid., Exhibit 117-J.

[412] Ibid., Exhibit 117- A – C.

[413] Ibid., Exhibit 117-K.

[414] Ibid., Exhibit 117– L – M.

[415] Ibid., Exhibit 117-L.

[416] Federal Trade Commission, Exhibit 118-B.

[417] Ibid.

[418] Ibid., 118-B-C.

[419] Ibid., 118-C.

[420] Ibid., Exhibit 117-O.

[421] Ibid.

[422] Ibid.

[423] Ibid., Exhibit 117-P.

[424] Ingram to American Bantam, Car Company, 6 November 1940, United States National Archives, College Park Maryland, Federal Trade Commission, Exhibit 116-C.

[425] Ingram to Quartermaster General, 6 November 1940, United States National Archives, College Park Maryland.

[426] John B. Cooley to General R. C. Moore, 6 November 1940, United States National Archives, College Park Maryland.

[427] E. B. Gregory to William S. Knudsen, 7 November 1940, United States National Archives, College Park Maryland.

[428] Quartermaster Corp. to American Bantam Car Company, 25 November 1940, United States National Archives, College Park Maryland.

[429] Federal Trade Commission, Exhibit 91-F.

[430] Ibid., 91 – 92.

[431] Ibid., Exhibit 120-A – B.

[432] Federal Trade Commission, Exhibit 119-C.

[433] Ibid.

[434] Ibid., 348.

[435] Ibid., Exhibit 120-C, D, F, E.

[436] Ibid., Exhibit 122-A.

[437] Ibid., Exhibit 121-B.

[438] Ibid., Exhibit 121-D.

[439] Ibid., Exhibit 121-E.

[440] Ibid.

[441] Ibid., Exhibit 121-F, I, J.

[442] Ibid., Exhibit 121-J-K.

[443] Ibid., 1383.

[444] Albert Wade Wells, Hail To The Jeep, (New York, New York: Harper & Brothers, 1946), 21.

[445] William Dick to Quartermaster General, 7 January 1941, United States National Archives, College Park, Maryland.

[446] Ibid.

[447] Sub-Committee on Motor Transport to The Quartermaster Corps Technical Committee, 14 January 1941, United States National Archives, College Park, Maryland.

[448] Ibid.

[449] Ibid.

[450] Ibid.

[451] Van Deusen to Adjutant General, 21 January 1941, , United States National Archives, College Park, Maryland.

[452] Federal Trade Commission, Brief of Counsel for the Commission, 13, United States National Archives, College Park, Maryland.

[453] Eugene Rice to George C. Marshall, 21 January 1941, United States National Archives, College Park, Maryland.

[454] Federal Trade Commission, Exhibit 161-A-B.

[455] Ibid., Exhibit 161-B.

[456] Ibid.

[457] Ibid.

[458] Federal Trade Commission, Exhibit 110-C.

[459] Ibid.

[460] Ibid.

[461] Federal Trade Commission, Exhibit 111-A –B.

[462] Ibid.

[463] Ibid., Exhibit 111-B.

[464] Ibid.

[465] Ibid., Exhibit 111-C.

[466] War Department, Subject: Willys-Overland 1/4 –Ton, 4x4, Truck, 7 February 1941, United States National Archives College Park, Maryland.

[467] Federal Trade Commission, Exhibit 165-A.

[468] Ibid.

[469] Ibid.

[470] Federal Trade Commission, Exhibit 125-A.

[471] Ibid.

[472] Ibid.

[473] Ingram to Willys-Overland Motors, Inc., 11 February 1941, United States National Archives, College Park, Maryland.

[474] Federal Trade Commission, Exhibit 246-A.

[475] Federal Trade Commission, 203.

[476] Federal Trade Commission, 151 – 156.

[477] Federal Trade Commission, 1070 – 1071.

[478] Federal Trade Commission, Brief of Counsel For The Commission, 17-18.

[479] MilitaryHistoryNow.com, "What the Hell is a 'Jeep'? — How Did America's Famous Military 4×4 Get Its Name?" 30 November, 2018

[480] https://en.wikipedia.org/wiki/Jeep

[481] Foster and Tilden, 64.

[482] https://en.wikipedia.org/wiki/Willys_MB

[483] Ibid.

[484] Ibid.

[485] Foster and Tilden, 71.

[486] Underwood, 35 – 36.

[487] Ibid., 36.

[488] Ibi5d., 37.

[489] Foster and Tilden, 80 – 119.

[490] Ibid., 92.

[491] Ibid., 108- 119.

[492] Ibid., 113.

[493] Ibid., 117-119.

[494] Allpar., 13.

[495] Ibid.

[496] https://en.wikipedia.org/wiki/Ford_jeep

[497] Ibid.

[498] Holger Eckhertz, D Day Through German Eyes: Eyewitness Accounts by German Soldiers of June 6th 1944, DTZ History Publishers, 90.

Index

A

Adams, General E.S., 191

Adjutant General, 41, 52, 76, 81, 82, 83, 84, 105, 106, 111, 180, 185, 188, 190, 191, 192, 193, 6, 7, 9, 10, 13, 17

American Austin, 31, 32, 33, 34, 35, 36, 37, 39, 107, 120, 125, 2, 5, 12

American Bantam Car Company, 28, 35, 36, 37, 38, 58, 61, 62, 65, 67, 68, 77, 81, 89, 94, 102, 106, 110, 111, 113, 115, 120, 121, 136, 211, 212, 214, 219, 11, 13

Appeasement, 24, 25

Artillery, 45, 57, 61, 64, 92, 102, 103, 104, 106

Atwood, Lieutenant Colonel, 85, 86, 89, 103

Austin, Sir Herbert, 31, 32, 33, 34, 35, 36, 37, 39, 43, 49, 50, 52, 120, 2, 5, 11, 12, 13

Austria, 25

Axle, Front, 74, 86, 90, 91, 110, 124, 127, 205, 207, 208, 209, 210, 211, 212, 213, 214, 217, 219

B

Bantam Reconnaissance Car, 126, 128, 129, 133, 202

Bartow, Georgia, 34, 35, 36

Beasley, Mr., 85, 86, 87, 88, 103

Bid Endorsement, 115

Biggers, John D., 186, 188, 193

Brown, Robert, 85, 86, 87, 88, 89, 95, 97, 98, 99, 104, 105, 126, 133, 215

Butler, Pennsylvania, 28, 30, 32, 33, 36, 37, 38, 58, 60, 63, 67, 70, 82, 84, 85, 87, 90, 94, 95, 98, 104, 106, 107, 108, 109, 110, 111, 113, 115, 116, 117, 119, 120, 122, 124, 125, 126, 127, 128, 131, 135, 136, 211, 214, 215, 3, 11, 12

C

Canaday, Ward, 141, 142

Cavalry, 43, 44, 45, 57, 58, 59, 61, 64, 77, 81, 82, 85, 92, 99, 102, 103, 104, 106, 133, 7, 9, 10

Continental Engine, 122

Crist, Harold C., 36, 37, 38, 84, 85, 86, 89, 98, 99, 108, 119, 120, 121, 122, 123, 124, 128, 129, 130, 135, 3, 12, 13

Czechoslovakia, 25

D

Dowd, Mr., 95

E

England, 23, 25, 31, 32, 107

Engler, Geroge, 95, 97

Evans, Roy, 33, 34, 35, 36, 37, 38, 39, 58, 59, 62, 64, 69, 112, 124

F

Fenn, Frank, 60, 61, 62, 67, 70, 81, 82, 84, 86, 89, 98, 101, 104, 105, 107, 108, 109, 110, 112, 117, 120, 121, 124, 125, 127, 129, 130, 134, 218, 7

Final Inspection Report on Pilot Model, 136

Ford, Motor Car Company, 32, 45, 47, 53, 67, 69, 107, 112, 129

France, 21, 24, 25, 26, 29, 32, 62, 64

Frazer, Joseph W., 141, 145, 146, 147, 150, 151, 152, 153, 154, 194

G

Gill, Reuben O., 34, 35, 59, 60, 67

Great Britain, 22

Gregory, General Edmund B., 175, 177, 180, 183, 184, 185, 186, 191, 193, 17

H

Hall, Fred, 86, 89, 108, 124, 125, 126

Hamilton, Lieutenant Homer G., 44, 45, 46, 61

Hausmann, Irvine G., 170, 188

Hempfling, Chester, 120, 121, 122, 123, 124, 2, 12

Hitler, Adolf, 24, 25, 26, 27, 57, 65

Holabird, Camp, 60, 62, 65, 72, 73, 82, 89, 90, 92, 93, 94, 95, 96, 97, 98, 99, 105, 106, 109, 110, 111, 112, 117, 126, 127, 128, 129, 132, 133, 137, 202, 210, 7, 9, 10, 11

Howie Machine-Gun Carrier, 43, 46, 52, 61, 3, 6

I

Infantry, 41, 42, 43, 45, 46, 47, 49, 50, 52, 53, 54, 55, 56, 57, 58, 59, 61, 64, 67, 71, 72, 73, 74, 75, 77, 78, 81, 825, 83, 84, 85, 90, 92, 93, 94, 97, 99, 101, 102, 103, 104, 106, 113, 3, 6, 7, 9, 10

Ingram, Colonel, 152, 153, 154, 175, 176, 177, 185, 186, 187, 194, 11, 16, 17, 18

Inspection Report on Pilot Model, 136, 220

J

Japan, 24

K

Kellogg-Briand Pact, 23

Kenower, Donald, 170, 188

Knudsen, William S., 107, 108

Kramer, Clarence, 171, 172

Kubelwagen, 58

L

Lawes, Major Herbert J., 60, 61, 62, 112, 129, 130, 132, 134, 7, 9

League of Nations, 22, 24

Lee, Colonel W. C., 74

Lewis, Robert, 68, 108, 125, 126, 127, 128

Light Reconnaissance and Command Car, 91, 92, 101, 102, 103, 104, 115, 136, 206, 216, 220

Locarno Treaty, 23

London Conference, 23

Lynch, General George A., 70, 72, 74, 75, 76, 77

M

Marmon Harrington, 47, 58, 72, 93, 94

Marshall, General George C., 104, 106

Moore, General R. C., 70, 82, 83, 183, 185, 186, 187, 191, 192, 193, 17

Mosely, Captain Eugene, 132

N

National Defense Act, 27

Nazi Germany, 25

O

Ordnance, 44, 53, 59, 64, 71, 72, 78, 79, 81, 82, 83, 84, 85, 89, 92, 96, 102, 103, 104, 105, 2, 8, 9, 10

Ordnance Technical Committee, 79, 81, 82, 83, 84, 102, 103

Oseth, Colonel Ingomar, 71, 72, 73, 74, 75, 76, 77, 78, 79, 81, 82, 83, 93, 94, 95, 96, 97, 99, 104, 113

P

Parts Analysis, 130

Payne, Commander Charles "Harry", 68, 69, 70, 71, 73, 74, 75, 76, 77, 81, 82, 84, 94, 96, 97, 105, 107, 108, 109, 112, 113, 132, 222, 10

Pilot Model, 110, 111, 117, 130, 136, 137, 215, 216, 219

Poland, 25, 29

Probst, Karl K., 107, 108, 109, 112, 119, 121, 123, 124, 125, 127, 128, 129, 132, 133, 136, 207, 222, 3, 11, 12, 13

Prototype, Jeep, 36, 47, 60, 62, 64

Q

QM 08370, 99

Quartermaster Corp., 43, 46, 53, 59, 60, 61, 62, 63, 64, 65, 70, 72, 75, 77, 78, 81, 82, 83, 85, 90, 92, 93, 94,

96, 99, 101, 102, 103, 104, 105, 106, 109, 111, 112, 113, 116, 117, 131, 137, 204, 206, 210, 2, 6, 7, 9, 10, 11, 13

R

Reconstruction Finance Corporation, 37

Rhineland, 25

Rice, Eugene M., 142, 151, 152, 153, 175, 176, 177, 184, 185, 186, 187, 190, 191, 192, 195, 17

Roeder, Dale, 172, 173

Roos, Delmar G., 142, 143, 144, 145, 146, 147, 148, 149, 152, 153, 154, 157, 158, 159, 160, 161, 162, 163, 165, 166, 167, 170, 187, 191, 194, 195, 196, 11

Roosevelt, Franklin D., 24, 28, 29, 35, 37, 69, 3, 12

Ross, Sergeant, 131, 135

S

Stimson, Henry L., 177

T

Tompkins, Major, 81, 82, 85, 86, 95, 96, 97, 103

Turner, Ralph, 120, 121, 122, 124, 131, 135, 136, 3, 12

U

United States Army, ix, xvii, xix, 21, 27, 37, 39, 40, 41, 57, 61, 67, 73, 81, 94, 111, 113, 126, 148, 180, 2, 4, 7, 8, 6

V

Van Deusen, Colonel Edwin S., 78, 92, 93, 94, 95, 96, 101, 104

Versailles, 21, 25

W

Washington Naval Treaty, 23

Willys Pilot Model, xv, 233, 235, 236, 237, 238, 239

Willys' Response to ES-475 Requirements, 222

Willys-Overland, vii, ix, xv, xvii, xx, 63, 67, 107, 111,
112, 137, 139, 140, 141, 142, 144, 145, 146, 148, 150, 151, 152, 154, 157, 158, 159, 160, 161, 165, 176, 179, 180, 181, 182, 183, 184, 189, 190, 191, 192, 193, 198, 203, 212, 226, 229, 3, 6, 8, 9, 10, 11, 13, 18

Willys-Overland Motors, Inc. ¼-Ton, 4x4 Truck (, 226

About the Author

Paul Bruno has spent twenty years researching, writing and studying early Jeep history. He has spent countless hours and treasure to tell this story to the world, first for the big screen and now twice in book form. After visiting key sites in the story, and years of research, including at the United States National Archives, he combined his knowledge of project management and history into the 2014 book, *Project Management in History: The First Jeep*. After additional research he completed *The Original Jeeps* in 2020 which further tells the story of early Jeep history and continues his journey into the depths of this important inspirational work of human ingenuity.

Paul has more than 30 years of experience in the fields of project management and information technology. He holds bachelor's degrees in management and computer software, as well as master's degrees in business administration and history.

Other Books by the Author: *Project Management in History: The First Jeep*

Articles and Historical Works:

The Cole-Malley Scandal: Nevada's Political System Revealed, Nevada Historical Society Quarterly, Summer 2007.

Governor James G. Scruhgam and Nevada's First Highway Construction Boom: 1923 – 1927, Nevada Historical Society Quarterly, 2012.

PM History Lessons (5 Titles): published by Projectmanagement.com
The Jeep ∼ *Gettysburg* ∼ *Escape from the USSR* ∼
Battle of Saratoga ∼ *D-Day*

About the Publisher

Manuel Freedman, known as Max, has been writing since the 1950's. Currently he writes, produces and coaches screenwriters in the movie industry in Los Angeles, as well as publishes books. *The Original Jeeps* is his ninth participation as author, publisher and/or editor in a non-fiction title.

Before starting his media company, Mr. Freedman ran his own advertising and publishing company. There he authored and edited five college-level textbooks for Adobe Systems, which were translated into eight languages and distributed in 35 countries. Three of them are on the subject of computer-based filmmaking; the other two on publishing. He was born in St. Louis, Missouri, and is a graduate of Stanford University where he was the recipient of a writing scholarship.

Other Books Published by the Publisher:

The First Jeep by Paul R. Bruno ∼ *The Great Unconformity* by Kate Troll
A'Mused by Sandy Coccia ∼ *Line of Communications* by Sondra Garner

Premise of this Volume

The spring and summer of 1940 witnessed the resounding defeats of the French army and British Expeditionary Force at the hands of modernized German troops, designed to take advantage of the latest advances in technology. These included mobile vehicles and tanks used in formation to blast through enemy lines, as well as combined ground and air tactics. The evacuation of the British from Dunkirk and the final defeat of their French allies in June 1940 left only a thin line of English fighter planes between that island nation and total defeat.

Meanwhile, leaders of the United States Army, decimated by demobilization after World War I and budget cuts during the Great Depression, knew they were completely unprepared for this new type of mobile warfare called "blitzkrieg," a German term meaning "lightning war." Though experts in the U.S. Army had worked from the end of World War I to develop a combination light weapons carrier and command and reconnaissance vehicle, no perfect model had yet been developed by 1940. In June of that same year, the Army compiled a list of requirements for a revolutionary new truck to replace the mule as the Army's primary method of moving troops and small payloads.

The Original Jeeps tells the story of the American Bantam Car Company, Willys Overland-Motors, Inc. and the Ford Motor Company, the three firms who dared to meet the challenge to build pilot models of this extraordinary new vehicle. The efforts by these automotive pioneers represent an astounding story of grit, determination and never-say-die courage that inspires, and ended in the creation of a legend: the Jeep.

Made in the USA
Middletown, DE
16 September 2020